Let A Shepherd Be Your Guide

Jacob Nathaniel Shepherd

WESTBOW
PRESS
A DIVISION OF THOMAS NELSON

WestBow Press books may be ordered through booksellers or by contacting:

WestBow Press
A Division of Thomas Nelson
1663 Liberty Drive
Bloomington, IN 47403
www.westbowpress.com
1-(866) 928-1240

ISBN: 978-1-4497-81033- (sc)
ISBN: 978-1-4497-8105-7 (hc)
ISBN: 978-1-4497-8104-0 (e)

Library of Congress Control Number: 2012924323

Printed in the United States of America

WestBow Press rev. date: 01/17/2013

Let A Shepherd Be Your Guide
My Signature Poem

Let a Shepherd be your guide and stay above the fray.
That's how you can be so sure that you won't lose your way.
Follow Jesus on that narrow path and watch just where He goes.
Please don't do as others do and never step on His toes!

Jesus travels far and wide, He's always on the move.
He's watching out for those in need, to share with them His love.
If you're down and out and need His help, be sure to let Him know.
He will soon be at your side with His blessings to bestow!

There is no greater love than His, it's there for one and all.
He's travelling around the universe and waiting for a call.
If some poor soul has lost his way and doesn't know what to do,
Jesus wants to make his day and He will pull him through!

Down here on earth we sometimes feel that we are so secure.
We have Aflac, Geico, triple A, and many more for sure.
We don't hesitate to call on them in fact we use them all.
We pay these folks a tidy sum for instant help to be there when we call!

I often call on Jesus when I need some good advice.
I get down on my knees and pray to Him in Paradise.
Even though I know He's busy He always takes the time
To listen to me while I make my case and doesn't charge a dime!

I thank my lucky stars each day for Jesus knows my name.
He knows that I'm a sinner but loves me just the same.
When I confess to Him that I've gone wrong, it happens every day,
He says to me so lovingly "Don't worry child, you didn't forget to pray!"

Introduction

I began writing poetry about five years ago when the first poem I wrote had a good reception from all the folks in my Church. I had written that poem to present as part of the Stewardship Campaign.

In my long lifetime of 89 years, I have packed a multitude of information into my memory cells, and so far they are remaining quite intact, and as a result, I have a very handy slate of things to write about. My primary interest in life is and has been for a long time my love for Jesus Christ and how He was prepared by God to lead us all into Heaven when our earthly journey is finished. However, my long life has also enabled me to be involved in a myriad of enterprises and interests, which gives me a generous supply of subjects just waiting to be poetically magnified.

I choose to do my story telling through the medium of poetry, and I believe in rhyming, metrically sound verses, and can generally tell a story in six verses of four lines each. The large majority of my poems are Christian in content, based on my love and devotion to Jesus. However, my total collection covers a real variety of subjects.

I have an e-mail lineup of approximately 100 who receive my poems as soon as they are written. In addition, I speak regularly to five or six local Assisted Living Homes, and the metric quality of my poems makes for good vocal presentation. My poems are very readable and I published a small devotional book a year ago which was received quite well locally.

This new book is largely about my love for Jesus, and how we should live in order to receive His Blessing and acceptance into Heaven when we finish our earthly journey. There is a poem for every day of the year, with special content poems on all holidays. Not all of the poems are religious, nor is the reader bound to follow the daily order. In fact if you desire, you can read any poem in the book on any day, finding a proper devotion as you see fit, following Jesus' declaration that we all have "free will!" I have included my interpretation of the Lord's Prayer in the beginning pages to be used in a devotional!

Enhance your devotional with a Hymn from the center of the book!

Book Summary

You will feel the inspiration of Jesus when you read the poems in this book.
The poet points to a lifelong love of limericks as the influence behind his poetic
endeavors......they are religious largely inspired by his Christian upbringing
. Although his first poem was written at the age of 82, a desire to share his
love for Jesus poetically has resulted in a large collection of poems not only
about Jesus but also about everyday events in the long life of a dedicated
Christian . The poet follows strict rules in that all the poems rhyme and
are so constructed that they make excellent lyrical and metrical subjects for
reading to others. You may be so inclined but if not, try it.....you'll like it!

Contents *January*

1. First Things First 1
2. A Broken Heart...2
3. A New Year Is Underway...3
4. A Plan For Today...4
5. A Prayer For A Friend..5
6. A Triple Crown Affair..6
7. A Valuable Asset...7
8. There's A Fork In The Road To Eternity......................8
9. All Through The Years..9
10. An Ode To Pastor Sam...10
11. Are We All Wet or What?..11
12. Are We In Trouble...12
13. Are We Sorry?..13
14. Time Is Of The Essence..14
15. Are You Being Responsible...15
16. Are You In Touch..16
17. Are You Ready...17
18. Are You Still In Doubt?...18
19. Are You Worthy...19
20. As I See It..20
21. I'm Sure Moses Is Proud Of Martin...........................21
22. Pray With Confidence...22
23. Be On Guard...23
24. Be Prepared, Don't Be Scared....................................24
25. Be Sure Your Soul Is Always Ready............................25
26. Beware But Be Aware..26
27. Beyond The Pearly Gates..27
28. Can We Dodge The Bullet?...28
29. Can You Pass The Test?...29
30. Jesus And His Friends...30
31. C'est La Vie...31

First Things First

The first day of the year is here again so we must begin anew
To make our plans and resolutions for things we want to do.
We lived up to what we resolved last year, did not skip a one.
Some of them required persistence but most of them were fun!

It feels real good to reach our goals, to hold our head up high.
Don't resolve to reach the moon unless you expect to fly.
Even then you may fall short and have to change your plans,
But if you're bound to travel pick out some nearby foreign lands!

If you're like me you've been abroad but you haven't seen it all.
Most of your travels are limited to the nearby downtown mall.
Pick out a resort and pack your bag, be sure to take your phone.
Always include your significant other, you dare not travel alone!

Most of us won't have to travel for we have things to do at home.
Just ask the "speaker of the house" and you won't have to roam.
These are made to order projects but don't fit your "bucket list,"
But once your mate outlines everything she won't have to insist!

Oh yes, our home is certainly our castle and we like for it to be,
The envy of the neighborhood and a delight for all to see.
When visitors come and enter the door, the tour will then begin.
Just be sure you've put your playthings away, that would be a sin!

When the day is over, I think I'm through, resolutions are all made.
Next year is going to be a struggle, I'm sure some of them will fade.
Home Depot and Lowe's will send me invitations, come back for more,
I'll be parking on their doorstep waiting for them to open the door!

A Broken Heart

Have you ever had a broken heart, one that would not mend?
Sometimes it makes you feel so bad you wish the world would end.
Don't despair, there is a cure, but it may take a while.
While you're healing, play the field, don't let it cramp your style!

Victims of a broken heart sometimes can't take the heat.
Drastic measures won't help the cause, you must accept defeat.
The object of a failed romance is better left alone.
Stay out of sight and for goodness sake, stay off the telephone!

The only treatment that I know about comes to us from above.
It is the real live loving touch of Jesus with His love.
He takes our wounded heart with Him and gives it tender care.
When He returns it with His love, it's now in good repair!

Most broken hearts are victims of a badly failed affair.
We're better off to take our lumps, it's really not so rare.
Find a lonesome someone who's a victim too, and get back on the ball.
When one door closes it is true, another opens, you won't miss out at all!

I know for sure without a doubt, that Jesus plays a hand.
He keeps in touch with all our moves and helps us when He can.
Don't ever be afraid to call on Him, He loves to be of aid,
And all of those with broken hearts will remember the price He paid!

Broken hearts and broken dreams are somewhat much the same.
They both result from sad affairs, it's hard to place the blame.
It's best if we will just admit, if we want to survive,
After all that we've been through, we're lucky to be alive!

A New Year Is Underway

It's the third day of the new year, things seem to be on track.
Resolutions that we made are set in stone, there is no turning back.
Hold on, you say, you need more time, can you have another day?
Just ask the Judge, He's up in Heaven, get on your knees and pray!

Today is one of those crucial times when plans are being made.
We all will doubtless need some help, where can we get some aid?
Don't let yourself be misled by the forces that seek your doom,
Just follow the Master of our fate, He's in that "Upper Room!"

The greatest power the world has ever known is now at our command.
We have access this very day to the King of the "Promised Land."
Don't feel you must do the planning all alone, He is by your side.
Don't be afraid to ask for help for Jesus wants to be your guide!

When I look back upon my life and view where I have been,
I'm still around by the Grace of God, for Jesus is my friend.
I've made some decisions that were wrong and I see in afterthought,
That without Jesus helping me, much damage I could have wrought!

I offer thanks right here and now to Jesus and all my friends.
Some wonderful folks have "gone aloft" to a life that never ends.
To all of us, as we begin this New Year, let's take Jesus by the hand .
He'll lead our precious USA to the future with good leaders in command!

Some folks say I mix my religion with too much politics,
But you can be sure that I haven't joined a bunch of heretics.
I always pray that Jesus will help our leaders keep our nation whole,
While He continues to provide to each of us, salvation of our soul!

January 4.

A Plan For Today

Speak to Jesus right away when you wake up each day,
Let Him know you're still around, He'll hear you when you pray.
Tell Him all about your problems and ask for His advice.
Don't wait until your troubles mount and you can't pay the price!

Jesus wants us all to lead a life that's free of sin,
So we must always let Him know the kind of fix we're in.
It would work much better if we'd just tell Him in advance
What it is we're about to do and what's the circumstance!

Everyone should know and be aware that Jesus knows our plan
And we should also know that He'll always help us if He can.
Tell Jesus what you're striving for and ask if He approves.
There may be a better way, He says, if you just make some moves!

Jesus was a carpenter, a working man like me.
I'm sure He was a crafty man, there in Galilee.
He doesn't speak a lot about those days when He was young.
We've heard much more about the cross on which He hung!

I love to talk with Jesus and hear Him call my name.
Without His love and good advice life would not have been the same.
I've always tried to do what's right, to help some others too.
I'm thankful that Jesus has been close by to tell me what to do!

It's wonderful to have the Lord to tell me I'm okay.
Without the love He's shown for me I wouldn't be here today.
I need to pray to let Him know that He is still my King.
I love you Lord with all my heart and thanks for everything!

January 5.

A Prayer For A Friend

Dedicated to the family of Bruce John Cartier

Goodbye Bruce my very dear friend.
You have reached a very glorious end.
You can bet we'll miss your smiling face,
But you are now at home in a wonderful place!

I'm sure that dear Jesus took your hand,
And led you down that road to the Promised Land.
In the twinkling of an eye He cured your ills.
No longer must you take those pills!

There comes a time when we all must go.
Our days must end down here below.
We leave behind our family and friends,
But we go to that land where life never ends!

We never know when our time will come.
Today for many, tomorrow for some.
They are waiting in Heaven for us to arrive.
All our friends who've died and gone are now alive!

We who love Jesus are said to be born again.
At that birth He takes away all our sin.
We start life anew in the Promised Land,
Where Jesus will greet us with a helping hand!

So Bruce, I really don't want to say "goodbye."
That word always upsets and makes me cry.
So I'll just say once more, "so long my friend,
It's just the beginning and not the end!

January 6.

A Triple Crown Affair

I've been around the world and back but I like it here at home.
As I've aged I've settled down and am not so inclined to roam,
But yes, I still like to travel to see things I've heard about.
I do like to sleep in my own bed, of that there is no doubt!

A major perk of travelling is the chance to make new friends.
You broaden your horizon and of course friendship never ends.
Sometimes new friends I make are friends of friends I've had before.
Renewing contacts that had been lost bring back days of yore!

Let's all admit right here and now we like to think about the past.
We keep scrapbooks about our yesterdays for memories fade so fast.
We pause to reminisce as we come to a happy smiling face.
It may be someone who's now in Heaven, their memory you can't erase!

We've just returned from a wonderful trip to the mountains of our state.
Chetola Lodge in Blowing Rock, the venue, and it was first rate,
To celebrate the birthday of an American Icon, Bob Timberlake his name,
Known around the world for his talents which have brought him fame!

This was an "Our State Magazine" affair, for which they're famous too.
They like to feature "home grown" things of interest to me and you.
This magazine should be a coffee table staple in everybody's home.
If you read it cover to cover then you won't need to roam!

Bring all the ingredients together in one place and you have all you need.
"Home grown" Bob Timberlake, worthy of honor in our state indeed.
Chetola Lodge was last week the most interesting place to be,
Sponsored by "Our State Magazine" known from the mountains to the sea!

A Valuable Asset

I find it hard to write about and yet it's as simple as can be.
A very valuable thing it's true and it's given to us free.
It's handed to us every day and we all will get the same.
Use it or lose it is a rule and we all must play the game!

You cannot put it in the bank you have to use it now.
Making plans for using it is tough, it isn't when but how.
You can sit and let it multiply but it will only melt away.
Just like that ice cube always does once it leaves the tray!

Our package of this asset is given to us early every day.
It behooves us well to get up early and start to make it pay.
A sleepy head is penalized and pays a hefty price.
Participation is required and it's not like shooting dice!

Although everyone has the same amount some say it's not enough
For them to finish what they started they often need more stuff.
Complaints arise, you've heard them all, it's usually an excuse,
But when you really boil it down it has to do with use!

Although the packages that we all get have equal content therein,
Some folks just waste the contents and don't know how to begin.
You see them sitting on a park bench throwing their assets away.
For some this is a way of life and they pursue it day by day!

This asset that we are given every day comes to us from above.
It's worth much more than its weight in gold and comes to us with love.
We never know how much is left in our account it's not for us to say.
When we've used up all our T I M E we'll go to Heaven to stay!

January 8.

There's A Fork In The Road To Eternity

The devil is alive and well he's loading transports bound for hell.
Don't buy a ticket, he's got so many he needs to sell,
That he'll soon be giving them away just to suck you in.
If you accept, you're on the hook, heading for a life of sin!

Please don't buy his bill of goods keep searching for a better choice.
Somewhere in the marketplace you're bound to hear the Master's voice.
That soothing tone is crystal clear and a sweet message it conveys.
This is something you can accept and it offers brighter days!

The devil won't give up without a fight, on that one you can bet.
He's got lots of things to offer that you haven't even seen just yet.
He's putting more agents on the job but offering the same old pitch.
Just sign your name on the dotted line my friend and we will make you rich!

To so many folks that's an offer too good for them to refuse.
They figure, "Oh what the hell, what have I got to lose?"
They board the first transport that comes along and soon are on their way.
It's not too long before they discover that someone always has to pay!

In the meantime Jesus is hard at work using a very different approach.
He is offering a different class of goods that's certified above reproach.
When you sign in with Him you soon will earn your set of wings,
And when you first set foot in Heaven's gate the Hallelujah Chorus sings!

We all do have a choice you know, which fork in the road do we take.
One fork is the wide open road to hell, please don't make that mistake.
Please take the narrow one that leads uphill, let Jesus take your hand.
You see, that becomes the "golden road" that leads us to the Promised Land!

All Through The Years

I know that Jesus wants me to write about His love for us.
It's all about that perfect love that raised us from the dust.
Jesus learned His lessons well and knew what He must do,
To teach us all that God is love and that fact we know is true!

Mankind began with Adam, his story we know quite well.
We can trace his family until today, there is a lot to tell.
The Old Testament is his record book, it contains his family tree.
A new book started when Jesus came, another of God's decree!

Jesus studied the Old Testament and spoke of things to come.
He talked about His Father's love and about our Heavenly home.
He formed a tight-knit group of men, Apostles they were called.
When they gathered to hear Him speak crowds were quite enthralled!

Jesus had but three short years to get His story told.
His followers loved to hear Him speak about the men of old.
They formed a fellowship that will never die, it flourishes today,
And we still celebrate His lowly birth, it's known as Christmas day!

The New Testament tells the story of Jesus' life on earth.
I've never heard a single soul refute the story of His birth.
Our Holy Bible, the Old, The New, the greatest story ever told,
Continues to sustain us every day, it's worth its weight in gold!

If you want to have a happy life then place your trust in Him,
The one that God sent as a Babe to take away our sin.
Don't let the evil forces of this world change your good outlook.
You can always find an answer in the Bible, that very precious book!

January 10.

An Ode To Pastor Sam

I like to think of days gone by when I was just a kid.
Life for everyone was pleasant then and we enjoyed what we did.
It's true we had some problems but all were within our reach.
If we could make it through the week we'd get to hear Sam Sox preach!

Now Pastor Sam was my dearest friend, he taught me quite a lot.
He was my mentor in many ways his advice was the best I ever got.
My Mom and Dad, they loved him too, for he was a friend to all.
Never too busy to sit and chat, always at your "beck and call"!

Sam and I played lots of golf, it was our favorite sport.
Neither of us were very good, that's true I must report,
But we would always do our best to play a decent game.
The good thing was we were at fault, there was no one else to blame!

This man Sam was big and strong and swung a mighty club.
His technique was quite unique and resulted in many a flub.
My inept attempt to shoot a "bird" was short of every need.
While I uttered a modest curse word Sam's strongest was "garden seed"!

Sam used that epithet quite freely and I found it quite okay.
I've used it too in my entire life and I still use it even today.
It keeps me from saying things that Jesus would never condone,
And I find it helps express a certain point of view even if I'm alone!

I look forward to seeing Pastor Sam when I reach Heaven's shore.
I hope that he'll be real nearby when I walk through the door.
I'm sure he joins with all the Saints to aid Jesus in the fight
To help all of us still here on earth to reach Heaven by doing what is right!

January 11.

Are We All Wet or What?

I feel a need to write today but don't know what to say.
It's not that I'm at a loss for words I've never been that way.
I'd prefer to talk about those things that I love best,
Like family and friends, sunshine and flowers that all bring happiness!

With all the rain that's come our way we're waterlogged for sure.
Our ponds are full, the grass is green the drought now has a cure.
As Noah surveys the scene he'll remember days aboard the Ark,
When he was waiting for the rain to stop so they could disembark!

Our plight is certainly nowhere near as dire as those days long ago,
But we will have some cases here and there of suffering and woe.
If the rain continues as it has it's possible that it will flood.
We won't beat Noah's record, not even close, but we'll have lots of mud!

Let's look upon the good sides of the heavy rains we've had.
We've already erased the deficit which makes us all real glad.
When rays of sunshine are shining through and flowers digest the rain,
The beauty of our gardens will give us reasons to smile once again!

The poet has said that God did not promise sun without rain,
Nor flower strewn pathways leading to joy without pain,
But He sent His Son Jesus as a gift to all mankind,
The greatest gift that anyone would ever be able to find!

We must be truly thankful for every part of God's plan,
The sunshine and the rain that benefits our fellow man,
And Jesus is now with God in Heaven preparing our future home,
So we'll have a beautiful place there with Him when we cease to roam!

January 12.

Are We In Trouble

Don't forget to say "Thank You Lord" before you end your day,
For every day is a gift from Him for which we do not pay.
He paid the price upon the Cross to save us all from sin,
And all He expects of us is to hear us say "Thank You" again!

Our leaders cannot solve our problems but do not seek our advice.
They always think they know best and let the poor folks pay the price.
Decisions are often bought and paid for by those who have the gold,
While the needy folks who could use some help are left out in the cold!

Okay, there are two sides to everything, but influence paves the way.
It's cash upon the barrelhead if you have something worthwhile to say.
It seems that those who have the most are inclined to want much more.
Too bad if you can't pay your way, you can't get in the door!

Our country is falling behind the rest of the world at large.
Our industrial might fled abroad which is why they are now in charge.
Our labor force has lost its power and the workers are losing their clout.
It seems that the new industrial credo is "let them do without!"

Unemployment rules the roost our government must foot the bill.
A mighty struggle is taking place down there on Capitol Hill.
The have's won't pay their fair share so have not's are forced to pay.
There is no equality there at all, that's not the American way!

We can't maintain the present course which is already very bad,
I saw it happen once before when I was just a lad.
Our leaders can reverse the course if they will just do what's right.
Otherwise our Nation will go down the drain and fade into the night!

January 13.

Are We Sorry?

Who was the man who nailed Him to the "tree?"
Can't you just imagine the pain there had to be?
Not just the pain for Jesus, which was real,
But for the man who placed the nails we ask how did he feel?

I'm sure that poor man suffered regardless of his fate.
Jesus asked God to forgive him, He wasn't one to hate.
I like to think that man felt sorry for what he had to do,
That when Jesus died he removed the nails, he felt he needed to!

Jesus died on that cross as payment for "our" sin.
All of us who believe in Him are the ones who always win.
For over two thousand years the story has been told.
It's a wonderful true story and one that never gets old!

Sometimes we are just like him, the man who placed the nails.
We cause pain for Jesus and we're the one who fails.
We ask for His forgiveness, get on our knees and pray,
And that is what we need to do today and every day!

January 14.

Time Is Of The Essence

We know that time is fleeting Lord, at the very best.
There seems we hardly have enough time to get our needed rest,
But we always have the time when there's somewhere we must go,
And we all do seem to have enough time as we're rushing to and fro!

We might ask, "Whats the need for all this haste?"
If we move around too fast there'll be a lot of waste.
We all must slow down so we can catch our breath.
You know that at the speed of light we'd be scared to death!

In our world today we have all these possessions we call "things",
But we are still missing the peace and quiet that moving slowly brings.
Would we be better off if we all knew how to fly?
I'm sure there would be a lot of mishaps and folks would surely die!

As you move about each day do others slow you down?
Has it gotten to the point where you never go downtown?
Traffic too is such a hassle that the lines are long and slow.
Many times you have the feeling that you'd rather stay home than go!

However, go you must for you're always out of this or that.
The shopping center is real nearby, just fifteen minutes flat.
You're there and back before you know you didn't lose much time.
That's good because it's fleeting Lord and to lose it is a crime!

We need to savor every day Lord which You give us as a gift.
We need to say hello to all our friends since it might give them a lift.
Plan each day to use it wisely with the freedom that it poses,
But never forget the most important of all, "take time to smell the roses!"

January 15.

Are You Being Responsible

The beauty of the earth today is almost beyond compare.
There's nothing else quite like it that I know of anywhere.
I look around at my domain and see the pretty flowers.
It's hard for me sometimes to believe that they are really ours!

I know however that Rosemary, my sweet wife, has begun her day.
She's out there in the garden patch where she loves to pay
Her respects to Jesus as she moves from bush to vine,
Inspecting all those beautiful flowers that give her peace of mind!

She's one of those who knows what to do and has a magic touch.
She knows just how much pruning to do and never does too much.
At the end of the day in the setting sun the garden is pristine.
I'm sure that Jesus loves to rest His eyes upon that beautiful scene!

I feel privileged and fortunate too, to live in this wonderland,
Where we have such beautiful scenes under our command.
It concerns me quite a bit to see our littered countryside,
Where many folks are too inclined to spread trash far and wide!

That's one price we have to pay for the freedom that we know.
We have laws that are easily broken by Tom and Bill and Joe.
They're not mean, they just don't care, they're busy with other things.
They throw their coffee cup aside as if it was equipped with wings!

Each of us must do our part to preserve our beautiful land.
We must be sure that we don't let disposal of trash get out of hand.
Mow your lawn and trim your hedge until it looks like new.
Your neighbors and the passers-by will be real proud of you!

January 16.

Are You In Touch

When you feel you just can't go on don't even think that you're alone.
The help you need is always near and your Best Friend is the One.
He's never too busy to talk to you that's one thing He loves to do.
So bow your head and tell Him what you need and it will soon come true!

It doesn't matter what's troubling you for the devil is always at work too.
He doesn't want you to live in peace and has things to offer you.
He likes to strike if you're feeling low when you have doubt of where to go.
He'll fight Jesus for your soul, it's up to you to tell him "no"!

Life can be beautiful but life can be sad we have choices to make each day.
We're always choosing what we think is best but how to know who's to say.
We don't have to be in trouble to ask Jesus to come to our aid.
He's always close by and always willing to bless the plans we've made!

Our life on earth is but a training ground for eternity, by and by.
We'll all be transformed when our time comes in the twinkling of an eye.
From birth to death a series of circumstance determine our destiny,
But we must make those choices that tell what our life will be!

It's been said that "no man is an island" and it's true we're not alone.
Too often when we need some help we run to the nearest phone.
I have found in my many years that my best help comes in prayer.
When I bow my head to pray and call His Name He's right there!

Some folks hear me talk or read my poems and say that I'm naïve.
They say that what they hear me say is not what they believe.
Just let me say right now, "I'm no Saint" and I don't profess to be
Anything but a friend of Jesus who'll join Him in Heaven for eternity!

Are You Ready

When I hear birds singing in the tree, I thank Thee Lord.
On days when I stay busy as a bee, I thank Thee Lord.
If I can move about without much pain, I thank Thee Lord.
For all the very welcome rain, I thank Thee Lord!

If we kneel and praise the Lord all day it wouldn't pay the bill.
You see we'll never thank Him near enough, that is until
That glorious day we see Him face to Face and He says "I forgive,"
And we can thank Him with all our love and settle down to live!

There is no way we can imagine what awaits us when we die.
We travel light, no bags to pack it's in the "twinkling of an eye."
I cannot describe what we will see my words will fail the test,
But I know that Heaven is where I want to spend my eternal rest!

Some few folks have had a glimpse of Heaven and then returned.
They have written books that tell the story of all the things they learned.
I know that everything they tell about is part of Jesus' story.
I love to read their account of seeing Him and Heaven in all its glory!

Let's face it folks we're not equipped to understand it all.
As human beings with no spiritual power we must wait for Jesus' call.
I'm sure He can see us well even when we try to hide.
That's how He can meet our need so quickly standing by our side!

So, never fear, He's always near, be sure to stay in touch.
Just don't forget to say your prayers, He loves us very much.
Never forget our destination and let Jesus know we care,
So when they call the roll in Heaven, we'll be sure that we are there!

Birthday of #3 Grandson Dawson Bristol   1996
Birthday of #6 Grandson Christian Opitz   2001

January 18.

Are You Still In Doubt?

We all crave confirmation of all the things that we believe.
When someone returns from Heaven our fears are much relieved.
Don Piper has written books about his trip and that's enough for me.
I'm convinced that "Heaven Is Real" where my soul will spend eternity!

Anyone who still has doubts should read his books and then
Renew their pledge to Jesus who will save their soul from sin.
Meantime we all must do our best to help all those in need,
For Jesus says it is our duty to do our part to end the world of greed!

We are given our entire life to accept Jesus as our friend.
It bothers me to see those folks who don't believe and deny Him to the end.
Will they get a "final chance" before the Judge to say "please let me in?"
The fires of hell are stoked with souls of many who weren't forgiven of sin!

I know some will say, "Who are you to tell me what I must believe?"
Well, dear friend, it's my Christian duty to pay for the mercy I receive.
It's quite true that we cannot "earn" our way to Heaven, it's not for sale,
But every soul we help Jesus save will surely reduce our "bail!"

The Scales of Justice are used to measure the sentence we will receive.
You'll find that many are seeking "Justice", they're ones who don't believe,
But those of us who know the truth seek "Mercy" for our soul.
Salvation for all of us is why Christ died and should always be our goal!

I still have a question about that "final chance" but some will wait to see.
I prefer to give my soul to Jesus now to guarantee "eternity"
In Heaven with Him in the comfort of the home which He prepared
For those of us who believe in Him and show we really cared!

January 19.

Are You Worthy

When I think of Jesus' Love my cares just float away.
Even though I'm not wealthy I can't let that ruin my day.
I can pay my bills on time and that will help my credit score.
I'm just as happy as most of those who are worth a whole lot more!

Being wealthy is not a sin but "loving" money is taboo.
The proper use of what you have is the only way to do.
Rich or poor, all dead men are the same which may not be bad.
Jesus cares not what you had but what you did with what you had!

No one on earth would be hungry if the wealth was spread around,
But thousands die every day because there was no food to be found.
Ones who die of hunger will go to Heaven and Jesus will feed their soul.
The rich may not be happy in Heaven, they're lost without their gold!

God did not put us here on earth without a guide for how to live.
The Bible tells us in many ways how much we are to give.
He feeds the birds in the air and fish in the sea, humans have free will,
In many ways we don't worry about the cost until we receive the bill!

Our election process is tainted by all the money that one spends.
Sometimes the outcome is bought outright, it just all depends.
Can they get by and hide the source, they will if they can.
We'll never know, come what may, who was the better man!

Tickets to Heaven are not for sale, not at any price.
You must earn your way, in fact by being extremely nice.
It doesn't matter how much you have but how much you give away.
That's the only way to make that trip and that is how you pay.

As I See It

What would I do without Jesus I'd be lost for sure.
I couldn't make it out of bed without looking for a cure.
There is no way that I could get along without Him as my Guide.
I'd be as blind as a bat if He was not always at my side!

You say you don't believe in God, I sure pity you my friend.
Where will you go to spend eternity when you reach the end?
Oh, eternity is a myth, you say, when you die you're dead.
Not for me, it's not the end, for I see great things ahead!

I want to walk and talk with Jesus and have Him hold my hand.
He's promised me that He will lead me to the "Promised Land."
Now that's the place I want to go, it's there in Heaven you see.
That's where my Heavenly Home will be, prepared by Him for me!

It's there I'll sit and talk with both my Grandpa's, I know they're friends.
A most wonderful part of being in Heaven is that life there never ends.
You see, eternity means "forever" and that gives us plenty of time,
To see all our family and old friends, my, won't that be sublime?

We can also work with Jesus in helping others to make the grade,
Just like all those Saints who helped me in life for which I've not repaid,
And all of us can join the choir for music always fills the air.
It's the most wonderful place we can imagine and it awaits us there!

My thoughts of Heaven I know fall short, much nicer 'twill be by far,
And it awaits us, one and all, when we have "crossed the bar."
I say to everyone I know, "get ready for that day,
When we all will meet again in Heaven and we'll be there to stay"!

I'm Sure Moses Is Proud Of Martin

Martin Luther King, Jr. was a black man, his soul was white as snow.
Jesus washed it clean in His own Blood two thousand years ago.
Martin sacrificed his life, as Jesus did, for members of mankind.
A greater hero of his own people would be difficult to find!

I'm sure Martin is busy now helping Jesus bring folks into the fold.
To bring all folks to Heaven when they die is a very worthy goal.
They were both completely color blind when looking at someone's skin.
They're major objective, "fair play for all" and "saving souls from sin!"

Martin was a worldly player along with Mandela and Tutu.
He fought for equal treatment of all who had them to look up to.
Martin put himself in harm's way with no thought of a real danger.
In the end his life here on earth was ended by actions of a stranger!

Martin, Jr.'s legacy is found in the eloquence of his word.
His memory is alive forever through the powerful speeches we heard.
None could tell a story better than Martin when he began to preach.
The crowd who gathered to hear was as far as the eye could reach!

The USA is a better place because of Martin's dedication.
Slavery and oppression are in the past and we have better education.
Barack Obama as President was possible because of Martin's work.
There's no discrimination on the job now based on race, it's no perk!

When you think of heroes look no further than Selma, Alabama,
Then look to Washington, D.C. where you'll find Barack Obama.
No longer a matter of civil rights we all now respect each other.
Black and white men are no longer reluctant to be called "brother!"

Martin Luther King Day

Pray With Confidence

Where would we be without the Lord?
He taught us all from God's own word.
He's there to lead us through each day.
All we're required to do is pray!

Don't be afraid to say your prayers.
It's just us talking to the "Man" upstairs!
Jesus loves to hear us pray.
He'd be happy to listen if we prayed all day!

Some folks are eloquent when they're on their knees,
But most are humble and have simple pleas.
It doesn't matter much "just how" you pray,
Just tell Jesus what's on your mind today!

Gather up all the cares that fill your heart.
He'll lighten your load right from the start.
It may not be easy for you to begin.
Just remember, He'll cleanse your heart from sin!

Your day will be brighter with God on your side.
You can smile and relax, hold your head up with pride.
Remember that He's with you wherever you go.
He'll be there to guide you if you need to know!

Beginning your day with a prayer on your mind,
You'll get a head start and won't fall behind.
Keep up the friendship you've established with God.
If your name's in His Book, that won't seem so odd!

Be On Guard

God alone has tender mercy for protection of your soul.
He sent His Son, Dear Jesus Christ to lead us to our goal.
No one but Jesus is free of sin and we weren't born that way.
Our Mom and Dad conceived in sin and so we all must pay!

When Jesus died upon the cross it was His sacrifice.
The greatest gift we've ever had and Jesus paid the price.
We must entrust our lives to Him, He will save our soul.
No matter that we sin each day, if we repent He will make us whole!

Satan takes the "other" side and offers us the world.
He'll take us on a jolly ride that sets our hearts awhirl.
We must all reject Satan's plan, as Jesus did as well.
Satan's recruiting a brand new crew to stoke the fires of Hell!

Our world is such a sinful place we have to stay on guard.
Enticements come in every form and invade our own backyard,
So we must give our lives to Jesus and let Him lead the way,
He's always waiting for us to call, that's why He taught us how to pray!

Don't be bashful, don't be shy, we'll all meet Jesus by and by.
We can't delay, must not be late, none of us know when we will die.
We must all be well prepared, confess our sins and ask that we be spared.
Jesus Himself will speak with God, they'll both be happy that we cared!

We must never forget, considering all, that the world's a wonderful place.
God made it all in just one week, a beautiful home for the human race.
Jesus came to show the way and had compassion for us all.
Now it's up to us to show respect, for this beautiful terrestrial ball!

Be Prepared, Don't Be Scared

Brighter days are coming and there's bound to be a change.
Get your house in order and if needbe please rearrange.
Take advantage of the coming boom, sweep losses out the door.
It's going to be a jolly ride say those who're keeping score!

There's more money afloat in the USA than there has ever been.
It's in the hands of very few but I see a changing trend.
Midas once had tons of gold but it proved to be his downfall.
Our wealthy folks will soon see the light and begin to help us all!

There's nothing like a "wake-up" call to open up some eyes.
The status quo has naught to offer, that certainly is no surprise.
Our money supply must be put to work, that's how it earns its keep.
While that money invested is helping others more earnings it will reap!

Nothing stirs the business pot like pay checks being spent.
Jack and Jill can buy a house instead of paying rent.
A real estate boom will reach new heights, never seen before.
People will be anxious to go shopping again after being so poor!

There'll be a trading frenzy in the market I can feel it in my bones.
Retirement funds will climb again and rescue our dear Dow Jones.
Double dips will be turning flips as an upside paves the way.
When rich folks put their wealth to work, that will save the day!

How do we get this message out to those who must take the lead?
Word of mouth from the bottom up is just the thing we need.
So speak to those who pull the "strings" that will plant the seed.
I mean "purse strings" which must be opened to do away with greed!

January 25.

Be Sure Your Soul Is Always Ready

Our soul departs our body the very moment that we die.
We're not aware of travelling but we move quickly through the sky.
When our soul arrives at Heaven's Gate we'll see folks that we know.
Soon thereafter we'll talk with Jesus who will tell us where to go!

We know that He has prepared a place for all of us to live.
We'll be there for eternity and we should all be ready to give
All our love and time and talent to Jesus, who will take our hand,
And lead us to our Heavenly Home there in the "Promised Land!"

There'll be so much for us to do, we never will get bored.
There's always something to be done, you just ask the Lord.
Heaven is such a beautiful place and everyone does their share.
We all will have everything we need and there's no greed anywhere!

Our soul remains a target of the devil as long as we're alive.
He tempts us all with dreams of wealth which never does arrive.
Too many people starve to death while others count their gold.
The souls of those who starve will rest in Heaven before they're very old!

We spend a lot of money on our health to keep our body strong.
We overlook the nurturing of our soul when we help others get along.
I've got mine, that's all I need, seems to be the newest creed.
Our souls be damned, that game that's played and fills us up with greed!

You better not tinker with your soul for that is God's Domain.
We must be ready at all times for we may not long remain
Here on the earth with all its faults and with the devil still at large.
So get prepared, yes, today my friend, and let Jesus be in charge!

January 26.

Beware But Be Aware

I like to express my thoughts in rhyme.
It always helps me to pass the time.
I like to tell those stories too
About dear Jesus who loves me and you!

I write my poems so that all will see
That there's a place in Heaven for you and me.
I'm looking forward to being up there
The wonders of Jesus for us to share!

Are you having trouble believing it's true?
You just don't feel that it applies to you?
It's time dear friend that you must choose,
You have Heaven to gain and nothing to lose!

The problems on our earth are proof that the devil is at large,
Trying to win our souls to show that he's the one in charge.
The devil promotes the greed and the greedy pollute our land,
Producing disasters all around like the one that's now at hand!

God is love and it's so true, that says it plain and clear.
The devil on the other hand deals in things that we should fear.
The devil brings on the dirty work and takes a mighty toll.
Oh yes, the devil interferes as we search for oil and coal!

Please don't despair, make your choice, which one to select.
Also keep in mind at all times the best ones to elect.
You see, our leaders are the ones we look to every day,
But Jesus is the leader of everyone, the one to whom we pray!

January 27.

Beyond The Pearly Gates

There is nothing that can compare
With love we'll find out there,
In that lovely place that lies
Beyond the "Pearly Gates!"

Jesus told us all about that place
While He was here on earth,
And said that He would take us there,
When we each had met our fates!

I wish that I could have been
Among those folks of old,
Who saw dear Jesus in the flesh
And heard the stories He told!

He talked of Heaven in glowing terms.
He sure described it well,
And said that if we followed Him
He'd take us there to dwell!

God Himself is always there
Upon His Throne of Gold.
Along with Jesus, His dear Son
And all the Saints of old!

Now I don't know 'bout you my friend,
But I want you to know,
That I am working hard to be
Among those that get to go!

January 28.

Can We Dodge The Bullet?

No one eats as well as I, my wife just loves to cook.
She knows the recipes by heart and doesn't need a book.
She memorized her favorite dishes and adds a personal touch.
The Good Lord blesses all our food and I always eat too much!

Jesus tells me that it's a sin and I need to cut way back.
If I don't get things under control I'll have a heart attack.
When Rosemary serves, I lose my nerve and I dig right in.
I pray that Jesus will smell the food and forgive me of my sin!

I do try to think of others when we sit down to eat.
I always say a prayer to Jesus and offer Him a seat.
"Come Lord Jesus be our guest" and please bless our food.
This gets us started right and gets us in the mood!

There's nothing that can erase the thoughts of all the hungry people.
We have them here in our own town in sight of our church steeple.
We do try to feed the poor, but many starve each day.
An awful lot of food is wasted there must be a better way!

Today our country is in trouble we're really on the brink.
Some fat cats don't pay their way and we're drowning in red ink.
Desperate people do desperate things, I just hope we can sustain
A modicum of civil control when our country goes down the drain!

Never in our history has so much been in the hands of so few.
They're not using it to help mankind which God asks them to do.
I'd sure hate to be in Jesus' shoes and have to be the judge,
And be the One to call the shot to make those people budge!

Can You Pass The Test?

Our life down here on earth is just a testing ground.
Jesus wants to know if we're the kind He wants to have around.
Our life in Heaven will never end so we must pass His test,
And that means that we must resolve to always do our best!

The story goes that George Washington never told a lie.
I have to say, "Good for him, he did much better than I,"
But I know that for sure, Jesus was the One Who never lied.
He lived an absolutely "Perfect Life" and for our life He died!

You can be sure that all of Jesus' words were clad in solid gold,
And worth more to those who do believe than what the rich folks hold.
Ten Commandments formed His Creed He practiced what He preached,
And when He died upon the Cross His sacrifice for us was reached!

Another test that Jesus used was the beautiful Golden Rule.
If you use it every day, it becomes a very useful tool.
He taught very many other things that also were tried and true.
If you want to follow Him you'll know just what you must do!

When Jesus spoke, the crowds approved and blessed His Holy Name.
They listened to His every Word and that is precisely why He came,
To teach the lowly rank and file all about God's Love,
And let them know what they must do to go to Heaven above!

So ask yourself, here and now, will you be able to pass the test?
Can Jesus count on you each day to do your very best?
He has a place awaiting us in Heaven, you know He said it's true.
I have a place for everyone and that certainly means me and you!

Jesus And His Friends

It will not matter if or where I'm buried, I'll be long gone by then.
My soul will be in Heaven where my new life will begin.
Our earthly body is a fragile shell and wasn't meant to last.
It truly has no further use once our days on earth are past!

Just be realistic and face the facts, who wants to hang around?
I know that I am going to Heaven so don't put me in the ground.
I look forward to meeting the Saints and hearing their tales of woe.
Those things they wrote of Biblical days continue to guide us here below!

I want to talk with Saint Paul about his shipwreck on the sea.
He landed on the island of Malta, a pleasant place to be.
He taught the natives about dear Jesus, they're strong believers today.
I spent three years there myself, I lived near Saint Paul's Bay!

I hope I get to speak with Jesus and thank Him for His Love.
He gave His life that we might join Him up in Heaven above.
He died so young, just thirty-three, and yet He lives today.
God sacrificed His Only Son, to show all of us the way!

The good things that we learned about the Bible from those Saints of old,
They were the things that they learned from the stories that Jesus told.
They also told stories of their travels which were far and wide.
As they travelled they were never alone for Jesus was by their side!

The Crucifixion was not the end but the beginning of Jesus' reign.
He sent the Disciples off on their missions to teach not loss but gain.
That's why they're known as Christian Saints and worthy of our praise.
They were the ones who taught mankind to pray for better days!

January 31.

C'est La Vie

Life is neat when you don't cheat but do the things you should.
No need to worry about your past if you've been real good.
Think about the little things, they're often left undone,
And don't forget to thank the Lord, the most important one!

A person who's happy with their life has little to regret.
Don't spend your time by being sad and trying to forget.
Just put on a happy face and hold your head up high.
Let people know you're not concerned if death is drawing nigh!

We move along from day to day and try to keep in touch,
With all our friends who're still around, the ones we love so much.
To shake their hand and see them smile, a sunbeam 'tis for sure.
God blesses all our friendships and helps them to endure!

When we are young and in our prime we often fail to pray.
It seems we just don't have the time and put it off today.
We need to plan more, well ahead, and have some time to rest.
Can't burn the candle from both ends, we'll wind up too depressed!

We must remember, life is tough, unless we plan ahead.
We're always behind and playing catch-up until we fall in bed.
Make a list of things to do and end it with a prayer.
When you're done you'll have the time to sit in your easy chair!

God gives us everyone the same amount of time each day.
He doesn't tell us how to use it, that's for us to say.
He does expect that we will use it for the good of one and all,
To be a help to all mankind on this terrestrial ball!

Contents February

1. Cheer Up And Smile 33
2. Come What May, Every Day Is Welcome 34
3. Conjecture 35
4. Day By Day..36
5. Dear Jesus Is My Hero..37
6. Are You Really Independent 38
7. Did You Cut Down The Cherry Tree..39
8. Divine Protection..40
9. Do We Have The Will..41
10. Do You Believe..42
11. Do You Have The Time..43
12. Following Jesus..44
13. Does Jesus Know Your Plans 45
14. For My Lovely Valentine 46
15. Heavenly Valentines 47
16. Don't Be Ashamed To Ask For Help 48
17. Don't Let The Devil Make You Do It 49
18. Don't Let Worries Worry You 50
19. Dedicated to The Honorable Barack Hussein Obama Our New President.....51
20. The Hazards of Leadership 52
21. Every Day Is Decision Time 53
22. Footsteps In The Sand 54
23. Forgiveness..55
24. Give The Devil His Due And Nothing Else..56
25. God Is..57
26. God Is Still In Charge 58
27. Dreams Of Friends..59
28. Put On Your Happy Face 60

February 1.

Cheer Up And Smile

There is nothing that is much worse than feeling sorry for yourself,
Just place your worries in Jesus' hands get them off that shelf,
Where you have kept them all stacked up, not knowing what to do.
He will help you make a plan that will be the best for you!

You know it's true that we all think that we can do it all.
I suppose it's just a source of pride when we don't have to call
On someone else to solve our problems, but when we face defeat
We find that our best efforts aren't enough and we just can't compete!

We shouldn't wait until we're in trouble to ask Jesus for His aid.
He'd love to help us in our daily lives with all the plans we've made.
Don't let yourself get overwhelmed ask Jesus to get involved.
With His help it won't be long before all your problems are resolved!

Jesus won't try to do your job or to take your place at all,
But He is always willing to help you out, so if need be just call.
He wants us all to be self-reliant and be as happy as we can.
Then we'll have a smiling face when we reach the Promised Land!

It's really sad when I think of all the misery in this world.
Much of it is self-inflicted by a mind that's in a whirl.
Try not let yourself be overcome by things that make you dizzy,
Your "honey do" list should be loaded up with things to keep you busy!

So let me say, in other words, please don't feel sorry for your plight.
Just think of those poor homeless folks who slept outdoors last night.
Say a prayer for all of them and thank Jesus when you pray.
It's because of His great love for us that we're where we are today!

Come What May, Every Day Is Welcome

Do you always see the brighter side or do you wallow in the mud?
When you see problems starting to form can you nip them in the bud?
Not many people have that knack of smiling through the tears,
But it can help you enjoy your day as you greet your advancing years!

None of us like to admit it but we all are growing old.
We do have certain aches and pains but we try to be real bold,
And brag about the fact that we're better off than most.
The fact that we are still alive and kicking is something of which we boast!

At our age, if you've got hair, it's bound to be snow white.
Of course, you can dye it if you wish but it's like day and night.
Some of us don't have much hair but a beautiful head of skin.
We give it lots of tender care but that don't help the fix we're in!

Now if you're vain and want to hide you can wear a fine toupee
But don't dare bend over for anything for that will ruin your day.
It's best to let nature take its course and you can always smile.
In fact no one will notice that you're bald after a little while!

It's best that we have no regrets and remember the good ole days.
Think about all the fun we've had in lots and lots of ways.
Of course we can't always do the things we used to do,
But we can certainly enjoy having a lot of fun trying to!

Be proud of who you are today and help someone if you can.
Live your life to aid mankind you'll be a better man.
The rest of your life can prove to be the best you've ever had,
And you can relax and enjoy your day for it won't be so bad!

February 3.

Conjecture

When we say there is no God, we're taking things too far.
That means we must accept the blame for being like we are.
I cannot be so naïve to think that I'm smart enough to be
Creative and capable of producing a lovely weeping willow tree!

I was allowed to plant seven seeds producing souls on this Earth.
What Adam started I prolonged and presided at their birth.
I take no credit beyond the planting, their Mother tilled the soil.
She tended the garden in which they grew, spending days of toil!

I've been around 'lo these many years but never produced a chicken.
Yes, they're awfully good when fried, they're really finger lickin'.
All the things that we enjoy as we occupy this planet Earth,
Were created by someone else who no doubt knew their worth!

There's bound to be someone somewhere who's always been in charge
Of every single thing that happens and I'll say "by and large."
We cannot fathom nor can we produce our needs even day by day.
The very mystery of it all escapes us and we accept it come what may!

I know I'm rambling and I know that happens also when we don't believe.
There is no center to our universe if we cannot conceive,
That there is a power, I call it God, who ties it all together,
And that makes us, me and you, one might say, "birds of a feather"!

Beautiful flowers flood our gardens now, most pleasant things to see,
I'm sure that most of us often wonder, how they come to be.
I looked around and finally found the most beautiful one, the "rose."
I'd like to take the credit for that one but only God can create those!

Day By Day

Don't let your footsteps lead you astray.
Trust in the Lord, He'll show you the way.
Too often we feel there's no way out
And so we choose to sit and pout!

Rest assured there's always hope,
Even though it's hard to cope,
So call on God when the road looks dim,
For you can always count on Him!

In early morn when you arise,
Go outdoors and search the skies.
Ask the Lord to chart your day,
You'll be surprised what He might say!

"Precious child just do what's right,
And you can sleep well every night."
It's not hard to make a choice,
Should you mis-step you'll hear His voice!

Don't give up if the going gets tough,
The help you'll get will be enough,
To start you down that well known road,
The one that leads to the Lord's abode!

Should you fail to make the grade
And need to seek His further aid,
Remember that He's never far away,
And He's glad to help you save your day!

Dear Jesus Is My Hero

Dear Jesus is my hero, my savior and my friend
He's guided me through all my days and forgiven all my sin.
I place my trust in Jesus each morn when I awake,
I know that He will lead me on the paths that I must take.

Oh Jesus, help and guide me in all I do today,
Don't let me faint nor falter, and please don't let me stray.
The world is full of pitfalls, don't let me fall therein,
Just keep me on the straightest path that leads away from sin.

Oh Jesus bring me someone, who needs my help today,
I'll work to solve their problems, and send them on their way.
So many folks are needy and have no place to go.
Take all I have and share it, with lots of love also.

Oh Jesus let me listen as you speak to me again,
You grant me strength and courage that keeps me free of sin.
I love to hear your whisper falling softly on my ear,
It will provide me comfort, throughout the coming year.

Are You Really Independent

Some folks say that "you can't see the forest for the trees."
That's like saying that "you can't make honey without any bees."
We all know that the trees are what make the forest come alive,
And the bees will come with the honey if we furnish them with a hive!

Dependence is a word that all of us humans ought to know.
We've been dependent since we were born it's something we don't outgrow.
Our Founding Fathers declared that we were "independent" in 1776,
But if we were truly "independent" today we'd surely be in a fix!

We're all dependent on something or someone, that's the American way.
That's true because we're never really alone, it changes day to day.
We're always striving to become "independent" and make it on our own,
But almost all of us choose to marry just to keep from being alone!

One thing depends on another to make the world go 'round.
We all depend on our radios so that we can hear the sound.
We depend on gasoline to run our trucks and of course our cars.
At the price we pay for it today, you'd think that it comes in from Mars!

The air we breathe, the water we drink, all come from a natural source.
We humans pollute our natural resources and we have no real remorse.
We chop down all our forests, that's why we have so few trees,
And most of our production plants have now moved overseas!

In our schools we put God into a drawer and tell Him to be quiet.
Yet He's the One that we all depend on when things don't go just right.
I guess you'd say that we're all mixed up it's either sink or swim.
The time has come my friend that we must act and put our trust in Him!

Did You Cut Down The Cherry Tree

I like to think I'm doing good for someone somewhere today
So I must be extra careful in choosing the words to say.
I don't like to step on toes or hurt someone's feelings too
So I must tread a very narrow path and consider what to do!

I don't know what others think but I have made my choice.
It's true we don't all think alike and some will raise their voice.
You can't believe everything you hear for some folks do tell lies.
Filter all the input to uncover the truth of the wherefore's and why's!

Oh yes there are many folks who will lie right to your face.
In fact, some will do most anything to help them win a race.
It's good we have a secret ballot to weed these liars out,
And that my friend is what our elections are really all about!

Line up all the candidates and yes, put them in a row.
Give them each a chance to speak so we can see how much they know.
Most will show their weakest points and lose favor with the crowd.
There are some who have done things of which we're very proud!

All of us like to think that our elections are always fair and square,
But sometimes evidence comes to light that voter fraud is there.
Oh yes votes are often bought and sold with outcome rigged of course.
Most are not surprised when the fraud is traced back to its source!

As in everything in daily life there's good and bad at play.
We all must mind our p's and q's and be careful what we say.
We're in the midst of an important election and wonder who will win.
Let's hope that no one tries to steal this election once again.

Divine Protection

It's easy to follow the road I took when I look back today.
There is no doubt that God was there to help me find my way.
I didn't know Him as well then but I knew He was my friend.
He always led me to a starting point where He thought I should begin!

The drums of war were loud and clear, Uncle Sam said "I want you!"
My deathly fear of "trench warfare" led me to ask, "What else can I do?"
No Navy for me, I couldn't swim, and my best friend died at "Pearl."
Another friend was flying high in a P-38 in a war torn part of the world!

Parental permission was hard to get, Mom feared for me to fly.
I begged and begged 'til she gave in, the tear stained form took time to dry.
Mental and physical tests were tough but I "aced" them both with flair,
In fact I finished the testing early and was sworn in "then and there!"

Uniforms and regimentation was something I liked a lot.
Learning to fly was easy for me and I was told that I was "hot."
I got special training to fly the big ones, the queens of the bomber fleet.
It was true, to fly the B-17, you could never make it with "cold feet!"

I arrived with my crew in the European warzone in November forty-four.
I was assigned to fly a B-17 named "Bottle Baby" fully fitted for war.
The sky was active with enemy fighters and deadly bursts of flak.
For 25 missions over Germany we survived while many didn't come back!

I often wondered why I was spared while others "bought the farm."
I felt the on-board presence of the Spirit who kept us from deadly harm.
He's never left me since those days and has filled my life with love.
I thank Jesus every day for directing me from above!

February 9.

Do We Have The Will

Sometimes I get the feeling that today is not my day.
I can't put my finger on the cause, so I must bow and pray.
Jesus always has an answer and shares with me a plan.
He asks me to pray for all my friends and help them if I can!

When I begin to think of other's who're in a sinking boat,
I know it's time for me to jump in and help keep them afloat.
It's time that everyone right now must share that bit of trouble,
So we all must do our best to overcome a definite bursting bubble!

I have no answer to our problems our Congress caused it all.
They would not act together like a team and then they dropped the ball.
No team will ever win the game unless they reach the goal.
You cannot stand around and argue and let troubles galore unfold!

We know for sure that Jesus watches every move we make.
He helps us to make those moves that we know are "for Jesus' sake,"
And that means we'll do all we can to help all those in need.
With Jesus watching and writing in His Book, all about our good deed!

Meanwhile, Congress fails to act they think they know what's best,
Give more tax breaks to the rich, to hell with all the rest.
That kind of action doesn't work it doesn't help at all,
A house divided as they are is truly bound to fall!

So what can we, the common folk, do to stem the tide?
We must join hands and field a team with Jesus on our side,
And we must always keep in mind, what would Jesus do?
If we'll just do what we know is best then we'll come shining through!

February 10.

Do You Believe

There are a lot of things in life that we don't understand.
We go about our daily lives and do those things we planned.
We feel quite good when day is done and we lay down to rest.
Too often we do not give thanks for having been so blessed!

One thing that I cannot understand is how some don't believe in God.
How these unfortunate souls receive the help they need is to me quite odd.
They don't have anyone on whom to call when they are down and out,
But Jesus comes to help them cope though they don't yet know He's about!

You see folks whether or not you believe in Him He never gives up on you,
And even if you don't believe, He lets the dreams you have come true.
So you can go through your entire life and feel you've done quite well,
But wait a minute, eternity for you is just ahead and you might go to hell!

Jesus is the judge of all, the good, the bad, and all those in between.
It's not that He doesn't love us all, even those who are real mean.
Jesus faces the devil every day while fighting for all our souls.
He wants everyone to believe in Him and to reach all of their goals!

I learned about the way the devil works while I was just a kid.
I was always very much afraid of him and worried about things I did,
But I loved Jesus with all my heart and knew He'd save my soul.
I don't know how I could do without knowing Him now that I am old!

I'd like to say to anyone who doesn't believe that it's not too late to change.
Close your eyes and pray right now, Jesus is always within range.
The moment He takes your hand and says "Welcome my dearest friend,"
You'll feel the Spirit enter your heart as He saves your soul from sin!

Do You Have The Time

We could do so many things if we just had the time, we say.
We all have the very same amount of time, twenty-four hours a day,
But how you choose to use your time differs by who you are.
Wise ones make good use of time and some even become a star!

Some folks "piddle around" a lot and never get much done.
Others spend too much of their time trying to have some fun.
When we don't make judicious use of time its loss is no one's gain.
We never recover wasted time it's always down the drain!

There are those who sit and watch the clock, wondering what to do.
They would be much better off to close their eyes and catch a wink or two.
You can refresh your "bank of time" and it will serve you well.
Don't try to live on "borrowed time", it paves the road to hell!

Schedules are the bane of life but depend on time you see.
Without a start and ending time what would a schedule be?
Nothing but a useless waste of time that helps to pass the day
And makes you wonder where all the time went for which we always pay!

Do something useful with your time don't let it go to waste.
If you aren't working, start a hobby, one that suits your taste.
You can spend your time in reading books or writing if you choose.
You may even help someone out, it's known as paying your dues!

I spend a lot of time in writing, like the poem you're reading now.
Some folks say they'd like to write, but they just don't know how.
You'll never know until you've tried what you can really do.
"Time is of the essence and something good can still come true!"

Birthdate of #5 Grandson, Luke Opitz   1996

Following Jesus

I like Jesus for my guide He's so well prepared.
A day can't pass that I don't think of things that we have shared.
With Jesus as the leader and me in line behind
There is nothing that we can't do for members of mankind!

I like to follow Jesus for there's always lots to do.
He goes where there are needy folks just like me and you.
It's wonderful to be with Him and listen while He talks.
He's always thinking how He can help and ponders while he walks!

If you would like to join the group, well it's not hard to do.
Just let Him know you'd like to help He'll sign you to the crew.
Then you and I can be a team and follow where He leads.
We never have to travel far there are so many needs!

Almost all have heard of Him but some are not inclined
To want to join His group and follow Him and some are merely blind.
So it is up to those of us whose love for Him is strong,
To tell the story of His love and help others join the throng!

It's hard for some to believe in Him a presence they can't see.
You must have a faith that's strong, it brings reality.
When you think of Jesus He makes His presence known.
The Spirit comes and takes your hand and you become His own!

The Trinity of the Father, Son and Spirit, they all deserve our love.
They work real hard to save our soul, they come down from above.
When I feel low and down and out I take the time to pray.
I know that when the answer comes it will make my day!

February 13.

Does Jesus Know Your Plans

This has been a hectic week for me but we'll soon see it through.
Life always has its ups and downs so that is nothing new.
Gods promise was that He would help but we would have to ask,
So what I ask of Him today is "Please make me equal to the task!"

It's so strange how our fortunes float, how they ebb and flow.
We never know where life will lead but each of us must go
Where destiny calls and without fear, accept His helping Hand,
For without Him there is no way to reach the "Promised Land!"

Long range plans are wonderful, but really it's just a "plan,"
We must live our lives "one day at a time" and do the best we can.
If the need arises we must alter the course but be sure to stay on track.
Carefully choose your words and deeds there's no way to take them back!

When I wake up every morning and put my feet upon the floor,
I don my robe and slippers and walk right out my front door.
I'm heading for the greatest Altar in the world, the early morning sky,
And in that great expanse, clouds and all, I see Jesus there on high!

Good morning Jesus, good morning Lord, it's me your loyal friend.
Another beautiful day has dawned and I need Your help again,
But first I want to thank You for your help during all the days gone by.
You led me through the bad and good from Your Home there in the sky!

I pray a special prayer today for all the leaders of our land.
Our Nation was founded with the help of Gods Almighty Hand.
We're at a crossroads Lord and we're not sure which way to go,
But we know that You are still in charge and that's all we need to know!

Ash Wednesday

February 14.

For My Lovely Valentine

Valentines are the kind of things that we want to keep.
They are precious words of love we dream of in our sleep,
But when they come from the one we love on that special day,
It makes our hearts go "pitter-patter" in a lovely way!

This valentine is for that "special" one, who stole my heart and then
Gave me her hand in marriage and promised to love me to the end!
We both have kept our promises and our lives have been sublime.
God keeps our feet on level ground with no mountains we must climb!

This life is for each of us, so special it's easy for us to see.
Not many people have such luck in love, when it is number three.
We fully accept that it was divine, that Jesus played a hand.
He even helped us find the spot to live in our earthly promised land!

We've been together six wonderful years and so much has transpired.
My health has been so good and my life has been so inspired.
With my love to feed my ego and Jesus to feed my brains,
I write a poem almost every day, unless that day it rains!

You see my sweetheart is a gardener and loves to work outside.
She has a beautiful flower garden and tends it with much pride.
When it's raining she changes course and works on cards instead,
And we both do all the puzzles 'til Sudoku rattles in our head!

My lovely valentine today surprised me with a treat.
She invited me to go with her to my favorite place to eat.
While I'm convinced in my own mind she's the greatest cook around,
We both enjoyed our valentine tryst and now have settled down!

Valentine's Day

February 15.

Heavenly Valentines

My seven beautiful valentines were all sent down to me.
They each came as a little babe, like Jesus used to be.
Each one came as a gift from God, to build a family.
God knew for sure that they would make a beautiful family tree!

God poured His heart into each one and used His "Angel Flight."
They were wrapped in swaddling clothes and tied up good and tight.
These bundles were sent by "Special D" just for their Mom and me.
Each one was welcomed with open arms into the family!

Jesus knew that we'd be happy to receive a precious girl or boy,
And He was right, we wanted both, sweet babies to enjoy.
Each one received much special care, each was a favorite one.
As the family grew in size and love, we had a lot of fun!

Each baby came with special gifts and talents all their own.
They each developed in their own way until they all were grown.
Their Mother and I knew that we were specially picked to be,
And thankfully blessed to raise this wonderful family!

So much talent and intellect now grace this lovely group of seven.
It just shows to all the world the wonders of God's Heaven,
From whence we came and in due time will return.
God sent Jesus as a tiny babe and from this we all must learn!

I write this poem to each of you and I hope you feel the same,
That I was chosen to be the one to give each of you my name.
I know that Jesus will join me now to send much love to you,
As we send our special love and thanks to your Mom, Joann Learu!

"With all my love, Dad"
2/14/2010

February 16.

Don't Be Ashamed To Ask For Help

When you find yourself in trouble and don't know where to turn,
Don't turn to drink and drugs and things that cause concern.
You may get "hooked" and cannot stop no matter how you try,
And you may even feel so bad you wish that you could die!

If you're smart, and most folks are, there's a better way to go.
It consists of merely using common sense and learning to say "no."
There's plenty of help just standing by who want to get involved.
If you will listen to their advice your problem may be solved!

Who is this help you want to know and what do I need to do?
First of all there's family and their main concern is you.
Unfortunately we turn away from those that love us most.
I can do it without their help is something of which we boast!

When family calls on friends to help things may improve a bit,
But it's too bad when they get fed up and really want to quit.
So we often find ourselves in a bind when no one seems to care,
But don't give up though things look bad for someone else is there!

Too often we don't think of Jesus but He always knows the score.
He's always ready to help us out He can do so much more.
He's not afraid to pitch right in and take us by the hand.
If we let Him, He will lead us from the depths back on to "dry" land!

A failing that we humans have is that of controlling our desires.
Eating, drinking, smoking and running around are the start of the fires.
These things that get us hooked, in moderation may seem okay.
Let Jesus help you with your control, He'll be there every day!

February 17.

Don't Let The Devil Make You Do It

The devil may be knocking at your door, don't ever let him in.
He's loaded up you can be sure with every kind of sin.
Oh he is crafty, persistent too, that's not so hard to see.
He brought along his playthings to entice you and me!

The devil doesn't pick and choose he's after everyone.
He's got a great big bag of tricks he'll try each until he's done.
Don't let his lures attract you they'll do a lot of harm.
If you just once fall for his bait, he'll pour on all his charm!

You may not always recognize the devil, that is true,
And you may not always be aware that he is after you.
So be a little cautious and suspicious if it's too good,
This mastermind of the sublime invented Hollywood!

Where do you go for help when you know he's on your trail?
Sometimes you'll find it's awful hard to get him off your tail.
There's only one that we all trust who we have learned to know.
If we ask Jesus to intervene he'll strike a knockout blow!

The devil found he could not bend Jesus, one on one.
He offered Him attractive deals, Jesus told him begone.
This lesson we should ne'er forget, call Jesus when in need.
He will help us stay the course, from danger we'll be freed!

So if your doorbell rings late at night and you don't know who's there,
Be careful, cautious, move real slow, the devil's everywhere.
Say a short prayer to the Lord, don't wait to get caught dead,
Then turn off all the lights and hop right back into bed!

February 18.

Dedicated to The Honorable Barack Hussein Obama Our New President

I have the greatest admiration for a man I've never met.
God sent this man into our lives, and we shall n'er forget,
That God believes and we agree, this man comes with a creed.
He's been preparing his entire life to fill our Nation's need!

He won the post to lead us all, he fought a valiant fight.
When others failed, he prevailed, and now he has the right,
To call the "shots" and make the plans, for all that he must do.
His courage is invincible, it's "steely" through and through!

There are those who felt that he, could never pass the test.
Who could not walk where he has trod, and could not be the best.
But with God's help and prayers beside, his life an open book,
He stepped in front and led the race, oh what a trip he took!

Today he'll take that solemn oath, with vows to serve us well,
With hand upon the Bible, his faith to show and tell.
Then he'll make his speech, to all nations far and wide,
And every single citizen, he'll fill us all with pride!

Barack Obama looks to God, for strength to stay the course.
With much to do, so little time, he goes right to the source.
He never fails to ask for help, gives credit where it's due,
He's now our newest President, he'll serve both me and you!

Thank You God for being there, when we're in need of prayer.
While the world looks on and their leaders are all aware,
They all will hear the sound of bells as our sweet "freedoms" ring,
And also our new President begins to do his thing!

President's Day

Don't Let Worries Worry You

Worry never solves a problem but it can cause a lot of grief.
We should always turn to prayer instead as we seek relief.
Jesus said, "Do not worry but put your trust in me,
And I will give you what you need to be worry free!"

Human beings are prone to worry because it seems the thing to do.
Yet, in itself it solves naught at all and causes havoc too.
Erase the very thought of worry and put on a happy face.
Leave your worries on the doorstep for that's a better place!

I won't worry that you will worry if you won't worry about me.
If we will use that approach then maybe we'll be worry free.
If the two of us are not worried then we can rest assured,
If neither of us have a need to worry then maybe we are cured!

We know that Jesus heals the sick and takes away our sin.
He tells us not to worry about the mess the world is in.
If we will place our trust in Him and help Him help our fellow man,
Then this world can be a happy place and we can smile again!

Can you get through an entire day without having worries on your mind?
Will you be truly happy with the solutions to your problems that you find?
We'll be a long way down the road to making this a better place to live,
When we all wake up and realize that we all have much love to give!

When you erase all worries from your brow and replace them with a glow,
Just let friends see the brightness of your smile which will let them know,
That Jesus is alive and well and dwells within your soul,
You can leave those worries on the doorstep and that should be your goal!

February 20.

The Hazards of Leadership

I don't know what I would do if I was President.
I'm glad Barack Obama's there I think he was Heaven sent.
He's spending time to get things right and doesn't act on whim,
He seeks advice from those he trusts and then we hear from him!

Not all our enemies are in foreign lands we have them in our midst.
They are trying to destroy our Presidents plan, they really do insist.
He has already done a lot of good and things are looking up,
If those who hinder would only help and quit trying to disrupt!

We take pride in being Americans for being brave and free,
And yet we're often torn apart and divided by hostility.
We must be prudent and cautious too, to safeguard all our beliefs.
Let's not let ugly forces take the helm with few troops but many chiefs!

The airwaves of our land echo the drumbeat of "big lies,"
From dawn to dusk these prophets of doom show hatred in their eyes.
Their major target is our President they'd like to do him in,
Not only do they dislike his goals they hate the color of his skin!

Oh yes our Constitution speaks of the equality of all men,
And yet it's hard for a white man to have a black man for a friend.
I sometimes wonder what Jesus would say now about the human race.
I don't recall that He ever talked about the color of one's face!

The hate groups also like to divide by what each one of us believes.
They think they are the chosen ones while all the rest are thieves.
Their actions often make me think that they're the devil in disguise.
We must do whatever it takes to be acceptable in dear Jesus' eyes!

February 21.

Every Day Is Decision Time

There is Someone up in Heaven who's watching over you.
There is no way that you can hide, He sees everything you do.
There is someone else who's watching too, but from way on down below.
These two are fighting for our very soul, we must choose which way to go!

We all face many decisions as we make our way each day.
Each one is important to our future, who shall I obey?
Some decisions seem so simple, yet temptation is so strong,
If we're not careful we may give in and wind up doing wrong!

Fear not, I say, though we have sinned, Jesus will forgive.
We can't escape, we must ask for the help that only He can give.
Remember that Jesus gave His life to save us from our sin.
In this daily game of life the sinner will never win!

Still each day we face the fact that decisions must be made.
The devil shows us the glossy side and calls a club a spade.
If we're to follow Jesus we'll choose the Savior's way.
He'll help us make that decision when we kneel down to pray!

There are none among us who have not sinned, the devil is hard at work.
In this world of ours today so many dangers continue to lurk.
We must begin each day by asking Jesus to be our guide
And make our decisions knowing that He is on our side!

We all are born in sin and have a lifetime to wheel and deal.
There is but one Judge in the Heavenly Court of Appeal.
In that Heavenly Court, mankind's justice gives way to love,
And the Judge's love gives way to "mercy" in the Promised Land above!

February 22.

Footsteps In The Sand

Don't let your footsteps lead you astray.
Trust in the Lord, He'll show you the way.
Too often we feel there's no way out
And so we choose to sit and pout!

Rest assured there's always hope,
Even though it's hard to cope,
So call on God when the road looks dim,
For you can always count on Him!

In early morn when you arise,
Go outdoors and search the skies.
Ask the Lord to chart your day,
You'll be surprised what He might say!

"Precious child just do what's right,
And you can sleep well every night."
It's not hard to make a choice,
Should you mis-step you'll hear His voice!

Don't give up if the going gets tough,
The help you'll get will be enough,
To start you down that well known road,
The one that leads to the Lord's abode!

Should you fail to make the grade
And need to seek His further aid,
Remember that He's never far away,
And He's glad to help you save your day!

February 23.

Forgiveness

Is your life an open book or do you try to hide
All those things you'd best forget 'bout which you've often lied.
If you could only clean the slate and start off fresh again.
There is a way that this can be, just listen well my friend!

Accept dear Jesus as your guide and follow Him each day.
He'll lead you down a different path and will not let you stray.
God sent Him, His only Son, to save us all from sin.
Do not forget this lovely thought, He wants to be your friend!

Jesus came to earth a babe, a very beloved Son.
He came to us a gift from God, the long expected one.
He travelled o'er the countryside, to teach and preach of love,
And every day He knelt to pray and talked with God above!

Everywhere that Jesus went the crowd sat in the dust.
They loved to hear Him preach about His Father's love for us.
There was a huge crowd looking on when John, His cousin, spoke
And baptized Jesus in the Jordan along with other folk!

If you can place your trust in Jesus and accept Him as your friend,
You'll find that He will clean the slate and forgive you of your sin.
No longer will you need to hide and you will always know
That God forgave for Jesus' sake and your soul is white as snow!

From now on in your daily life you can be real secure
That Jesus is still helping you to keep your soul real pure.
Don't hesitate to kneel and pray to thank Him for His love,
And you will know He's alive and well and watching from above!

February 24.

Give The Devil His Due And Nothing Else

We don't talk much about Gods greatest foe, I'm speaking of the devil,
But let's admit he's always around and never on the level.
We all have contact with him every day we need to stay on guard,
For some of his offerings are very attractive, to resist is very hard!

There are many religions on the earth but only one devil you see.
He's the master of our globe's vast underworld, as mean as he can be.
Of all the people who've ever lived he had the greatest ego of them all.
He challenged God for His own throne which caused his own downfall!

When God sent his only Son to earth to save the human race,
The devil saw Jesus as a threat and with his guile met Him face to face.
He offered riches and world power too if Jesus would just bow down,
But Jesus did not accept the devil's plan and ran him out of town!

The devil doesn't operate alone he has recruits of many kind.
They're at work at any time and place trying their best to find
Those folks who have no love for Jesus, they're all around you know,
And they're the ones the devil wants to stoke the fires below!

Jesus still fights the daily battle to keep the devil at bay.
He wants all of us to come to heaven, not go the other way.
Just stay on your best behavior, say all your prayers as well.
When the devil and his force arrives just send them all back to hell!

February 25.

God Is

There are those who believe there is no God and they insist,
If that were true in anyway, we wouldn't even exist.
None of us will ever know how God came to be.
He was, He is, and will still be God at eternity!

Those folks who don't believe in God, just what do they believe?
How do they reconcile that strange belief, it's hard to even conceive.
If you have no belief in God your life must be an empty shell,
And God has said if we don't believe in Him, we'll surely go to hell!

It's much harder to deny that God exists than let the truth be known.
Just open up your eyes and look around, God's love is freely shown,
In every flower, in every tree and in every bird that sings,
There is no way that human hands could ever create those things!

I thank God that He is out there controlling our Universe.
Mankind falls short in so many ways, some things we must reverse.
Too many folks who don't believe refuse to change their way.
They can't accept that there is a God and it's Him we must obey!

God loves us each and everyone and sent His Son to be our guide.
Jesus confirmed that God is love, then for our sins He died,
And when He left that hillside tomb, He went with God again.
We'll go there too if we believe, nothing to lose, everything to gain!

I'm speaking now to all those folks who deny that God is King.
If they'll dig deep enough into their hearts they'll hear the angels sing,
And from that moment on until the very day they die,
They'll worship God who is alive, a fact they won't deny!

God Is Still In Charge

No one dies before their time and no one knows that date,
And no one dies by accident but rather it's known as fate.
We all should stay in touch with Jesus every single day,
For we don't know the time nor place when we'll be called away!

God wants everyone to come to Heaven when their time has come.
That's why He sent Jesus, His Only Son to prepare our Heavenly home.
Furthermore, the Bible was written to teach us how to live.
Jesus wants to be your friend He has so much love to give!

Don't delay and wait too late to start training for your demise.
By waiting you may miss the boat and that would not be too wise.
Jesus is ready to save your soul and put your mind at rest,
So that when you have run the race you will have passed the test!

We're all smart enough to know that we must learn the ropes.
We will not be successful if we expect to live on hopes.
Jesus will help us get prepared and teach us what to say.
So it's important that we call on Him and talk with Him each day!

It's true that Jesus wants us to be happy while we're here on earth.
He sent us into a happy home, t'was not an accident, our birth.
Your loving Mother, God bless her soul, went through a real ordeal,
But she endured and forgot the pain, when she first heard you squeal!

So while we must not neglect our training for events on down the road,
We must overcome our hardships every day and not add them to our load.
Leave room to share love with our loved ones, put on a happy face,
For God sent us here to be happy members of the human race!

Dreams Of Friends

When I closed my eyes last night as I lay upon my bed,
Visions of some other days were dancing in my head.
I saw lots of my old friends just walking down the lane.
Most of them were doing well but some walked with a cane!

I spoke to each and called their name as they were passing by,
Hello George, hi there Jack and Sam, each of them said "hi."
And also there were some other folks, I cannot tell you who,
Who when I spoke to them just stared and said who the heck are you!

As I remember in the dream, I caught them by surprise,
But every single one of them looked me in the eyes.
They were searching through their brain, dredging up the past.
Most of them soon smiled and laughed as they remembered me at last!

Soon we all were telling tales it seemed like yesterday.
Some happy stories, some were sad, but each one had their say.
As things unfolded we all agreed that life had treated us well.
We talked and talked until it seemed there was nothing more to tell!

I don't know why I had that dream which was pleasant as it could be,
But what a thrill to see my friends, at least it was for me.
Of course I didn't see them all, I wondered about others too.
I hope I'll have another dream soon and see the rest of you!

I like to think this dream was like our trip to Heaven will be,
When we will greet all those we love, our friends and family.
I hope that all who read this poem will join me in my quest,
To be among the ones who get to be, Jesus' special guest!

February 28.

Put On Your Happy Face

Are you content with your life as it is today,
Or do you wish things were different in some fantastic way?
Not too sure what you'd change if you just had the chance?
Before you make a drastic move evaluate your circumstance!

You may be overlooking the most important things of all.
They may seem insignificant but they could cause you to fall.
Sometimes we let a very simple thing disrupt a tranquil scene.
If you would just take a bit more time then things could be serene!

Helter-skelter is a term I'm sure you've heard before.
It's a game the devil plays as he tries to get in your door.
The smoothest moments of your life can easily become a dread.
You must resist the devil's pitch before you wind up dead!

Now this is no idle threat the devil makes as he interferes.
He isn't content when you're smiling for he likes to see your tears.
A happy family life is something that he just cannot condone,
So don't let him back you into a corner where you'd be all alone!

The very darkest moments of our life come when the devil is nearby.
Jesus sees that trouble is brewing as he watches o'er us from the sky.
If we just look to Him day by day and let Him take us by the hand,
We can overcome the work of the devil and head for the "Promised Land!"

There's nothing else that can compare with the joy of a happy family life.
The man is fortunate indeed who finds a real helpmate for a wife.
The devil will try to stick his nose in where it truly does not belong,
But you must be content and yes, beware and smile and sing a happy song!

Contents March

1. God Loves To Mend A Broken Heart 62

2. Dreaming 63

3. God Will Show The Way 64

4. "Going Home" 65

5. Good Friends 66

6. How Green Is Your Valley 67

7. Goodbye Love 68

8. Goodbye Teddy 69

9. The Birthday Girl 70

10. Growing Up 71

11. Hail To The Queen, Goodnight Irene 72

12. Happiness Is Good For The Heart 73

13. Happy Birthday Jesus 74

14. Don't Be Afraid 75

15. Happy, Hopeful Or Both 76

16. Hard Times 77

17. Hard Times Again 78

18. Have A Nice Day 79

19. Heaven Bound 80

20. Heaven Help Us 81

21. Heaven Is Waiting 82

22. I Can Do It 83

23. Hello 84

24. Hello Jesus, Are You Free 85

25. Help Wanted 86

26. Here I Am Lord 87

27. He's My Brother 88

28. The Royal Wedding 89

29. Hooray For Hollywood 90

30. How Attitudes Change 91

31. Easter 92

March 1.

God Loves To Mend A Broken Heart

Broken dreams and broken hearts go hand in hand they say.
Jesus heals them with His love and makes them go away.
Two hearts that often beat as one are said to be "in love."
These matches are all made in Heaven and come down from above!

No one is perfect, that's for sure, but we all need to try.
Perfection is our goal of course, but it may be set too high.
We all must do the best we can and some day by and by,
An Angel of the Lord will come and teach us how to fly!

Life will not bring happiness if broken hearts are there.
You must get someone to bind them up with lots of tender care.
Two broken hearts that beat as one will soon be whole again,
And with His healing God sends love which always takes away the pain!

When Jesus puts His Logo on a match He wants it to succeed.
He wants to know that the two involved will meet each others need.
He doesn't push but takes His time to be sure the match will last.
He doesn't want a failure to occur, just because it moved too fast!

Relationships that fall apart were not built on love, I'm sure.
Appearances are often deceiving and it's likely they won't endure.
A healthy interest in similar things will bring togetherness,
Which along with compatibility are things that will bring success!

Dreaming

When it's time for me to die I know where I will go.
I'll be going up to Heaven, for Jesus told me so.
It won't be in a fancy car or in a big airplane,
I'll be walking with my Savior down a lovely garden lane!

I have no fear of dying for my future is all set.
No bags to pack, we leave it all there is no need to fret.
Out destination is well prepared to fill our every need,
With Jesus walking by my side I'm coming home indeed!

When we arrive at the Pearly Gates, St. Peter is standing there.
He says to Jesus, "Hello Master my dear friend, I've got some things to share."
Jesus answers like you to me, "Hello Pete what's on
your mind, I've brought another soul,"
That's when Peter says to me, "Welcome home our
friend Jake, your name is on our roll!"

I've never known such loving care as I received that day.
Jesus led me through the Gate and we proceeded along the way.
Family and friends from out of the past said "Hi" as we passed by,
I knew I'd see them later on so I did not say goodbye!

We arrived at a lovely park and Jesus said, "You're home,
You'll be here for eternity and you'll never have to roam."
He hugged me tight and said to me, "So long my dearest friend,
We'll be in touch from time to time, this life will never end!"

I can't describe the beauty of the place where I live now,
So beautiful that I know I'm dreaming and I'll wake up somehow.
I fall down on my knees to pray "Dear Lord, I'm ready to go!"
Some day my dreams will all come true for Jesus told me so!

March 3.

God Will Show The Way

Would this world be much different had you not come to be?
If your dad had married my mom would you be somewhat like me,
And if my dad had married your mom would I be somewhat like you?
Things would be different that's for sure, not knowing who is who?

Just think about it for a while are you real glad you're you?
Have you ever wished way down deep to change a thing or two?
You may be happy with who you are, but what if you were me
And you found your name was hanging on my family tree?

Creation and evolution are mighty words and had a part to play
In making this old world of ours just what it is today.
I like to think that I am kin in some way to everyone I know.
I know Adam was my "mega" grandpa for Jesus told me so!

The human race before the flood had changed from what God made.
Much like today the world had gone berserk and morals had decayed.
God selected one family to survive my "mega" grandpa got the call.
Noah began a new family tree and that one includes us all!

So here we are, much time has passed, and now we all are kin.
Black and white, red and yellow, no matter what shape you're in.
We all are creatures of our own tastes, as different as can be.
Now no one knows what is to come, we'll have to wait and see!

The future of the human race, the one that we know now,
Hangs in the balance seems to me and we don't know when or how.
Cataclysmic things are happening, are we approaching the end?
I've put my trust in Jesus Christ, how about you my friend?

March 4.

"Going Home"

No one knows when their time will come,
When Jesus calls our name.
So we must always be prepared,
Our presence to proclaim!

If you accept the love of Christ,
And live the life He taught,
He'll welcome you with open arms,
And rewards for battles fought!

You must not fear this "trip" abroad,
The last one that you'll take,
Christ has made His plans for you,
And Him you can't forsake!

Gather up your "Golden Deeds,"
Your troubles leave behind,
Make sure that Jesus knows you,
Just "one" of earth's mankind!

We'll miss the ones we leave on earth,
They'll follow when it's time.
We'll welcome those who've gone before,
Our life will be sublime!

Good Friends

Dedicated to Joan and Juan Rueda, October 10, 2009

We have two friends named Juan and Joan.
Lovelier folks we've never known.
When we're in need, we know they're there,
Just letting us know they really care!

They have an abode in Inland Greens,
Surrounded by trees and tranquil scenes.
They feed the birds, the squirrels, the ducks.
A lovely home worth a "million bucks!"

There's even a fox that comes to dine.
The food they furnish he likes just fine.
They see the world from their back door.
No one of us could ask for more!

Juan's a Columbian, and Cuban too.
Speaks perfect Spanish which he loves to do.
He's an ambassador and known all around.
He's got friends all over this town!

Joan's a Brit, an English Dame.
After World War II is when she came.
Her husband Ralph died some years ago.
She met Juan who makes her glow!

We're fortunate to have them as a friend.
Don't want our friendship to ever end.
With this poem I hope I'm heard,
I'll just say "ALOHA", their favorite word!

How Green Is Your Valley

Black clouds forming in the sky,
There'll be raindrops falling bye and bye,
Lightning flashes fill the air
Causing thunder everywhere!

We sometimes fail to recognize
This purest water from the skies,
Is another gift that comes our way,
Just one of many day to day!

We get some rain but sunshine too.
The sunshine comes with skies of blue.
This combination of sun and rain,
Makes seedlings sprout and fill with grain!

Without the rain there is no doubt
We would have a terrible drought.
A water supply is hard to find
While crops all perish on the vine!

There's not much that we ourselves can do,
But be thankful and conservative too.
Please don't waste our water supply.
Use it on the crops so they won't die!

We must be good stewards of planet earth.
Fight to preserve it for all we're worth.
There'll come a time when we'll all be glad
And thankful too for the good life we've had!

Goodbye Love

We all should savor every day
We have with those we love.
There comes a time when we must part.
The call comes from above!

We never know how long we have
Or when the call will come,
But Jesus guides our destiny.
It's He who calls us home!

We must prepare to say "goodbye"
Or we will miss the chance.
Give special thanks for every hour,
Thank God for our romance!

It's terribly hard to lose a mate
Whose lives we've shared so long.
We must accept, it is our fate
And prayers will make us strong!

Don't wait too long, please don't neglect
Your spouse, tell them that you care.
You may not know what they expect
But there's so much to share!

Too soon perhaps the time will come
When Jesus makes His call.
Our loved ones leave for their new home
And our tears begin to fall!

March 8.

Goodbye Teddy

Dedicated to the Kennedy family
in Memory of EdwardMooreKennedy

Sadness grips our hearts today,
They're laying our friend Ted away.
This patriarch of the Kennedy clan,
Has made his move to the "Promised Land!"

Friends have come from far and wide.
Tears have flowed as many cried.
He's been honored with words of praise.
To toast his life, our glass we raise!

No one was dedicated more than he.
It seems that this was meant to be,
For his three brothers gave their all,
While he survived to carry the ball!

He served our country with lots of pride,
Right up until the day he died.
He knew how to get things done.
When things were tough he usually won!

He was a champion of people's rights.
He got involved in desperate fights.
He was always there for the folks in need.
The down and out need me became his creed!

I'm sure that Ted will fit right in,
Up there in heaven where he'll soon begin,
Just doing what Jesus wants him to do,
And help other folks like me and you!

March 9.

The Birthday Girl

Today is a beautiful day for I have sunshine in my soul.
I do not need to see the sun to feel those rays of gold.
Though clouds outside fill the air and rain is sure to fall,
I feel the nearness of God's Love which comes to one and all!

Today's a special day for me my bride is adding a year.
Jesus helps us celebrate by letting us know He's near.
The festive nature of this day will make our spirits sing.
We'll light candles for the cake and thank God for everything!

Birthdays come but once a year wish we could have two,
But then we'd age much too fast and never have time to do
All the things that come with celebrating in a great big way,
So we'll be happy with the joy that brightens up our special day!

We realize how time is passing when birthdays roll around.
We won't admit we're getting old we'll look until we've found
That magic site, the fountain of youth, "what's that you say?"
"Stop looking, there is no fountain, you must keep young some other way!"

Try exercise and diet too, they're good at any age.
Don't worry about the way you look, you're not up on the stage,
But keep on plugging day by day, just one day at a time,
And just relax and take it easy, your day will be sublime!

The song says, "smile and the world smiles with you,"
So put on a happy face, you're among the chosen few.
Those who have sunshine in their hearts all day,
Knowing that Jesus will always hear them when they pray!

Birthdate Of Rosemary Maldony Shepherd, 1945

March 10.

Growing Up

God doesn't let us off the hook,
So we must always do things by the book.
We should then stick to protocol,
And do things right or not at all!

When we were in the second grade,
We were so proud of things we made.
We learned to read and then to write.
Our teacher said we were so bright!

As we progressed we learned it's true,
Our lives are shaped by what we do.
As I look back now, I wonder why,
There were some things I wouldn't try!

My teachers helped me move along.
I learned from them what's right and wrong.
My life was changed as I learned more,
I couldn't wait to know "what for?"

My school days ended in "thirty-nine,"
I'd been in school since "twenty-nine."
The depression years sure took their toll,
Although just a "kid" I felt so old!

God has always been my friend.
He stuck with me, His help to lend.
He opened up the world for me,
And helped me become what I should be!

Daylight Savings Time Begins Today

Hail To The Queen, Goodnight Irene

We dodged a bullet last night thanks only to the Lord.
The storm has passed but we haven't at all been bored.
We have no newspaper today so we have no puzzles there.
We googled up a few from internet which were only fair!

We missed the "Jumble" and the "Cryptogram" too,
But we had a good crossword and of course Sudoku.
The storm didn't damage our brain, no, not at all.
There's always a way that you can cope if you'll just play ball!

Hurricanes are "scary" but they do give you time to plan.
They are not like tornadoes which will kill you if they can.
They're also not like a thunderstorm which is over and done quite quick.
The buildup lasts for days and weeks and almost makes you sick!

The buildup for this storm was long and fit for a real life "queen."
It was given a name which we'll never forget, a classic gal, Irene.
She fit right in with others of lore, Hazel, Floyd and Fran.
We stayed home to greet Irene, but from those others we ran!

Evacuation is sometimes best and at times it must be done.
We stayed around to greet Irene because we thought it might be fun.
Our home is such a sturdy fort, always ready for a fight,
And it proved to be as we believed it kept us safe all night!

The wind was howling, trees were swaying, but we were well prepared.
If we had never seen this before we might have been quite scared.
The rain poured down by buckets full and the rain gauge overflowed,
But we survived with naught to fear in the comfort of our sweet abode!

March 12.

Happiness Is Good For The Heart

Happy thoughts fill my heart it's such a lovely day,
I had to let some others know just what I had to say.
My wife, dear one, said, "come look, the sun is very red."
A great big crimson ball of fire was shining overhead!

Down in Chile the sun is shining on a glorious sight.
Those miners who were trapped were saved, it was a victorious night.
It feels so good to have some happy news, my, that is a change.
Election "lies" and battle "cries" are driven out of range.

I hope that everyone of you can find something to make you smile.
Your smile will brighten someone's day for just a little while.
This world would be a better place if the smile replaced the frown,
And every single one of us could look up instead of feeling down!

Let's be honest and face the facts, we have a choice of how we feel.
We must overcome all thoughts of doom, might help if we would kneel
And simply ask the Lord for help, He's always been so kind.
I'm sure that He would be glad to help us find some "peace of mind!"

I must not let anything take my "happy thoughts" away,
And in my "good night" prayers I'll say, thanks for a lovely day.
I've found that to be happy it's not possible all alone,
And we can't throw away the daily "news" and the noisy telephone!

I'm going to do the best I can to let today bring lots of joy,
Not just to me but to everyone I know, every girl and boy.
I hope that everyone of you, my friends and all my family,
Will join in making our day today just as "happy as it can be!"

Happy Birthday Jesus

Today is Jesus' birthday when He is born in someone's heart.
Somewhere, someone will celebrate, for them a brand new start.
It's Happy Birthday Jesus every day and that includes today,
So let's all sing Happy Birthday Jesus now, as we bow to pray!

Birthdays are always happy times as we celebrate each one.
We count the candles on our cake it's all a lot of fun.
This happens only once a year, a long time in between.
We can celebrate with Jesus everyday just think what that would mean!

So many people are down and out and have no place to go.
They have no job, no food to eat their life is a tale of woe.
For them a birthday party for Jesus would brighten up their day.
This party doesn't cost at all, just bow your head and pray!

Jesus wants to help each one, to bless the poor and needy,
But our society today tends to favor those who are rich and greedy.
"If you've got the money, honey, they've got the time,"
But if you truly need some help they cannot spare a dime!

The custom of birthday gifts is something that's well known.
We must give our heart to Jesus, it's the most precious thing we own.
Our gift from Him comes every day, it's a love that never fails.
The greatest gift we ever receive, it's the story the Bible tells!

So it's okay to measure time by birthdays that have gone by,
But don't forget to say Happy Birthday Jesus, you know He's nearby,
And if you feel the urge and are so inclined, you can sing along,
For Jesus loves to sing as well, especially if it's a happy song!

Don't Be Afraid

Don't be afraid of Jesus, He's a regular guy.
He's always waiting for your call He likes to just say "Hi."
You may not know it but it's true, He knows us all by name.
You will recognize His voice, it always sounds the same!

"Good morning Jesus, it's me again" I said to Him today.
"I'm here to ask a favor Lord, I hope that that's okay."
"Of course it is my child" He said, "Tell Me what's your plan?"
When I told Him, He simply said, "I'll do everything I can!"

From that moment on I knew, deep within my heart,
That all the things I asked of Him would soon begin to start.
Sure enough it wasn't long until my plan was in full swing.
It was just as He had said, He took care of everything!

So if you find you're in a bind, don't know just what to do.
Don't hesitate to call on Him, He'll help to pull you through.
He knows all the ins and outs, the wherefores and the whys.
Jesus can still do miracles, that's where His power lies!

Someday you'll find, just like I said, that you can't do it all.
You're overwhelmed without a clue and don't know who to call.
Remember then the things I've said and get down on your knees.
It's time to ask for help from Jesus who will listen to your pleas!

What a thrill it is to know that we are not alone,
That there is someone real nearby that we don't have to phone.
Just bow your head and say "hello", He'll answer with His "Hi!"
And after He has heard your plea, you merely say, "Goodbye!"

March 15.

Happy, Hopeful Or Both

Should we rejoice, I think we should, the al-Qaeda king is dead.
Most people when they die go to Heaven, he went to hell instead.
This self-sworn enemy of the USA killed many in our land.
The well known enemy of Jesus is now the devil's second in command!

The devil now has extra help in fighting for our soul.
We can't let up on our vigilance for our defeat is still his goal.
He'll be lurking in the shadows with the devil at his back.
We must watch our every step and not let them attack!

We need to renew our pledge of allegiance to the Lord please do so today.
He needs to know that we're still on board, there can be no delay.
It's true that we have won a major battle but we must be on guard.
These two wicked princes of evil will hang out in our own backyard!

The Earth created by the Lord for us all is a very lovely place to be,
But the devil does the best he can to create lots of misery.
I'm sure he welcomes bin Laden to his team but we can't let them score.
While we have won this latest battle we by no means have won the war!

Jesus will be inviting us to continue our fight as well.
We must prevent this new partnership from selling products made in hell.
Our magnificent world already has its share of rampage on the run.
We can't let these "devils diplomats" convince us that it's all so much fun!

I went to war once years ago to fight a horde spawned by the devil.
I'm ready once again to pitch right in and fight these new forces of evil.
If everyone will join me in this fight I'm sure we will succeed
For if we're sincere it will clearly be a defeat for "crime and greed"!

March 16.

Hard Times

I think about my Mom and Dad they were so good to me.
We didn't have much of the worldly goods but we lived happily.
We persevered and each day was hard, depression took its toll.
We all pitched in to do our part and that kept us off the dole!

We learned a lot during those years which were filled with dread,
But we had a pleasant family life and a place to lay our head.
Friends and neighbors stuck together and helped each other out.
It's true, no one had a lot but we learned not to sit and pout!

Things have never been as hard since nineteen-twenty-nine.
The bubble burst for those with wealth who had been doing fine,
But when the bad stuff hit the fan those folk were not prepared.
The entire world was in a funk and it seemed that no one cared!

We struggled hard to make ends meet, Dad was very busy.
He tried his hand at many things and drove an old "tin-lizzie,"
A nineteen-twenty-seven Model T which Henry himself had made,
We saved all our nickels and dimes to help Dad make a trade!

Swayed by the beauty of the paint Dad bought an Essex Super-six.
It was powerful with real gears changed by floor-mounted sticks.
As slow as cold molasses it was to start but it moved fast when hot.
Time elapsed and things improved, but that Essex had gone to pot!

Dad then bought a Rockne sedan named after a guy named Knute.
I especially remember the "running boards", this car was kinda' cute.
The economy improved, we still struggled but I had learned to drive.
That year 1939 I finished school and got a job, we managed to survive!

March 17.

Hard Times Again

Mama always let me lick the bowl,
Starting when I was only three years old.
The best time was when she was baking cakes.
My oh my, but Mama sure had what it takes!

Now she was good at other things as well,
For she was crafty and made things to sell.
The depression years were hard on everyone,
'Til FDR arrived up there in Washington!

Mama helped my Dad in his business too,
A man of many talents knowing just what to do,
He created beautiful furniture from other people's trash,
He was also a good cook, making "depression era hash"!

Mom and Dad together made a very wonderful team.
They didn't let depression woes interrupt their dream.
They raised three kids but I was the only boy,
And you might say that I was my Dad's pride and joy!

World War II was a turning point and everyone had work to do.
Young men like me went to war, Dad's job was something new.
It qualified him for Social Security which later saved the day.
He was retired for many years and Social Security continued to pay!

We've been through another depression, it hasn't been good at all.
So many folks have been hurt as their fortunes continued to fall.
My Social Security has helped a lot as I have grown quite old,
But one thing hasn't changed a bit, I still like to lick the bowl!

St. Patrick's Day

March 18.

Have A Nice Day

It's early morning and I don't know what today will bring.
The sun will drive the fog away and we'll hear robins sing.
I've had my talk with Jesus and asked what I could do,
To make this world a better place for folks like me and you!

There is no better time to plan than early in the morn.
The sun is rising in the East as a beautiful new day is born.
Another gift from God's own Hand, given with His Love,
The rain has brought new life to earth, it came down from above!

I'm sure that there is no one of us who lack some things to do.
There's always something on our plate that needs attending to.
So check that list of "honey do's" and be sure that they get done.
If you're still alive, relax at "five", have a drink but stop at one!

It sure will be a busy day if things just go as planned.
You'll be moving all around and you'll need a helping hand.
Why not take Jesus with you everywhere you go?
Introduce Him to your friends He's someone we all should know!

Jesus will also help you with your chores He's quite a crafty Guy.
You'll be surprised how much gets done, my how the time does fly.
Jesus' presence will not hinder you, He doesn't interfere,
But if you find that you need help, you'll know that He is near!

So why not spend your day with Jesus, you will be surprised.
How much more you can accomplish it'll open up your eyes,
You won't need to say "goodbye", He'll stay there in your heart,
Just waiting for tomorrow to begin, and He'd sure like to play a part!

March 19.

Heaven Bound

The vastness of our universe has room for many souls.
Thousands from the Haitian earthquake are now on Heavens rolls.
Don't worry about there being room it all is God's domain.
The universe continues to expand while the earth's size will remain!

God has welcomed our departed to Heaven since the birth of mankind.
He sent His Son Jesus to tell us all about the wonders we would find
When it becomes time for us to leave our life here on the planet earth.
We'll join Jesus and the Saints and celebrate just as we did at His birth!

We all know that God created the earth for us all to occupy,
And you must know that the earth is just a cosmic speck floating in the sky.
The many millions of souls who have gone on aloft before
Will welcome us to Heavens door where we'll reside forevermore!

The story of Jesus' death and resurrection is known to all.
It lets us know that there is "life" after our final call.
We all must live our lives on earth in gratitude and service to others,
Doing all we can to help mankind, our sisters and our brothers!

Today the world is mourning for the thousands who have died.
Where were those mourners in the past when these thousands cried?
Haiti has been for many years among the neediest on the earth.
Their leaders have exploited everyone from their very time of birth!

The entire world should keep this tragic calamity in their mind
If and when they really think about the future of mankind.
We must remember that Jesus said that we should all "believe".
That's the major thing we all must do, our salvation to receive!

Heaven Help Us

Jesus wants to have a hand in everything we do.
Are you willing to stand aside a bit and let Him help you?
He doesn't want to be in charge, just likes to help a bit.
You'll find His help improves the work you'll never want to quit!

Jesus is a Master Craftsman for Joseph trained Him well.
If you need a problem solved you won't need to yell.
Just bow your head and call His Name, He'll soon be at your side.
Your problems soon will disappear for He'll help you to decide!

You may think I'm kidding but it's a fact He'll help things move along.
Always when He's involved things work smoothly and don't go wrong.
You'll be glad you called on Him and He'll be happy too.
A job well done pleases everyone when the work is through!

We all work hard our entire life to earn a decent living.
As citizens we pay our way and that includes some giving
To help the many who are down and out and need someone to care.
That fits right in with Jesus' plan He wants us all to share!

Some folks call this "socialism" and don't want to pay their way.
They have their wealth all stacked up and add to it each day.
They hide their worth to avoid the tax and fight to keep it all.
Our leaders can't agree to pay our bills our credit rating is bound to fall!

Both sides are guilty in their own way for the awful fix we're in.
Greed has played a major role and it's looked upon as sin.
I hope our nation can survive and not go down the drain.
Our least prepared will bear the burden, but we all will feel the pain!

March 21.

Heaven Is Waiting

Dedicated to my dear friend Evelyn Wilson Blizzard

I know there's joy in Heaven this very special day,
For our dear friend Evelyn Blizzard is even now on her way.
We will always miss her sweet smiling face,
But Herman is there awaiting and he's been saving her a place!

They both were such very dear friends of mine.
It's true that more wonderful folks you will never find.
They were in fact a most truly lovable pair.
I'm sure that Jesus will be happier now that she is there!

Evelyn has been lonely ever since Herman has been gone.
She really missed his funny jokes and being all alone.
She welcomed all of her dear friends who liked to pay a visit.
When you knocked upon her door she merely said "who is it"!

She never was too busy to sit and chat awhile.
I'd travel half-way around the globe just to see her smile.
She dearly loved all of her friends and she did have quite a few,
But she always made it very clear that she was happy to see you!

She's leaving her family now with a void that they can't fill.
The same is true at "Little Chapel" where she'll be missed until,
Jesus Himself sends the word and makes it known to all,
That Evelyn has arrived in Heaven and they are having a ball!

The "Pearly Gates" swung wide open when Evelyn had arrived,
And there with Saint Peter was Herman standing just inside.
The "Master Hugger" himself was happy as he gave her the works.
You see, being "Hugger in Chief" is just one of his many perks!

By their friend, Jacob Shepherd

March 22.

I Can Do It

One day at a time is fine and a very good way to go.
What will happen to us tomorrow is something we don't know.
So we only make plans for things that we must do today.
The rest of our life is not for us, but our Higher Power to say!

The fact that I'm alive today is a miracle there is no doubt.
My Higher Power pulled me through often when I'd been counted out.
Everyone has a story to tell of what their life was like before.
Folks who're deep in trouble now would like to hear much more!

My program leads me to believe that there is a life beyond.
I joined with others just like me and we formed a common bond.
We're all alike in many ways and that we can accept.
Making changes where we should, at that we're all adept!

Serenity, wisdom, courage and change are words I understand.
Those words have helped me every day to do the things I've planned.
That little prayer I say each day helps me to fill my need.
As long as I do not forget to pray I'm sure I will succeed!

The Twelve Steps and the Golden Rule all come from God's domain.
They are the tools that we must use to help relieve the pain.
We'd like to have just one more drink, then we'd stop for sure.
That's when we realize that we can't stop, that there really is no cure!

Help me Jesus, help me Lord, and all who are just like me.
I know that you are listening and I know you'll hear my plea.
I cannot quit I must admit, can't do it on my own.
But with my Higher Power's help and AA I won't be all alone!

Author's Note: I am not an alcoholic, but I have admired the work
and success of AA program for a long time. Active participation
as a member of the Board of Directors of a prominent treatment
center for many years helped me to be sympathetic yet realistic
in helping family members and friends deal with ravages of
what we all now know as a disease.

Hello

Are you among the friendly folk who love to say "hello."
Who don't mind stopping just to chat when you are on the go.
You'll never know how much it means to someone passing by,
For you to speak some friendly words or merely just say "Hi"!

Too many times we miss the chance to make a person's day.
Perhaps we're at a loss for words and don't know what to say,
But more than likely we're thinking of our problems large and small,
And we don't realize that someone else may have no friends at all!

Walking down the avenue one day, the day a perfect "ten"
I'd tried to contact all my friends but none of them were in,
So here I was alone, adrift, I didn't know what to do.
If only someone rushing by would say a word or two!

I stopped to think and realized that I was the one at fault.
I was not doing what I should, not doing what I ought.
So I began to look around at others passing by.
Soon I saw a likely soul, approached him and said "Hi"!

The object of my bold approach sure was a friendly guy.
He looked at me and said "Hello, I'm glad that you said Hi,
You have helped restore my faith I thought that no one cared",
And from that moment on we talked about the things we shared!

That chance encounter on the street was one that saved my life.
You won't believe this but it's true his sister is now my wife.
If we had a lot more time there's more that I could tell,
But I'll merely share this "gem" with you my sister is his wife as well!

March 24.

Hello Jesus, Are You Free

When you have a problem do you ask Jesus for His Aid?
You can be assured that it'd be the best choice that you ever made.
You won't have to hem and haw and tell Him what to do.
You see, He's always well prepared to do what's best for you!

The human race has been around for 'lo these many years.
Jesus came into the world to help and calm our fears.
A freely-given gift from God, who sacrificed His Son,
Who let Him die upon the Cross as the Chosen One!

The world has prospered under God and mankind has achieved
A level of affluence that never would have been believed
By the early followers of Jesus, those wonderful Saints of old.
They helped to write the New Testament in precious words of gold!

We humans are never trouble-free and it wasn't meant to be.
The devil has been around forever and entices you and me.
He would like to "rule" mankind and always plays his hand.
All of us must resist his pitch on our way to the Promised Land!

Jesus is the Saving Grace of what ails mankind today.
Without His Help we'll never, as a Nation, see a brighter day.
We seem to think that "fighting for our rights" is the proper thing to do.
We need to think much more in terms of "what can I do for you?"

So when you have a problem, always call on Him.
He's not the kind to look the other way and let you sink or swim.
He'll join right in and help you with whatever is your task.
Just tell Him what the problem is and he'll do anything you ask!

Palm Sunday

Help Wanted

Is there something we can do to help to turn the tide?
We all have talents we can use and we'll have Jesus by our side.
I'm already working on my list, I can't wait to start.
There is so much that I can do if I work with all my heart!

Jesus has been my friend, my guide, for lo' these many years.
He wrapped His arms around me all those times when I shed those tears,
And yes, He was always nearby when I found myself in need.
He was the One who led the way each time I did someone a good deed!

I've watched our world go up and down, it's been a bumpy road,
But Jesus never let me down at all He helped me carry my load,
And every time that sadness hit me hard Jesus took my hand.
He looked me in the eye and squeezed my hand and helped me understand!

Jesus always calls me Jacob most people just call me Jake.
As Jesus equates me with His Bible friends it's almost more than I can take.
I'm glad that He thinks of me that way it really makes my day.
I'm so thankful for His love that it makes me want to pray!

So is there really something that we can do to let folks know we care.
I'm sure that Jesus will say "Right On" as our love for Him we share.
If we will help Him spread the word many folks can still be saved.
All who hear his message of forgiveness will be sorry they misbehaved!

When we sit down to watch the news we see so much to fear.
Natural disasters are very bad and seem to get even worse each year.
Mankind makes it worse again with destruction that's caused by war.
God Himself may end it all real soon it's already gone so far!

Here I Am Lord

No one knows when their time will come,
When Jesus calls our name.
So we must always be prepared,
Our presence to proclaim!

If you accept the love of Christ,
And live the life He taught,
He'll welcome you with open arms,
And rewards for battles fought!

You must not fear this "trip" abroad,
The last one that you'll take,
Christ has made His plans for you,
And Him you can't forsake!

Gather up your "Golden Deeds,"
Your troubles leave behind,
Make sure that Jesus knows you,
Just "one" of earth's mankind!

We'll miss the ones we leave on earth,
They'll follow when it's time.
We'll welcome those who've gone before,
Our life will be sublime!

He's My Brother

I awoke this morning with a "family" on my mind.
This was something new for me and was not the usual kind.
It was in fact about the "Fearsome Four" as Teddy rejoined them all.
I'm sure that Joe, Jr., Jack and Bobby will now throw Ted the ball!

All four of these young men were born to lead their fellow man.
They were from a real dynasty known as the "Kennedy" clan.
Papa Joe, a wealthy man, was ambitious but with reputation flawed.
He served as Ambassador to Great Britain before he was outlawed!

"Joe, Sr." settled all the family into an enclave near the sea.
That became the "launching pad" for their political activity.
"Joe, Jr.'s" Air Corp duty called when World War II began.
He died a hero when his plane exploded, ending big Joe's plan!

"Jack" was subject to many ills but managed to enlist.
He became a Navy hero, then ran for office since Papa did insist.
He worked up through the Senate ranks and became our President.
An able man who served us well 'til assassin's bullets made a sad event.

"Bobby" was a sailor and with the Navy sailed the sea,
But he too became involved and helped make history.
As Senator and AG for President Jack, he learned his lessons well.
A leading candidate for President, assassins bullets were his death knell!

"Teddy" was the youngest boy and youngest child of nine.
Senator for years, another Henry Clay, was also called a lion.
After many years of problem health he lost his final valiant fight.
This last member of the "Fearsome Four" finally turned out the light!

March 28.

The Royal Wedding

In London everything is at fever pitch that's wedding bells we hear.
Kate and William have spent nine years getting things in gear.
Yes, there have been ups and downs but they both persevered,
They've now reached the chosen date, their vows will be revered!

It will be the biggest show since Prince Charles and Lady Di were wed.
The Mother of William was a beautiful bride as Kate will be it's said.
They're both quite young and so much in love, it's obvious to all.
The Brits all love these colorful affairs it's the Royal protocol!

When Prince Charles and Lady Diane were wed, we were on the scene.
My family and I were in London and we wanted to see the Queen.
The pageantry was overwhelming but we tried to see it all.
Security was restrictive and much went on as we walked down the mall!

The citizens all demand that they be part of every show.
Folks pour in from around the world and land at Air Heathrow.
They catch the tube to Westminster and Spur road near the gate.
The Palace where the flag is flying and they want a glimpse of Kate!

On Thursday night the crowds are growing and moving to and fro.
It's obvious that everyone wants to be at the best place to see the show.
You cannot see it all unless you move around a lot and then,
There is so much going on that there is no way you can take it in!

After noon on Friday distantly you hear a mounting roar of the crowd.
The ceremony is over and official and the noise gets real loud.
Prince William and Princess Catherine appear and are now officially wed.
The crowds will celebrate and drink toasts all night and no one goes to bed!

March 29.

Hooray For Hollywood

Dedicated to my son John Hilary Shepherd, who has a Master's
Degree from American Film Institute and is a Screen Writer.

When it comes from Hollywood most likely it's make believe.
Films are made for every mood that the human can conceive,
But some few are really true and bring tears to your eyes.
They are tellers of tall tales and masters of disguise!

I have a very soft spot in my heart for victims of any kind.
I shed tears at the drop of a hat and no one seems to mind,
But when it's over and turns out well, I'm happy that I cried.
It shows my mate that I am human with a sentimental side!

I love to watch the awards programs, they put on quite a show.
There's glitter and some tension too with very few folks in the know.
Fame and heartbreak are in the envelopes, hidden from our eyes.
When it is opened it brings to some a confirmation, to others a surprise!

When I think about the happiness that winning always brings,
I also think of those who lost and are left waiting in the wings.
Those losers are building up their resume with casting calls to come.
There's no doubt that they will all stay busy with starring roles for some!

Every story that's told on screen will provide a lot of roles.
Many more grips work behind the scenes to help them reach their goals.
I've played some "extra" parts myself, it's fun but tiring too.
When all your friends see you on the screen they can't always tell it's you!

Hollywood is just a part of the world wide movie scene.
Wonderful stories from every land make it to the silver screen.
"Entertainment" is the important word its center is "tinsel town!"
I'm sure that all of them will work real hard, not to let us down!

Good Friday

March 30.

How Attitudes Change

Negative thoughts are in the air,
I feel them moving here and there.
I can't say why I feel so blue.
That is why I've come to You!

You always help me when I'm down.
You make me smile instead of frown.
You'll find me now upon my knees,
Asking You to help me please!

The devil is casting his net around,
To catch poor souls when they are down.
I'm not taking the bait today,
Opting instead to kneel and pray!

I know You'll help, You always do,
Especially when I'm feeling blue.
Those negative thoughts have moved offshore.
They're just not active anymore!

I'm searching now for beautiful things,
A gentle breeze, a bird that sings.
This helps me see the brighter side,
The one with which I'm satisfied!

You've helped me find just what I need,
So I no longer have to plead.
Thank You Jesus for everything You do,
Now I am happy and the "sky" is blue!

March 31.

Easter

When Jesus died upon the cross mankind lost their best friend.
Thank God it was a short term loss, but they didn't know that then.
They shuddered as they watched Him die, an awful thing to see.
As they placed Him in the tomb their thoughts were of eternity!

The broken body of our Lord lay in the darkness of the tomb.
He was as helpless as the day God placed Him in the Virgin's womb.
On this lonely Sabbath day the friends of Jesus knelt to pray.
They didn't know what else to do they needed Him to lead the way!

Early on that Sunday morn, the first day of the week,
Mary Magdalene to Mary said, "Come let us go seek
Jesus our Master Who's in the tomb, let's see just where He lay."
They hurried now toward the tomb, 'twas at the break of day!

As they passed the garden wall the sun's rays bathed the tomb.
Since the stone was rolled away they looked into an "empty" room.
A young man dressed in 'dazzling white' was watching o'er the scene.
Jesus Christ had disappeared, was nowhere to be seen!

The young man said, "He is not here He's risen and is free,
Go tell His Disciples He'll meet them soon in Galilee."
As they ran to tell His friends Jesus appeared to them and said,
"Don't be afraid, it's really Me, I've risen from the dead!"

Jesus met for forty days with His Disciples and had a lot to say,
"Go ye into all the world and preach the Gospel every day!"
When His time came, He said "Goodbye" and ascended into the sky!
He was born a gift from God, to save us all He had to die!

Contents *April*

1. All Fools Day 94

2. How Old Are You 95

3. Grandsons 96

4. I Remember You 97

5. I Have A Friend In Heaven 98

6. I Hear The Voice Of Jesus 99

7. I Like To Laugh...100

8. No One But God Can Save Your Soul............................101

9. I Love To Sing of Jesus 102

10. I Remember When..103

11. I Wish I Knew The Answers 104

12. I Wonder...105

13. If At First You Don't Succeed.......................................106

14. Imagination...107

15. In Memory of My Dear Friend George Borg..................108

16. Is It Judgement Day? 109

17. Is It The Truth?..110

18. Isn't It Wonderful 111

19. It Was Fun...112

20. It's Always Up To God...113

21. It's Apple Blossom Time 114

22. It's Just A Word 115

23. It's Mother's Morning Out 116

24. It's Never Too Late 117

25. It's Not A Dream..118

26. It's Not Over 'Til It's Over...119

27. It's Not Too Late..120

28. It's Not Up To Us...121

29. It's Time For Action..122

30. Jesus And Billy 123

April 1.

All Fools Day

There is no fool like a real old fool, or so the saying goes,
But fools don't live to be real old and I am one who knows.
Today is known as All Fools Day around the world you see.
Some fool will seek to play a prank on us then they'll laugh with glee!

Now for that prank to work its will, you have to bite and then,
The perpetrator slaps his knee and shouts, "April Fool" again.
Okay, I will admit, most All Fools pranks are funny, at first they are.
So don't persist and do re-runs, it might even leave a scar!

You see it's true that some folks just can't take a joke,
But others will buy most anything, even a pig that's in a poke.
The pranks that surface on All Fools Day I'm sure you know them all,
But folks forget it's All Fools Day and for those pranks they fall!

Don't put salt in my coffee cup but the sugar will be okay.
When I sit down for breakfast I forget it's All Fools Day.
All those pranks that will be pulled today will bring a lot of fun.
To be sure there may be nothing new, we've used them every one!

Its not hard to find a young fool but old ones are few and far between.
I bet that all the young ones think that I am being mean,
But by the time you reach my age, you've been through the mill.
If there's something you haven't seen it won't be long before you will!

Young fools, old fools, all kinds of fools, today is All Fools Day.
People are having fun of all kind with pranks they love to play.
So when it's time for bed tonight let's hope that all can say,
I made some people laugh today and that has made my day!

How Old Are You

Don't ever think you know it all there's always something new.
You never get too old to learn and change your point of view.
Your life can change from "dull" to being "fun" again,
So always keep an open mind to let new things enter in!

Do you never think of getting old but then lie about your age?
When you look into a mirror does it send you into a rage?
The wrinkles show and magnify, you cannot hide the truth.
Let's face it folks, don't hide the fact we're getting long in the tooth!

Now I'm speaking from a very personal point of view.
I can only speak for me and I dare not try to speak for you.
I'm quite proud of my age you see, it doesn't bother me.
That God has let me live this long makes me happy as can be!

Make every day that you're alive count for something good.
It there's something you want to do, don't say "I wish I could."
Just go ahead and do it and enjoy it while you may,
For no one knows when this might be their very "final" day!

Never worry about your death but be ready when it arrives.
It's the very one who doesn't worry that most often survives.
Don't let thoughts of dying get you down, it's something we all must do.
If you'll just put your trust in Jesus, He'll take good care of you!

So get busy learning something new and start a new career.
Dig out all those projects you've put aside for a brand new day is here.
If you're lonely then call a friend for they may be lonely too,
But never, ever, say those words, "I don't have a thing to do!"

April 3.

Grandsons

Grandsons are solid proof that God is certainly good.
I'd like to have a dozen more, oh how I wish I could.
The six I have are wonderful and a great little group.
Not quite enough for football but enough to have a Scout Troop!

Diversity is certainly essential in any kind of team,
And no one has a monopoly on just how to stay on the beam,
So when they're all in town and we sit down together,
The cacophony proves to everyone they're not "birds of a feather!"

Of course, some are good at this and some are good at that,
I'm sure that someone within the group knows how to swing a bat.
Each one is good at something special that the others don't know about.
They all excel in their own way, of that there is no doubt!

I held each one of these precious boys when they were just minutes old,
The chance I had to kiss them then was worth a pot of gold.
Tender, sweet and squalling too, I whispered in their ear,
Welcome to our family and Grandpa's glad you're here!

As each of you go through life and strike out on your own,
Always remember your family ties, you'll never be alone.
Respect your elders with your love and all of your peers as well.
In return they'll be glad to help you so that you will never fail!

I want each one of you to know that you're special in your own way.
Don't be afraid to compete and give your very best each day.
Marry a sweet little girl, have lots of kids, be sure to wipe their noses.
Above all else I've said I must say, "take time to smell the roses!"

April 4.

I Remember You

Who are these many people who are always passing me by?
Some seem to know me when we meet up "eye to eye",
But when I search into my brain, I do not find their mug.
I'm always happy when one of them gives me a real big hug!

I must admit it's sometimes hard to remember everyone's face.
I try real hard and almost always remember a time and place,
Which leads me right into my valued name and faces file,
And I find a friend from long ago I had not seen in quite a while!

What joy it is to reminisce about all those years gone by.
This coming from a dear old friend who managed to catch my eye,
So I'm always watching in the crowds of people passing by,
Hoping that I'll spot a friend who like me has a roving eye!

Sometimes I see a familiar face but cannot remember the name.
I would like to look away, but too late, I have to play the game.
Which one will remember first, where we met and when.
Neither one remembers where but we have a mutual friend!

So we now have a conversation about that friend who we both know.
A scenario begins to emerge and soon we both can show
That neither of us has lost their mind, we do remember where.
We were at a big "to-do" and there were many people there!

Now we talk about that big "to-do" and what have you done since?
We find that we do have similar tastes and that makes a lot of sense.
By now we have become good friends we'll remember the time and place.
Should we meet again in a crowd, I'm sure I'll remember their face!

April 5.

I Have A Friend In Heaven

I have a friend in Heaven,
The one that we all know,
I talk with Him and He with me,
I know he loves me so!

I have a friend in Heaven,
His earthly days were spent,
To teach us all that "GOD IS LOVE",
We learned just what that meant!

I have a friend in Heaven,
He died that we might know,
The path that we must follow,
As home to Heaven we go!

I have a friend in Heaven,
He rose and lives today,
He's always there if I should call,
He always makes my day!

I have a friend in Heaven,
He gave His life for me,
Not just for me, but one and all,
And soon in Heaven we'll be!

JESUS, our friend in Heaven,
Requires not much from me,
Our friendship is alive and well,
His faithful Steward I'll be!

I Hear The Voice Of Jesus

I am not a preacher and I don't pretend to be,
But one day Jesus came and said, "would you speak for Me?"
I said "of course I will, I know you trained me well,
And maybe I can save someone who's headed straight for hell"!

So I would like to say right now what I have come to know,
That Jesus is our friend indeed and really loves us so.
Why not open up your heart today and let Him walk right in?
There is no doubt that He would like to save you from your sin!

Now as I said, I don't preach but I do write poetry,
To tell folks of my dearest friend and of His love for me.
I like to share with everyone the story of God's love.
How He sent His only Son to earth from Heaven up above!

I've heard good preachers in my life, Samuel Sox and Billy Graham,
My very favorite one of course was dear old Pastor Sam.
He wanted me to follow him and preach about our friend,
But Uncle Sam and World War II soon brought that to an end!

I've always tried to live my life so that I do not have to fear.
I hope my words will comfort some, whose death is drawing near.
I feel the nearness of God's love as I write this today.
I hear the voice of Jesus as He tells me what to say!

I've lost some real dear friends within the recent past.
Jesus comes to comfort us so that the hurt won't last,
And also just to let us know that our friends are with Him now.
What a blessing it is to know that Jesus keeps His solemn vow!

I Like To Laugh

Laughter is the medicine that all of us should use.
Smiling is a form of laughter which no one can refuse,
So put on your happy face and grin as you pass by.
The world would be a better place if no one had to cry!

A funny joke will make you chuckle if there's nothing else that will,
Although a rather bawdy limerick will sometimes fill the bill,
So you must always be discreet when telling dirty jokes,
Especially in a crowd that's mixed and you don't know the folks!

I like to make folks laugh, I really do, it brightens up the day.
A heavy heart may shed its load and pending tears will go away
When someone tells a funny story that everyone can enjoy.
So polish up your repertoire with jokes you can employ!

Don't try to tell a funny joke unless you know it well,
The punch line is the major part of every joke you tell.
If you forget the punch line in front of a crowd of folks,
You will find that you've become for sure the "butt" of all your jokes!

We can't be funny all the time for life is serious too.
Sometimes we cannot laugh at all, for there's too much for us to do.
We put aside the jokes and such and then we settle down,
But please don't ever replace your pretty smile with an ugly frown!

I'm sure you know some folks who just don't know how to smile.
Oh yes, they're the very ones who cry while walking down the aisle.
Happiness and laughter should be the goal you seek each day,
And that is how we all should live for there is no better way!

April 8.

No One But God Can Save Your Soul

God is the Master of the Universe it's huge and has no end.
He sent Dear Jesus, His Precious Son to die for mankind's sin.
Jesus told us what we must do to join Him up in Heaven.
His twelve disciples spread the word 'til Judas fell and left eleven!

God says there are only two possible places to go when we die on earth.
He sent Jesus to tell us all about it and so we celebrate His Birth.
No other religion has that connection and that's a crying shame.
In fact there are many places on the earth they don't know His Name!

We all must do our very best to lead folks to the Lord.
We can't all be in the pulpit but we can surely spread the word.
We know the devil is always actively opposing Jesus' plan.
We must reject his gaudy schemes and save those folks we can!

Now some folks do not believe in God so they have little to tell.
For them for sure there is no Heaven but for them there's always hell.
It's not up to me to condemn their souls I'd save them if I could.
I'd like to take them with me to Heaven and if I could I would!

About those folks who don't believe, are they afraid to die?
Do they say that someway they'll beat the odds and on this they rely
And when they die and reach the gate no-one knows their name.
They must accept that they're at fault and there's no one else to blame!

What can we do to save those folks who say they don't believe?
Are they reluctant to accept any help that they might receive?
I'm sure Jesus wants us all to return to Heaven from whence we came,
So anything we can do to save a wayward soul would only be fair game!

I Love To Sing of Jesus

I love to sing of Jesus and what He means to me.
It helps me curb my sinful ways, can even set me free.
Thank God for sending Jesus to save us all from sin.
We need to praise Him everyday so let us now begin!

I hear the music ringing now, from all the hymns I love.
It's heavenly music, that's for sure, it's coming from above.
Raise your voices everyone, be sure it's loud and clear.
As we sing, we think of Him and wish that He was here!

Sing hallelujah, praise the Lord, He is our God and King.
We all must thank Him everyday, He gives us everything!
Praise God from whom all blessings flow, praise His Holy name.
Once we place our trust in Him, we'll never be the same!

When we arise each early morn we start the day off right.
We thank the Lord for all His love which kept us through the night.
With God and Jesus watching us, the Holy Spirit too,
No one could ask for better care, it's what we all must do!

As we sit down for our morning meal we bow our heads in prayer.
We thank the Lord for all our food and for His tender care.
All through the day as we accept His help for everything we do,
Let's ne'er forget to offer thanks and ask Him to see us through!

April 10.

I Remember When

I often think of all the days when I was just a kid.
It's great remembering all the fun we had and all the things we did
I often wonder too what happened to my buddies tried and true
I'd like to gather all of them around and guess just who is who!

You'd think of course that we could always recognize a face,
But oftimes after years have passed and we're in a different place
You wrack your brain and clear the webs so that you can see,
And all the while you wonder why that person doesn't know me!

We stand around and kick the clods and hang our head in shame,
Does it happen to us all, can't remember our best friends name?
Then, guess what, our wives speak up and quickly save the day.
Why not just introduce yourselves, you'll have a lot to say!

Where would we be without those gals to tell us what to do?
I'll tell you where I'd be for sure but I don't know about you.
I'd be looking for a mate, someone to love and hold my hand.
I know for sure I wasn't meant to be alone and that I understand!

It's really sad but years go by and time does take its toll.
For those of us lucky to survive we hate to admit we're old.
Some fortunate ones still have a mate but some are now alone.
They wander around and would be lost without their mobile phone!

Oh well, it's true, life is great, each day brings something new.
If we can just make it out of bed there's something we can do.
But first, please don't let's forget, Thank God for everyday.
He's right there in Heaven listening in He'll help you on your way!

Birthdate of my Dad, Jacob N. Shepherd, 1884

April 11.

I Wish I Knew The Answers

When Jesus died upon the Cross, people then weren't aware
That He would be so beloved by so many everywhere.
The story of His death and resurrection spread far and wide.
His Apostles carried the message around the world like a rising tide!

The Creed relates that He spent three days in hell before He arose.
What He was doing during those three days no one really knows.
I like to think that He was fighting with the devil for His very soul.
The fact that He won that fight proves that He can make us whole!

Having seen the burning brimstone torment those folks in hell
Made Jesus more determined than ever that His Story He must tell.
He worked real hard from the beginning and He still works hard today
To bring salvation to everyone and for that we should daily pray!

Do not believe the devil when he tries his best to lure you in.
The truth of the matter is that his wares are loaded down with sin.
Do not accept his promises that he has just what you need.
He'll have no trouble selling his bill of goods to those who bask in greed!

We would all be better off to spend our days working with the poor.
There are so many down and out who've been pushed out the door.
They have no way to make a living and don't know what to do.
There but for the wonderful Grace of God go folks like me and you!

Those folks without a place to lay their head are always on Jesus' mind.
I can imagine He's saying to Himself, "What's happened to mankind?"
They're hoarding their wealth and worldly goods like it's a ticket to ride
A "Golden Chariot" up to Heaven, but it all disappeared when they died!

April 12.

I Wonder

Do we become Angels when we die?
I mean will we have wings with which to fly?
It's my belief that Angels are a special breed,
Developed by God for His manifold need!

We shouldn't be surprised by the UFO.
Just more of God's troops keeping watch here below.
When you get to Heaven you may be in luck.
You may be flying a UFO instead of driving a truck!

It's hard for us humans to fathom those wonders above.
We must remember that Jesus became a man to share His love.
His experience on earth furnished insight for Heavenly living.
His return to His Heavenly throne became a time of giving!

God is beginning to share His creations with us here on earth.
So much has been passed on to us since the time of His birth.
We first developed electricity from the powerful lightning bolt,
And nuclear power was first envisioned from a sunbeam's jolt!

So much has happened since the world's creation.
If God dropped Adam into our midst imagine his elation.
I think that our first glimpse of Heaven will also be a surprise,
So all of us should be prepared for God to finally open our eyes!

I don't mean for this message to cause anyone to worry.
While things here on earth change daily, God's in no hurry.
Thousands of years have passed since this world was born.
Let's try to keep mankind's damages from looking weary and worn.

If At First You Don't Succeed.................

Do you ever have those days when nothing seems to work?
The pieces of the puzzle don't fit and you almost go berserk,
So you go back and start again and move things all around.
Before long the problem is solved, the solution you have found!

When you stop to analyze the trouble that you had at first
It seems perhaps a lack of forethought may have made things worse,
So you sit and ponder over all those early moves you made.
It's quite clear that you were wrong with the early plans you laid!

It's good to have an early morning chat with the Man upstairs.
He can help you start the day off right because He really cares
About you and all those plans you made to have a perfect day.
It's always wise to seek His Help so please take the time to pray!

Once you are up and running and you've got things underway
You like to keep your plans on track and finish them today,
For we don't know what tomorrow may bring, that's too far ahead.
Let's hope that we have lots of pep and hop right out of bed!

I think it's best if we don't plan too doggone far ahead.
If we find ourselves with too big a load we'll fall behind instead.
We're always playing catch-up and nothing gets done of course.
We find ourselves leaving things undone and causing much remorse!

So get up early and leave plenty of time to get things started right.
A good night's sleep will rid you of those worries that you had last night,
And best of all you follow your plan and overcome the trouble it poses.
The work is completed as planned and there's now "time to smell the roses"!

April 14.

Imagination

If you were in my shoes today what would you like to say.
I need a subject to start me off, to get me on my way.
Sometimes it's like that, don't know why, but yet,
I'll soon be writing something good, on that I'd place a bet!

Imagination plays a role in all we do each day.
We have a task that must be solved and it won't go away.
We think we know what we should do and that is really great,
But just before we get started we decide, let's just let it wait!

You see we imagined somewhere deep inside there must be a better way
To solve that task that we must do but we'll let it rest today,
And by tomorrow I'm thinking now, I'll surely be ready to go,
So there's no rush, just put it aside, I can do it later you know!

Another dawn, another day, we've got lots of things to do.
What about that task we put aside, can we put it in the queue?
Well, I don't know why not, we should have time today.
My imagination is working overtime, but things should be okay!

The sun is setting in the west, I haven't had much luck.
All those things I wanted to do, I'm going to need a truck.
It sure is funny how things pile up you never will get through,
And that's just the way things work out when you've got things to do!

The week's gone by and you're still at work when someone asks,
You've been working really hard did you finish all your tasks?
You wonder why they should ask so you merely answer, I imagine so,
Imagination always comes in handy when you don't really know!

April 15.

In Memory of My Dear Friend George Borg

I often think of Malta and my friends so far away.
The memories of those happy times remain with me today.
There were so many guys and gals, they all were helpful too.
That's why I was successful in the things I had to do!

The first day I was in their midst I met a guy named George.
He became my dearest friend whom others called Mister Borg.
Without his help it's clear to me I could not have done my best.
He was my voice, my ears, my crutch he helped me pass the test!

George was married to Lina whom he loved both body and soul.
They produced three wonderful kids a good life was their goal.
Joann and Maria, beautiful girls, and Joseph like his dad.
Sweet grandkids soon came along and Grandpa George was glad!

When time arrived for me to leave I left George Borg as boss.
He did so well with my old job there was no threat of loss.
He ran those plants for many years they always did quite well.
Until one day the axe did fall, the decision made to sell!

George was free now but tallyho, the government knew him well.
They put him to work at once, the job he got was swell.
A nice big office was a perk, he had a staff of course.
He had the kind of job where he could aid the labor force!

George was taken from our midst when Jesus called him home.
He left a void we cannot fill no matter where we roam.
Let all family and friends be sure there will be no debates.
Rest assured that George will greet us all at the "Pearly Gates"!

April 16.

Is It Judgement Day?

T'would be a grave mistake for us to know the date of Judgement Day.
The when and where we'll meet our end is up to God to say.
He may not have decided yet just when He wants to end it all.
There may be some bigger plans in store for this terrestrial ball!

God wants us to enjoy life and to live in harmony.
So many do not have that choice, being at war constantly.
Eternity is a long, long time and we must be prepared
To be a friend to all mankind as our life in Heaven is shared!

If you think it's hard to get along in this world that we know,
There will be many adjustments to be made in the land where we will go.
I'm not sure we'll have our choice of where we go in the "Promised Land,"
But no need to worry for Jesus will be leading us by the hand!

Getting comfortable with others is something that may be hard to do.
We must realize that we may not live alone nor would we even want to.
Since Heaven has existed for many years and will prevail forever,
Then family ties are something that we may never have to sever!

We all know that Heaven is a part of God's big master plan.
It's referred to lovingly by those who believe as the "Promised Land."
I try my best to live my life in order that I may hope to go,
Whenever Jesus feels it's time for me to give up my life down here below!

When I die the world won't end, but for me it will.
I'll transfer residence from earth to Heaven, my home above to fill.
I will not worry about the date, it's not for me to know.
If Jesus thought it was my business He would have told me so!

April 17.

Is It The Truth?

Some folks have a way of saying just what's on their mind.
Others beat around the bush and tell stories of all kind.
If everyone would just speak up and tell you what they mean,
The world would be a better place if everyone came clean!

I try to keep an open mind and always speak the truth.
Don't try to mislead anyone for that would be uncouth.
Any time you tell a lie you damage your own soul,
And when you try to cover up you dig a deeper hole!

Any lie that one might tell they might call it "lily white"
Will influence everything they do until they go to bed at night,
And then they wonder why it is that sleep won't come at all.
It's hard to get true "peace of mind" when you have dropped the ball!

You never gain a thing in life by lying to hide the facts.
It's awfully hard to cover up and hide dishonest acts.
Folks who live deceitful lives rarely get ahead.
They spend a lot of time saying things they never should have said!

It's not so hard to tell the truth in everything we do.
That way we never have to lie about something that was untrue.
For lies beget more lies and soon the truth is buried deep.
And like I've often said before no one will get to sleep!

Make a promise to yourself and start today off right.
Just tell the truth in everything and you'll sleep good tonight.
The wonderful thing about it all as everyone can see,
That great big smile upon your face "the truth has set you free!"

April 18.

Isn't It Wonderful

Jesus wants us all to know that He is close at hand.
He is always there awaiting in the Promised Land.
Should you find yourself in need without a place to go,
Just place your burden in His Hands with your tale of woe!

You see, Jesus has quick access to the Greatest Force of all.
He's in constant touch with God The Father and doesn't have to call.
The Two of Them will take your burden and sprinkle it with love,
And then the Angels' own express will return it from above!

I'm a firm believer in all the stories from the New Testament.
God sent Jesus, His Only Son, to earth, and His whole life was spent
Preparing Himself to teach us all about what God has in store
For those of us who believe in Him and vow to sin no more!

When Jesus died upon the Cross, two thousand years ago
His friends all thought that all was lost and they had no place to go.
Much like us today, they couldn't believe the stories that He told,
Especially the one that said He'd rise again, it was very bold!

But rise He did and now we know that He still lives today
And occupies the Place of Honor in that Land about which we pray.
He has prepared a wonderful place for us all to live with Him above,
And while still on earth if we believe, He showers us with His love!

I don't know much about other religions but the one I've been taught.
I only know that Jesus tells us to believe and do the things we ought.
He's the Only Son of God The Father, I give Them Both my love.
I know too that when I die, I'll go live with Them above!

It Was Fun

I like to think of the good ole' days when I was just a lad.
Sometimes it seems that those days were the best I ever had.
They were middle depression years and Daddy had no job.
We all pitched in to do our part and did not sit and sob!

I spent a lot of time at simple tasks to help my Mom and Dad.
Dad opened up a used furniture store, using talent that he had.
He could do most anything that could be done with hands.
A lesson that I learned from him was, you must do what life demands!

We lived in a neighborhood where there were lots of girls and boys.
There was always something going on that did not require the use of toys.
We played a lot of "tag" football and games like "hide and seek."
It seemed that some new kids moved into our area almost every week!

In those days we did not mix with blacks, but all others were fair game.
We called ourselves "the Chestnut Street gang" and this was our domain.
With Prentzas, Showfety, and Kontoulas, my name Shepherd did seem strange.
We were just a melting pot of sorts and never moved out of range!

We all attended school nearby in a city school of course.
Aycock School, grades one through six, was our education source.
Misses Irving, Pinkston, and Garlick too, were names that come to mind.
A better group of teachers I'm sure you'd never find!

I got my start in that arena and it has served me well.
When I look back at those good ole' days, there is a lot to tell.
The names of all those kids I knew are still emblazoned on my brain,
And I will always be very happy that I grew up in that domain!

It's Always Up To God

I seek the loving help of Jesus when I pray today.
There's someone special on my mind who's name I will not say.
A young man who's quite close to me and yet so far away,
I feel the best thing I can do is bow my head and pray!

I have special thoughts right now of this one of whom I speak.
I'm sure Jesus shares my concern and will furnish what I seek.
I'm praying that He will intervene where I dare not raise my voice.
Jesus is always willing to help us out when we have no other choice!

Sometimes we have to hold our tongue and not say what we think.
It's better to confirm those things we want to say using pen and ink.
When the time is right and He is ready, Jesus will make His move.
As Master of the Universe His actions He'll convey with undying love!

I look back many years into my life when I was in a similar spot.
My mentor wanted me to "preach" and spoke of it a lot,
But Jesus intervened and asked me to help to save our land.
I changed my plans and learned to fly so I could lend a hand!

I chose not to "preach" the Word when I returned from war,
But I've never lost my love for Jesus in fact I love Him even more.
I spread the story of His love for us everywhere I go.
It gives me pleasure to speak of Him to everyone I know!

April 21.

It's Apple Blossom Time

They say that you should eat an apple every single day,
Which will help you keep all the doctors far, far away.
I'm heading to the grocery store just to get some Golden Delicious.
They're not only very tasty but they are also very nutritious!

I like to eat real simple things that help me stay in shape,
But when I'm offered apple pie for me there's no escape.
Oh, I may dilly-dally for a bit, but my resolve just fades away,
And I will surely someway get my full quota of apples for today!

My Mother made delicious apple pie and she used apples from our tree.
When I gathered those apples for her apple pie, I always kept one for me.
I guess you'd say I joined the apple corps, for I became a fan,
And I've continued to eat lots of apples since I became a man!

I used to carry an apple from our tree to my teacher at Aycock School.
I may not have been the smartest kid but I was surely no one's fool,
And I knew the grades on my report card reflected many things,
Including my teachers feeling that I was an angel although I had no wings!

I still think that an apple is welcome in everybody's lunch.
Grapes would be real nice and would suffice but they come in a bunch.
So you'll find apples most everywhere and I was always glad to see
A juicy Red Delicious in the bottom of my lunch bag, waiting just for me!

Apples come with different names, much like people don't you see.
There's Granny Smith and Gravenstein and Gala, all hanging on a tree.
I've always liked the Empire, Fuji and Braeburn, they all are very good,
If you put Winesap or Jonagold into an apple pie, man thats delicious food!

Birthdate of #4 Daughter M. Christine Shepherd, 1971

114

April 22.

It's Just A Word

There is a word that we all know but we don't think about,
An ordinary word it may be but it has lots of clout,
For you can always make it fit wherever you need it most,
By adding only one more word to modify the "host!"

The "host" word is an easy word, we use it every day.
It helps us get our point across in almost every way.
You can't misspell the "host" word for it's simple as can be.
You also never change the sound but use it frequently!

I keep on beating 'round the bush and have not used the word.
I want to keep you guessing and you may think I'm absurd.
The "host" word can be used alone or can be modified
By any word you pick and choose until you're satisfied!

I don't want to give away, the "host" word you must guess.
An easy word we use a lot you know it more or less.
While you may not have guessed the word, it's put your mind to work.
You'll be thinking long and hard before you go berserk!

It's not a word you "have" to use, there are many just as good,
But this word always helps you out so you are understood.
Do you think you have the word, the one I'm looking for?
If you do then you are smart and I am just a bore!

I'm still looking for that word, I'm getting mighty close.
I've really had to rack my brain you'll say I've been verbose.
I hope that I can finish up by making this poem rhyme.
If I can't then you can say, "You've wasted lots of "time!"

April 23.

It's Mother's Morning Out

MMO at LCOB is dear to you and me.
The greatest group of "good ole gals" that you will ever see.
They give their time and energy it takes a lot of that,
To give those Moms a morning free so they can sit and chat!

Wonderful ladies, one and all, God blessed each one you see,
With His special kind of love which they give so patiently.
Jesus has reserved a special place in Heaven just for them.
The love they show for those dear kids is love they have for Him!

The nursery's equipped just like at home, for babies to get their rest.
They'll get a lot of loving care, that's what MMO does best.
As they get older and move on up, they learn to pray and sing.
And in the playground open air, they can play and swing!

These lovely ladies are all well trained, to reprimand with tact.
They show a child who's being bad it's not the way to act.
So kids grow up at MMO with grace and love for all,
To share in prayer, learn a song, and run in Fellowship Hall!

When MMO ends for the day, a big decision must come.
Where will the gang have lunch today before going home?
It doesn't matter where they go, they've tried them all before,
So once the big decisions made, they all walk out the door!

Our thanks must go to everyone who's served and played a part
In MMO at LCOB, the church with a great big heart.
So I'll just say it all right now, and say it loud and clear,
Thank God for "Miss Linda" and her girls, so precious and so dear!

Dedicated with our love to Barbara Heath, May 1, 2009

Written by "Mr. Jake"

April 24.

It's Never Too Late

God bless those atheists who don't believe.
For those poor lost souls I truly grieve.
The long pathway through life that I have trod,
Would have failed completely without the presence of God!

Each new day that dawns brings with it God's love.
I thank Him with all my heart for watching from above,
For bringing to me and my loved ones, happiness and health,
And providing enough of life's blessings so we can share the wealth!

God also provides us daily, freedom from harm and danger.
When you need His help, you'll find that He's not a stranger.
There have been times in my life when my pathway was not clear,
But when I called on Him to lead the way I had nothing to fear!

So it is, for me at least, awfully difficult to see,
That if I didn't believe in God, where in the world would I be.
I plan to spend eternity in Heaven where God has His home.
When He needs me to help with someone else, I'll be free to roam!

You can tell me if you wish, that you don't believe.
How that is possible, I can't even conceive.
I'll do my best to convince you that you should change your mind,
For as a believer you'll be saved and not left behind!

Non-believers will not make it to Heaven, they go the other way.
Jesus agonizes over every lost soul that He's unable to sway.
I wish there was something more that I could do to retrieve,
These wayward atheists who are lost because they don't believe!

April 25.

It's Not A Dream

It's hard for me to understand how some folks don't believe in God.
I can understand man's love for his fellowman for that's where Jesus trod,
But Jesus went further down life's glory road to tell us of God's love,
And gave His life so that we might join Him in God's Heaven above!

It's hard to accept that when I die, I'll never see "some" loved ones again.
To think that when they die they'll just fade away, that's hard to explain.
As I approach the end of life my faith in God gets stronger by the day.
It's inconceivable that all I've learned will just wither and fade away!

We are hard to convince of the existence of something that we can't see.
We constantly ask ourselves, "How in the world can this be?"
Well, there's the answer, it's not in this world, it's up in Heaven above.
Now we don't know exactly where Heaven is but it's full of Jesus' Love!

It's also filled with all the Saints and all the folks who've gone on before.
Near death experiences have allowed a glimpse by many who want more.
They have the "proof" which some must have, it satisfies their mind
And opens up the doors to Heaven for all members of mankind!

As humans we all have faults of sorts, the devil sees to that.
He's jealous of our love for Jesus and wants to wage combat.
The devil leads so many astray some seem to like his wares.
I prefer to place my faith and all my love in that "Man upstairs"!

I have no doubt at all, oh yes I know that my Savior lives.
God confirms my faith each day, and my, what sweet comfort that gives.
I am no longer out seeking "proof" for that's already in my heart,
And if you have not yet accepted Jesus I hope you soon will start!

It's Not Over 'Til It's Over

Don't try to tell me I'm too old, I've never felt so good.
That's unusual I must admit so I'll just knock on wood.
I never cease to be amazed at things I find to do,
Like finding something new to write about when I write to you!

Now I won't run in the marathon, no sir, that is not my thing.
Not only that but to be sure my legs have lost their spring.
Oh, I can walk a couple of blocks before I feel the pain,
But then I stop and rest a bit and then I start out again!

Well, yes, I've had trouble with my eyes, doesn't everyone?
Don't hear too good either, but then I don't need a megaphone.
I use Medicare and all it offers to its fullest extent.
I thank God for that program, it was Heaven sent!

I don't want to bore anyone while speaking of my plight.
You see I'm one of the lucky ones for I have seen the light.
I know that Jesus cares for me, I know He always will.
When I'm tired of "keeping on" He'll total up my bill!

I'm wise enough to know one thing I'm here because of Him.
So many times through my long life it was either sink or swim.
Jesus always came to help me out and lent a helping hand,
And He patiently now is waiting to take me to the Promised Land!

No one reaches perfection as they travel down life's long road,
But they can always call on Jesus to help them carry their load.
I live in Peace and thank the Lord for each day that I'm around,
And I also know for sure that someday soon I'll be Heaven bound!

April 27.

It's Not Too Late

Wake up America, don't give up, for that time is close at hand.
I believe that Jesus will soon come again and He will take command.
King George II tried very hard to prove that he was the chosen one.
His reign sure showed that Republicans are not fit to have the throne!

King George I began the quest when he first took command.
His entire family helped his fight, they are a warrior clan.
Old King George was first to try to save the world by force,
But he stopped too soon, a big mistake, Saddam lived on of course!

Bill Clinton came from lowly roots with no heroes in his past.
He took the reins and set us on a path that was to last.
For two full terms our fortunes rose, we all were doing well.
The books were balanced for a change and then things went to hell!

The State of Texas was the first to fall for King George II's line.
Brother Jeb in Florida chimed in and said, "I think we're doing fine."
Then they met with King George I to plan a "palace coup."
They all agreed, this warrior group that it was the thing to do!

With the budget surplus moving up, the debt was coming down.
Republicans rubbed their greedy hands made plans to take the crown.
Clinton's peccadillos hurt their party though Gore was squeaky clean.
The votes when cast were in a tie, but the Bush court ruled supreme!

In early 2001 George II moved into the WH with his cast and crew.
They began to look around to see what damage they could do.
The "terror" attack on September eleven opened up the door.
Wasn't long before His Highness Sir King George led us into his war!

April 28.

It's Not Up To Us

We must not judge our fellowman, that's strictly God's domain.
Opinions yes, we all will have, from casting stones we must refrain.
A fine line runs between the two, be careful what you say.
If you feel inclined to cast a stone, stop long enough to pray!

When heroes and idols fall from grace and do things beyond belief,
Our first reaction is to cast a stone to get some form of relief,
But we must leave these things to God He'll know just what to do.
For only He knows the facts, no tabloid tales, but everything that's true!

I like to think I'm not judgmental, opinionated, yes.
Peccadilloes by my heroes hurt, that much I must confess.
I know I must forgive for I have been forgiven.
The life I lead in every way is now truly Jesus driven!

It's hard to find a part of our lives completely free of sin.
We go to church, we say our prayers, we give thanks, but then,
We fail to let the whole world know that Jesus is our friend.
We must always admit that we belong to Him, a rule we cannot bend!

When we review the road we've travelled during our life here on earth,
There will be lots of things we miss that happened since our birth,
But you can rest assured that Jesus has all the facts at hand,
For they were written in our Book of Life without fail at His command!

Everyone who expects to spend Eternity with Jesus must survive
The final judgment rendered in person as soon as we arrive,
But we must prepare well in advance for that final exam.
That'll be the first time we'll personally see the Greatest of all "I Am"!

April 29.

It's Time For Action

If our country stays on its course, we're going down the drain.
We keep sending money to foreign lands while our people feel the pain.
We never should have fought those wars yet we invaded them.
Our President misinformed us all and he was acting on a whim!

In the meantime, back at home, the country's surplus disappeared.
Big deficits were created to foot the bills, much worse than we all feared.
Eight long years of bloody wars caused our young men to fall like flies.
None of this had to be, it was all based on a pack of lies!

We've reached the point where we must act and we must be real bold.
It will be real hard to stem the rising tide caused when that bill of goods was sold.
The rich got richer as they reaped the whirlwind and they never paid their share.
It's time they realized that they must help and start paying a tax that's fair!

There is a move afoot to oust our President and it's based on "fairy tales."
The very same kind of approach that took us into war let's hope and pray it fails.
But now we all must bite the bullet and help our fellow man.
So many folks have lost their jobs, their homes, they really need a helping hand!

We must not let our Nation fail and become one based on greed,
Where dog eats dog, the rest go hungry, and there's nothing based on need.
The devil's forces vent their spleen over our radios day by day.
They preach a venomous hatred of our Government it's not the American way!

So what do we do to change the course, it's up to me and you.
We are the instruments of salvation that can pull our country through.
If you are willing to do your part and feel we must do what we must do,
Then hold your "peace" 'til 2012, and then vote for "you know who!"

Birthdate of #3 Son, John H. Shepherd,   1967

April 30.

Jesus And Billy

There will be much joy in Heaven when Jesus greets Billy Graham,
When Billy kneels at the foot of the One we know as the Great "I AM."
Billy has more friends in Heaven than anyone else on earth.
His arrival there will cause a stir, much like the Savior's birth!

Billy was born a mortal man, much like you and me.
He wanted to be a baseball player but that was not meant to be.
God saw in this young man something that His Son also had,
The Evangelism within his heart made Jesus mighty glad!

Billy recruited a mighty team, disciples you might say,
They followed him around the world to spread the word each day.
This team was dedicated to the Lord just like Peter, John and James.
Jesus knows them all very well so I need not call their names!

Kings and Queens and Presidents and millions of folks like me,
Have bowed their heads while Billy prayed and asked the Lord to be
Our Savior and the chosen One we seek to save us all from sin.
Billy led millions to the Cross where they were born again!

Millions of words have been written by and about this man.
There is no doubt that he has helped to execute God's plan.
A Library showcases the work he did while he was alive and well,
A magnificent display dedicated to all those folks who might have gone to hell!

Down through the many ages since Jesus lived on earth,
There have been many Holy men, most of humble birth.
Some were Saints, we know them well, Peter, Luke, John and Paul.
I believe that Jesus will declare "Saint Billy" the greatest of them all!

Contents May

1. That's How It Was 125

2. The Bee And The Rose 126

3. Jesus Shines As Does The Sun..................................127

4. That's Where Jesus Lives 128

5. The Battle Goes On...129

6. Let Jesus Help 130

7. Just Call On Jesus...131

8. Jesus Will Be The Final Judge 132

9. Just Relax And Let It Happen...................................133

10. Just Say Amen 134

11. Just Working On My Problems 135

12. HAPPY MOTHER'S DAY 136

    A Tribute To Mothers.. 137

    Mother's Day 138

13. Getting Ready For Mother's Day.............................139

14. Mother Dear Who's Now In Heaven 140

15. To Mom 141

16. Let The Spirit Take Your Hand 143

17. Let's All Be Friends With Jesus 144

18. Let's Get In The Mood With Music.........................145

19. Let's Have Fun 146

20. Let's Put Our House In Order 147

21. Let's Refuel Our Fuel Supply 148

22. Let's Save Old Glory..149

23. Let's Use What We Have 150

24. Life Is Wonderful 151

25. Life Moves On 152

26. Lost Souls..153

27. Memorial Day 2011 155

28. Memories On Memorial Day 156

29. Love Finds A Way 157

30. Jesus My Savior, Jesus My Friend............................158

31. Love In Bloom 159

May 1.

That's How It Was

When I was just a little boy my Mother said to me,
"Come say a prayer to Jesus, get down on your knee."
She taught me how to talk to Him, He was her friend said she,
And He became a friend of mine He's been so good to me!

Sue Ellie Rhyne, my teacher then, a lady in our church,
Shaped my life and others too, she taught us how to search
For all the finer things in life, no matter we were poor.
We had the love of all our friends and Jesus loved us more!

Pastor Shenk, who baptized me when I was six weeks old,
Poured blessed water on my head, it went straight to my soul.
I know that water came from God, He wanted it to stay.
I still can feel it in my heart, I'm sure it's there today!

Pastor Shenk confirmed me too, by then I was twelve years old.
I'd grown a bit and learned much more, I had a lofty goal.
Pastor Sam arrived, a simple man, who had a heart of gold.
He nurtured me and helped me plan a future that was bold!

When war engulfed our nation I was the perfect age.
Uncle Sam said "I want you," I had to turn the page.
No more my goal to preach the Word, I wanted now to fly.
I was too young but Mother signed, I did not want to lie!

I learned to fly a big, Boeing "B" seventeen.
It was a fantastic, capable flying machine.
It had four motors and a crew of ten.
We all looked to God to "save our skin!"

That we all survived was a gift straight from the Lord.
It had always been our feeling that He was also on board.
He saved me then, He watches o'er me today.
I'll always be so thankful, that Mother taught me to pray!

May 2.

The Bee And The Rose

There is a bee sitting on your nose,
I'm sure that he's looking for a rose.
He'll have to leave his lofty perch
And embark into a much wider search!

Don't worry a bee won't sting all on his own,
But be sure to leave him there alone.
Just give him time to go away,
Don't swat at him and make his day!

We know the bee is looking for something sweet,
And there's nothing sweet but awfully neat,
About a nose that's also looking for a rose,
So follow that bee wherever he goes!

Please don't disturb him while he feeds,
Upon that rose which satisfies his needs.
Right now he's happy and content,
And your nose can catch that wonderful scent!

So this just goes to show that things work out,
Don't get all upset and rant and shout,
Disturb the bee and invite his sting.
Just leave him be and he'll do his thing!

The bee is smart and knows full well,
That if he stings that's his death knell.
So let him search and find that rose,
And spread that scent for that poor nose!

Jesus Shines As Does The Sun

A gloomy morning without the sun, sure do miss its rays,
But I know it's shining somewhere, bringing beautiful days.
So I take heart and think of Jesus, He shines everywhere
And even though we cannot see Him, we know that He is there!

That's the beauty of the "Trinity" They surround us with Their love.
There's always rays that lift the gloom, shining from above.
So don't despair and let the gloom of weather get you down.
Pack your worries in your pocket and take a trip to town!

Jesus loves a happy face because He loves us so.
It makes Him sad when we feel bad our faces do not glow,
So when you speak to Him today..I'm sure you plan to pray,
Just tell Him what it is you need, He'll get it on the way!

Don't be discouraged if it takes a while for you to get results,
For Jesus may have to speak to others, the Saints that He consults.
Just bide your time and keep your cool, you must have things to do.
Don't worry about the time it takes, He'll be in touch with you!

Easter Day will soon be here and we must be prepared,
To once again sing Hallelujah because Jesus Christ was spared.
God sacrificed His Only Son, then raised Him from the tomb.
The greatest joy for all mankind since Jesus left His Mothers womb!

Gloomy days are soon dispelled when Jesus comes to mind.
It's such a thrill to think that He has come to save mankind.
I am so often overwhelmed when I think He knows my name,
But then I remember that was His mission and that is why He came!

May 4.

That's Where Jesus Lives

My future lies in Heaven when my earthly days are done,
Where so many of my friends and family have already gone.
I know that they'll be waiting for me somewhere near the gate
To welcome me with open arms but I just don't know the date!

I look forward to meeting Jesus for He's done so much for me.
He gave His life for all mankind so faithful we must be.
Someday we'll join the everlasting throng travelling hand in hand,
Moving down that beautiful road that leads into the Promised Land!

I recently read Don Piper's wonderful book, it took away the fear,
That I think most folks have when they know their time to go is near.
Everyone should read that book for I know that it is true.
Jesus sent Don Piper back to earth to tell his story to folks like me and you!

We read the Bible stories of the Saints and we learn a lot from them.
We must read all of Jesus' stories for we'll learn much more from Him.
For two thousand years He's been at work preparing our Heavenly abode.
I'm sure that it will be there waiting when we reach the end of the road!

The years that we have here on earth seem like they'll never end.
We're fortunate to have Jesus leading us for He's our dearest Friend.
If we just follow where He leads and take all of His advice,
We'll be rewarded for our good deeds and for treating people nice!

Many thanks and admiration to Don Piper for his book,
"90 Minutes in Heaven"

The Battle Goes On

Who's that knocking at my door?
Have I seen you there before?
If I open the door to let you in
Will you save my soul or urge me to sin?

It could be the devil in a disguise,
But it could be Jesus coming as a surprise.
Jesus would be coming to offer me some help,
But the devil would bring trouble to my very doorstep!

This battle goes on every day of the week
And sometimes diverts the very help that I seek,
And replaces it with lots of the devils shiny toys,
Which are sure to get the attention of all the girls and boys!

What should I do when I do go to the door?
I'll be prepared for sure for I've been there before.
I'd love to see Jesus and ask Him to come right in,
But if it is the devil then I'll shut the door on him again!

The devil is not welcome at all and knows that for sure,
But he still offers his gaudy baubles as a crafty lure.
I'm always at home if Jesus knocks and I usher Him right in,
He brings me lots of help each day and takes away the sin!

Since that battle never ends, I'm always on alert.
If I let down my guard then I'll be the one that's hurt.
So when I hear that knocking at my door today,
Before I answer it at all, I'll bow my head and pray!

May 6.

Let Jesus Help

Don't turn your back on Jesus, He can still see your face.
Do not try to hide from Him, there is no hiding place.
If you have a bone to pick, confront Him like a man.
Once He gets you straightened out, you'll be His biggest fan!

So many folks go through life with big troubles on their mind.
They never have the happiness that Jesus wants for all mankind.
If they could just accept the fact that Jesus is our King,
He'll ease their burden, cure their ills, take care of everything!

Sometimes it takes an entire life for folks to see the light.
It's not until they're faced with death that they begin to fight.
"Deathbed confessions" save many souls for Jesus hears them too.
Saving someone who was bound for hell is what He likes to do!

God appointed Jesus, who was His only beloved Son,
To be the savior of our souls and He's the only one.
False prophets of all kinds abound to lead mankind astray.
We must not let the devil's team stand in our savior's way!

The world at large is a wonderful place but fragile in many ways.
We must assist nature in a long range plan, one that really pays.
Earthquakes, storms and floods are natural events but do take a toll,
We can prevent the ravages caused by man which should be our goal!

We're merely caretakers of the earth and we just come and go.
God rules the entire universe, it's His creation as you well know.
We must show our thanks for all His gifts and take part in His plan,
Which includes our life on earth and our move to the Promised Land!

May 7.

Just Call On Jesus

Dear Lord I'm lost and need your advice.
I've been to bat and struck out twice.
I know that I must try again,
To try and fail is not a sin!

You should always try to do what's right.
You may not win but always fight.
Let Jesus know if you need His help.
He'll be glad to guide your step!

I'm down and out and in a bind.
My troubles now are a different kind
From those before which I could fix,
But now the devil's got new tricks!

I'm on my knees, my head is bowed.
I can wait and I'm not proud.
I know that You're busy with others too
Telling all what we must do!

When you get around to me,
I'll be waiting with a simple plea.
Just get me started down the road.
I know You'll always share my load!

I don't know why we wait so long,
To ask for help when things go wrong.
We all have learned from long ago,
That Jesus loves us, this we know!

May 8.

Jesus Will Be The Final Judge

Today begins another week and for that we should be glad.
We can make this one of the best that we have ever had.
Just settle down and thank the Lord for what He's done for you.
He's still working on your behalf to do what you asked Him to!

Jesus never abandons His children as each of us is known.
A "child of God" is what we are, even though we're grown.
He wants us all to have a happy life right here on the earth.
As children of the "King of Kings" we each had a "Royal Birth"!

I'm not rich, I've had to dig, but I can get along.
If our politics will just settle down we'll once again be strong.
Our country must do all it can to be helpful to one and all,
But it seems that there are always folks who just will not play ball!

When we fight among ourselves, the world abroad tunes in.
They're looking for us to lose our way, for our downfall to begin,
But, we the people, with Jesus' help, won't let that happen here.
We all have put our trust in God so we have naught to fear!

The next few months will tell the tale, who will win this fight.
There is no doubt that our President wants to do what's right.
Will he be allowed to do his job by those who've rigged the vote.
No matter which way the tide will turn, we all are in that boat!

Now you can make your voice heard, you have a choice to make.
Do what your heart tells you to there is so much at stake.
The winds of freedom are blowing I can feel them on my brow.
Whether we will sink or swim is up to us and what we do right now!

132

May 9.

Just Relax And Let It Happen

We put a seed into the ground from which a beautiful flower grows.
What makes it bloom with all its color, only Jesus knows.
Miracles happen every day in every garden spot,
Taken for "granted" by one and all who let it go to pot!

We overlook the beauty of the earth which God gives us for free.
Too often we're too occupied and don't take time to see
Nature as it works its will and paints a colorful scene.
We pay big bucks when someone puts that picture on the silver screen!

What makes us neglect our surroundings which nature sends our way?
We go through life with blinders on and struggle every day
To find that perfect work of art which we cannot afford,
And let the beauty of the world go by while feeling somewhat bored!

Most of us are smart enough with a fairly good I Q,
And yet I know I cannot make a flower, can you?
We keep looking all around while the world passes us by
And we miss one of God's beautiful scenes as sunrise gilds the sky!

Yes, then we lumber through the day without a single clue
Of where to go and can't decide just what it is we should do
To beautify our garden plot, so we try to find a way,
And miss that freely given beautiful sunset that ends every day!

Don't let's forget that nightfall has its beauty too,
And yes we're still hard at work to see what we can do.
To fill our hearts with beautiful scenes we saved for last the best.
A beautiful golden full moon in a cloudless sky rising in the west!

May 10.

Just Say Amen

I always like to say "Amen."
It's another way to say "thanks again."
It also means that "I approve."
Another way to show our love!

Some folks say, "It's just a word,"
But this one comes straight from the Lord.
Use it only as you know He would,
With lots of love, the way we should!

We often say things we don't mean.
"Just words" you say, although obscene.
Always think first, use some tact.
Be sure it's true, a proven fact!

Words like stones can break a heart.
Think long and hard before you start,
To say some things best left unsaid.
Say something sweet and kind instead!

There are many who talk too much.
They often get themselves "in dutch."
There are others who don't talk a bit.
They like to listen so they just sit!

Of course not all have things to say.
We use words even as we pray.
Think a lot about how to begin.
End up with thanks to God, just say "Amen!"

Just Working On My Problems

I'm glad that I've got problems, they keep me busy, see?
Without those problems on my mind, my gosh, where would I be?
Working on my problems keeps me busy most of every day,
And when I've solved one or two, I'm ready to "hit the hay!"

Now I've heard people say that they are trouble free.
I often wonder if they had problems, just 'tween you and me,
For problems could mean trouble, you know just what I mean.
It's good to stay out of trouble to keep our records clean!

So if you've got problems and troubles, you're in good company.
You've got things to do today and you'll be busy as a bee.
An idle mind will soon go blind, I think someone has said.
It's good to have some things to do, it gets us out of bed!

Down through the years mankind has prospered and made progress too.
You see when they had problems it gave them something to do.
Inventions are merely the result of another problem solved,
So get up early to work on your problems and let others get involved!

Problems, problems, we've all got problems, what are we to do?
We're not inventors, we're regular folks and we have troubles too.
We spend our time hoping to find the best way to proceed,
But finding solutions to our problems is our greatest need!

Our troubles create problems which keep us on the go.
The problems come when troubles keep us running to and fro.
Round and round our problems go, our troubles not far behind.
There's plenty there to keep me busy, see, for the answers I must find!

May 12.

HAPPY MOTHER'S DAY

Call her Mother, Mama, Mom or Ma, call her what you will,
Paying homage to this one we love gives us all a thrill.
We all should get down on our knees to show our true respect.
I wish that mine was still around I'd like to hug her neck!

To have a Mother that we love is something that we all share.
I sometimes think that we forget the pain that she must bear,
To bring us each, alive and well, into this world with love,
You can be sure that when we're born there's joy in Heaven above!

You see it's true that Jesus shares with us, the love for Mother dear.
There's bound to be a special place in Heaven where Jesus will appear
And place upon each Mother's head a crown which she deserves,
In honor of the leadership she gives to the family that she serves!

Every woman is not a Mother but every woman has a Mother.
They're all endowed with some traits that help them help each other.
So on this special Mother's Day, let's honor every woman,
For we know without them all, this world would not be human!

As a man I have been blessed by experiencing fatherhood.
Seven times my wife gave birth and we had quite a brood.
She's up in Heaven now and I know she wears her crown,
And while all her children honor her I know she's looking down!

Today, to all the Mothers still alive and those who've gone away,
Our wish for you from all of us is Happy Mother's Day!
We want to show our love for you, for that we can't be shy.
We miss you all so very much and we miss your "apple pie!"

A Tribute To Mothers

My Mom was such a gentle soul, she wouldn't hurt a fly.
It's been fifty long years now since we had to say goodbye.
She's been with Jesus all that time and that thought makes me glad.
I've missed her every day of course and that thought makes me sad!

There's only one day in the year when Mothers reign supreme,
But all the things that Mothers teach help keep us on the beam.
Even though my Mom's in Heaven, I know she thinks of me.
Not once a year but every day, her smile I still can see!

I like to think that all my friends who've died have gone to Heaven too.
I hope they get together with my Mom and talk of things we used to do.
She taught me how to talk with Jesus, she taught me what to say,
And every morning I bow in prayer because she taught me how to pray!

On Sunday, Mothers everywhere will be remembered on their day.
Every member of their family will have a lot to say,
With flowers and cards and sweet candies of all kinds,
Loving tributes that will let her know just what is on our minds!

Let's not forget those ladies who have never borne a child.
All women are known as the weaker sex which doesn't mean they're mild,
And so for Mom's and wives and daughters and all our girlfriends too,
Where would we menfolk be without someone to come home to?

I'm truly glad we reserve a day to honor the women of the world.
They may be Mothers but some are not but all were once a girl.
These giggling, bashful, lovely creatures with lots of curly hair,
Grow up to be the leading ladies of our dreams and of our love affair!

Mother's Day

There's something all of us have no matter who we are.
Kings and Queens and Presidents and every movie star,
Even Jesus, Lord of Lords, the Son of God you know,
Had this same thing that we all had which God Himself bestows!

I know by now you know for sure what I am speaking of,
The greatest gift God gives us all that comes with all His love.
Thank You God for my dear Mom, without her I wouldn't be.
Fashioned from her own flesh and blood to join the family tree!

Except for Mothers none really know, exactly what's involved,
To spend a full nine months until the birthing is resolved.
That's why they are a "special" group who have a lovely way,
Of accepting all our love and thanks that comes on Mother's Day!

A Mother is the first "hero" that every child will know.
She's there to help take our first steps we put on quite a show.
While she continues teaching us she becomes our first "best" friend
And keeps us out of trouble as she guides us through thick and thin!

Mother's day, a special day, the one we set aside,
To honor every Mother and our own with lots of pride.
Whether she is still alive or with God's Angels in the sky,
We'll honor her with all our love until the day we die!

Jesus' Mother was there with Him as He hung on the cross.
She knew that He was special but His death was such a loss.
I'm sure that She is now with Him receiving tender care,
And She is there to welcome home, Mothers from everywhere!

May 13.

Getting Ready For Mother's Day

Dedicated to the memory of Susie Ann Hornbuckle 1892-1961

There is no joy in any heart when "Mama" leaves the nest,
When Jesus calls "dear Mama" home for her eternal rest.
There must be in Heaven a special place for all the "Moms" to go.
I know it must be special too, for Jesus loved His beloved "Mama" so!

For every child that's born on earth "Mama" bears the pain.
Papa stands around and crows "look what I've done again."
Dear Jesus identifies well with "Mom" for He too bore much pain,
And died to save us all from sin, as He began His reign!

Every person who has been on earth has had a "Mom" it's true.
It all began with Eve, the first to bear the pain and bore not one but two,
And so it is, even today, that Mom's bear most of the load,
To build the families that we all know and keep things in the road!

We have, of course, a special day, we call it "Mother's Day."
T'would be no exaggeration to call every day "Mother's Day."
"Mom" works each day from dawn to dusk for very little pay,
And has to wait to get her due 'til that special day in May!

Never neglect your Mother and work hard to smooth her path.
Don't expect her to teach you how to spell or how to do your math,
Don't ever let her suffer needlessly but be sure she always has the best
Of everything that she should want or need to ease her day of rest!

We still have some time to go until that day in May.
While many of us have said our "Goodbye to Mom" we celebrate that day,
The one that honors all those Moms from "Eve to Susie Ann."
If your Mom is still alive then be sure to kiss her sweetly while you can!

May 14.

Mother Dear Who's Now In Heaven

Mother's Day brings other thoughts that fill our hearts with love.
How could we ever fail to think of that Sweet Jesus up above,
Who placed us in our Mother's arms, where we fell in love and then
Began a life long love affair, one which will never end!

Even when our Moms have gone we know where she will be.
She's resting up there in Heaven with Jesus don't you see.
She's one of those with Angel's wings, a crown upon her head.
She sends to us a message "Please don't cry I really am not dead!"

I have good memories of my Mom, they come from way back when.
She was not a raving beauty queen but beauty comes from within.
My Father thought she hung the moon and treated her with care.
I used to watch them hug and kiss a real live love affair!

Life goes on without my folks they're both in Heaven now,
And while I'm sure they're helping out I really don't know how.
I'd like to think of them in the choir but Dad couldn't carry a tune.
I'm sure that he is being useful too, perhaps "hanging out the moon!"

Reflection on my entire life comes easy on Mother's Day.
She was the one who got me started down life's long highway,
And while she's not here right now, her presence fills the air,
And I envision her in loving terms, in her "easy" chair!

So I take this moment to say thanks to Jesus for giving me this gift,
This lady who bore me through all the pain and gave my life a lift,
I'm sure that He's been good to her and I'm sure she's glad to be,
A member of the Heavenly Chorus that sings hymns to you and me!

Birthdate of My Mother, Suzi Hornbuckle Shepherd, 1892

May 15.

To Mom

The mother of my children was born to fill a special role.
Each time that she had given birth dear God refreshed her soul.
Each little child that came into our growing family,
Was met with love and tender care just as it was meant to be!

"Jay-Jay" was the first in line and became truly a number one.
A difficult labor for first time Mom brought forth this welcome son.
The Dad was listening, scared to death, afraid that she would die.
When it was over with both okay, all he could do was cry!

"Suzi-Beth" soon came along, a prettier doll you've never seen.
In a major hospital now, with plenty of gas, the birth was more routine.
Next in line but not far behind, number two son "Lewie" arrived.
His "strita" breathing caused funny sounds, but everyone survived!

After the trio, Mom's namesake, "Joann Yates", came to join the group.
Now with four in all, two girls, two boys, we really had quite a troop,
But we still had a way to go to finish up our clan.
There were two more slots to fill based on our original plan!

A bubbly, bouncing, baby boy, was what we had in mind,
But Jesus sent us "Becky Jo", the sweetest girl He could find.
A bright-eyed bundle of giggling joy, she brightened up our day.
Mom loved to get them all dressed up and take them out to play!

We changed hometowns and moved into a pleasant neighborhood.
With lots of kids in families just like us, it worked out very good.
Four more years passed by the boards, then "John Hilary" made a grand debut.
In all honesty and thanks to God, we thought that we were through!

John had four years as our baby boy and played that role in style.
In Heaven, Jesus found a precious tiny girl and kept her with Him awhile.
He searched His files to find a Mom, a special Mom you see.
He placed this tiny babe in our Mom's arms, we named her "MMC"!

MMC is short for Mary Mildred Christine, we call her "Kris" of course.
All these three names were family kin, there was no other source.
High School diplomas, exams and College degrees, all seven got their share.
Our Mom even took the time to get her own degree
at UNCG, and she just loved it there!

Mom was present at all five weddings and later held all six grandsons on her lap.
Too soon cancer reared its ugly head, treatment
took its toll and set a very deadly trap.
I'm sure that every baby now coming from Heaven has known her loving touch,
Jesus in His wisdom would have her in charge of "nursery row", this Mom we loved
SO VERY MUCH!

May 16.

Let The Spirit Take Your Hand

Jesus comes in Spirit form to call on us each day.
We must be ready when He calls so don't forget to pray.
Just open up your heart and let the sunshine enter in,
The Spirit rides the sunbeams and saves our soul from sin!

Many people glimpse the Spirit and recoil from fear of ghosts,
Through the Spirit, Jesus speaks "Fear not says He, I am the Holy Ghost.
We must be ready for His call, we don't know where or when,
But rest assured that He's nearby, He could be riding on the wind!

Let us remember that for the Spirit, our life is an open book.
We cannot hide a thing from Him, there's nowhere He can't look.
He sent us here as tiny babes, He knows us, warts and all,
He's watching everything we do and waiting for our call!

Don't be afraid to have some fun, Jesus loves a happy face.
He's sad indeed as misery abounds among the human race.
He battles daily with the devil who wants to do us in,
So all of us must do our part and turn away from sin!

If you feel the Spirit working in your life today,
Welcome Him with open arms and do not turn away.
He wants to shower you with His love so offer Him your hand,
He'll help you take the proper road that leads to the Promised Land!

We know that Jesus is in Heaven, some folks have seen Him there.
He sends the Spirit into our realm and He travels everywhere,
So when you feel the breezes blow and feel the sunshine on your face,
Just thank the Lord as you receive this evidence of God's Grace!

May 17.

Let's All Be Friends With Jesus

I know there is no greater love than Jesus has for me.
From early morn to late at night He's always sure to be,
Ready with a helping hand, if I should need to call,
And always waiting with open arms, should I begin to fall!

There have been so many times I didn't do the things I could,
When I didn't even do all those many things I should,
But Jesus still gave me His love and said that we were friends,
Which prompted me that I should act to quickly make amends!

I'm trying hard to right the wrongs, to do things as I should,
Making sure that when I act, I do things that are good.
I find that when I need His help, Jesus is always there,
And always willing to provide me with His tender, loving care!

If you are also one of us who sometimes go astray,
I hope that you will call on Jesus and turn to Him today.
He'll be very happy to assist in anything you need.
Very simply, say a prayer, and you won't have to plead!

He's been around so many years, He's seen it all of course.
He can help us solve our problems and save us from remorse.
All He requires is that we pray and share our love for Him,
With all our friends and fellowmen and just be kind to them!

I want all my friends to know Jesus as their friend.
What He does for me, He'll do for them, always without end.
So please listen, one and all, to what I have to say.
Let Jesus be your guide and friend, accept His love today!

Let's Get In The Mood With Music

A beautiful poem when set to music becomes a beautiful song.
When I hear music of that kind I could listen all day long.
I may not remember every word but the tune is in my heart.
When early morn is filled with music, I'm off to a wonderful start!

Almost every song I hear has special meaning in its own way.
Memories of a time and place which somehow seems like yesterday,
Visions of friends and loved ones pass before my eyes.
Beautiful music creates an atmosphere in which time really flies!

It's true that every romance has been influenced by a certain song.
"Our song" is the one that everyone listens for all the day long.
The words and music of that special song are sure embedded deep.
And that's why each song when played causes someones heart to leap!

I think it's known that music is the international language of love.
Around the world, words may differ but the music comes from above.
She may not know what you're saying but her heart goes "pitter-pat."
If I'm any judge it's "love in bloom" no matter where you're at!

Some of our most beautiful songs are those we hear in church.
We all have our favorites and for those we don't need to search.
We just open up our hymnbook at the proper page,
And join the choir in beautiful music, no matter what our age!

The world would be a better place if speeches were delivered in song.
Whatever the message and by whom in music they couldn't go wrong.
If talk shows were converted to music we could all swing and sway,
If dictators and tyrants sang opera superb, OhWhat a BeautifulDay!

Armed Forces Day

May 19.

Let's Have Fun

There is a word I like to use, that simple word is "fun."
It's a word we don't use a lot, unless we're having some.
You use it often with your kids when they go out to play.
This world would be a better place if we used it more each day!

When I hear someone use the word I always laugh and smile,
For if you're truly having "fun" you can relax a while.
Just tie up all your troubles in a knot and call up all your friends.
Get them all together at your place and hope it never ends!

Too often we don't take the time to enjoy the things we should.
We need to spend a lot more time doing things for our own good,
And what would be more likely than having lots of "fun?"
Of course it could be a simple thing like soaking up the sun!

So what if you miss a day at work, the boss says "where were you?"
You merely reply, you do not lie, "I had some things to do,"
And with a smile the boss just says, "you dog-gone son of a gun,"
I know all about those things too, you were just out having "fun!"

Days may come and days may go, we have to live a little.
There isn't any time to waste, no time to sit and whittle.
So make good use of every day but be sure to have some "fun."
You'll have more friends than ever and be the envy of everyone!

The root word "fun" can lead to many and one of these is "funny."
The relationship of those two words is not like "sun" and "sunny,"
But if you're really having "fun" while some may think it's "funny,"
Just say to them, you need some "fun," come along and be my honey!

Let's Put Our House In Order

If you think you've got it made you better look again.
Be sure you talk with Jesus, you have no dearer friend.
He'll check you out and set you straight on the "glory" road
And you don't have to carry further that extra heavy load!

We never reach perfection where we are free from sin.
The devil never gives up his goal of trying to suck us in.
Las Vegas beckons with both arms to lure you with their wares.
Just call on Jesus for His Help, He's One who really cares!

Jesus wants to save your soul no matter who you are.
You won't need your telephone for distance is no bar.
He's always listening for your call so say "hello" each day.
That's where the magic lies, it happens when you pray!

Some day the world is going to end but no one knows just when.
The earth is failing to support its people, for some starvation is the end.
Wars and threats of war are rampant from all sides.
Jesus won't be really happy until "peace on earth" abides!

Meanwhile the devil is working overtime giving out his samples.
Look all around you every day there are many sad examples.
The devil is seeking the downfall of the human race.
He is a very crafty salesman so don't tempt him face to face!

The leaders of our country have a lot of work to do
By trying to help the down and out who need a break or two.
Cooperation is the key they must use if they are to get along.
We must show the world that once again the USA can be very strong!

May 21.

Let's Refuel Our Fuel Supply

The world is such a beautiful place to live, and yet,
The mess we have down in the Gulf is as bad as it can get.
It seems that no one has the answers and even if they did,
They're the kind who would be holding out for the highest bid!

You and me, we like to see, that things are going well,
But those poor folks along the Gulf are in a living "hell."
We take pride and tell ourselves, there's nothing we can't do,
But we've unleashed the fury of nature itself and we're really in a stew!

I think God is testing us, there may be worse in store.
What will we do when winds of doom begin to come ashore?
We haven't learned that there are times when God Himself must act.
Man can't control the weather, earthquakes or volcanoes, that's a fact!

What to do, what do we do, that's the major question now?
God helps those who help themselves so we all must take a vow.
The one thing that "all" can do is pray, to God we all must plead.
Why not have a National Day of Prayer to express to God our need?

God puts the answer to our dilemma before our very eyes.
The sun shines every day on earth, the power's in the skies.
We've just begun to take the hint and harness rays of light,
And we have solved how we can use that power through the night!

God doth send the wind to blow, it is an energy source.
When it blows across a fan that turns it is a powerful force.
We must develop the sun and wind, their products are very clean.
Let's cut down on fossil fuels and keep our ecology green!

May 22.

Let's Save Old Glory

I know that I'm no prophet but I sure do love the Lord.
I love to write about my love for Him, hope you don't get bored.
I like to think I'm doing what He wishes me to do,
And that's to tell everyone I know so they will love Him too!

I think that some folks feel it's a weakness to call on Him.
For me my greatest strength comes from telling them
That there's no weakness in confessing all your sins,
For it's while you're on your knees with Jesus that new life begins!

This is not a sermon and I'm not preaching for that's not my way.
I'm just a poet who loves to tell what Jesus did for me today.
Take my word for it my friend , say the word "Jesus" and He'll be there.
The greatest gift that God gave to us and Jesus is everywhere!

My early morning talks with Jesus gets me started on the right track.
From that moment on during the day, I look ahead and don't look back.
What's done is done and God forgives me as Jesus leads the way.
Since I know Jesus is at my side, I make it through the day!

I'm fearful that our Nation may be losing the fight with Satan's team.
This sworn enemy of God has sent an army to kill our dream.
These skillful agents of doom invade our daily life.
Satan's fight to destroy Jesus creates a lot of strife!

We all must fight to protect the phrase, "In God we trust."
Wherever it appears on money or buildings, its salvation is a must.
This destructive effort by members of Satan's unholy team,
Must be defeated to preserve the foundations of our lifelong dream!

May 23.

Let's Use What We Have

God gave us the powers of the earth to use as we see fit.
We haven't yet harnessed those powers for our own benefit.
When those powers get heated up volcanoes will explode
Earthquakes and tsunamis join together and soon they dump their load!

It's very sad to see the damage caused by nature at its worst.
Hurricanes bring both wind and rain they race to get there first.
No matter which force wins that race the damage will be done,
And it's true we have little defense against the arrival of either one!

Mankind's battles are fought in different ways and we lose almost all.
Nations try to destroy their neighbors with the use of a uranium ball.
We use the powers that God provides to wreak havoc far and wide.
Too often there are no constructive gains that are made by either side!

We live in a world of plenty but we are overcome by greed.
Financiers battle to corner the market and forget all those in need.
Those powers that God provides for all mankind are used for someones gain.
Little children starve to death while so many ignore their pain!

Mankind's efforts should be employed to provide for everyone.
Politicians call it socialism when they're asked to help someone.
I can remember when I was young and neighbors helped each other,
But now it seems the shoe is on the other foot and neighbors do not bother!

We need to make more use of those things that come from God.
Solar power, water power, wind and atomic power all must be involved.
We can't give up but must control these things that nature provides,
And put it all to work for us instead of something that divides!

May 24.

Life Is Wonderful

I feel the need to say "hello" to Jesus Christ today.
To thank Him once again for listening to me when I pray.
I just don't know what I would ever do without,
My friend up there in Heaven to take away the doubt!

It seems to be so hard for some to say "hello" to Him,
Even when they're in a fix and must either sink or swim.
What they don't understand is He will keep us all afloat,
So it's important that we all repent and get into the boat!

Don't feel unworthy and don't be afraid to open up your heart,
For Jesus is awaiting I am sure, to have you play a part.
He'll give you all the slack you need, He won't pull your chain.
He's the gentlest soul you'll ever meet, you have a lot to gain!

Thank You Jesus for your love, and everything you give
To all us people here on earth, who need your help to live.
We try to be the masters of our fate and do what we must do,
Until we finally realize that we must depend on You!

When you see the sunrise at the dawning of the day,
Bow your head and say a prayer, let Jesus lead the way.
You won't go wrong if you accept His word and follow Him.
The devil's crowd will do their best to have you follow them!

The beauty of the day tells me that Jesus is around.
He's watching everything I do, He's never let me down.
I'm sure that He would like to be a part of what you do,
Just as He's always done for me, I'm sure He'll do for you!

May 25.

Life Moves On

Will you still love me when I get old,
When I can't hear, have teeth of gold,
Or will you feel you've done your part,
Pack up and leave and break my heart?

You see this story works both ways,
One side prospers the other pays.
It's also known as give and take
Since both must work for goodness sake!

Into each life some rain will fall.
It clears away some strife but not all.
We abide our time and the sun will shine.
A gift from God both yours and mine!

We follow the road wherever it leads.
The good Lord watches and fills our needs.
We never know what's up ahead,
So we must go where He has led!

I'm so thankful for Jesus' love.
He sends the rain and sunshine from above.
When I need someone to hold my hand
He comes with stories of the "promised land!"

I hope you see why I don't worry,
When Jesus comes He's in no hurry.
I pray to Him and thank Him every day.
He's never let me lose my way!

May 26.

Lost Souls

Jesus doesn't punish us but He remembers our misdeeds.
They're all recorded in His Book, that's all the proof He needs.
When we're ready to enter Heaven He'll open up His Book,
He'll turn it to the proper page and take a real good look!

We're standing before the fairest Judge the world has ever known.
We cannot hide our sins from Him He's watched us as we've grown.
Forgiveness is what we must seek with Mercy from the Judge!
We'll never make it past the bar if we're holding some kind of grudge!

There are some folks who'll say to the Judge, "I don't believe in God".
I'm sure a tear will drop from Jesus' eye but I'm sure that He won't nod,
He'll open up His Book and see the proper page filled with sins galore.
Some sinners seek no Mercy from the Judge and continue to sin some more!

Unfortunately it's true that some folks don't believe and never see the light.
Their belief is that there is no God and death will end their plight.
They're surprised to stand before a Judge and some will just not play ball.
To renounce Jesus as you look Him in the eye sure takes a lot of gall!

Some very few will have a change of heart as they stand before the Judge.
As they get down upon their knees and confess, Jesus doesn't even budge.
He loves to save misguided souls who've turned away from evil,
But too many will not seek forgiveness and just join up with the devil!

I get no joy in writing this, in fact it causes me some pain.
The hardest poem I've ever written and my tears come down like rain.
Just like Jesus I still love those who don't believe, I have no axe to grind.
The Judge will give us all a final chance, He is so wonderfully kind!

This is the 300th poem I have written since my first one,
"My Friend Jesus" written October 2006.
I must confess that because of the content, it is by far
the hardest one I have felt compelled to write.
Thank You Jesus!

May 27.

Memorial Day 2011

I personally was honored many years ago when Jesus saved my life.
He rode beside me in my plane and protected me from strife.
I pass all the honors on to those who didn't make it back.
I saw their planes explode right beside me when they were hit by flak!

All those in service who died in battle were welcomed by the Lord.
He didn't decorate them with medals but with a much deserved award.
A lovely Heavenly Home with Him was ready when they arrived,
Most of them were now much better off than if they had survived!

Too often I fear some overlook the ones they have left behind.
We need a separate Memorial Day for them to give them peace of mind.
They are the ones who suffered most they're always filled with grief.
Although it's true, this Memorial Day does bring a measure of relief!

I don't belittle in any way medals and honors bestowed upon the brave.
They are certainly measures of our Nations thanks which they can save,
But too many awards I'm afraid are just sitting on the shelf,
And it takes a special day to drag them out and decorate oneself!

The Good Lord knows that I appreciate the thanks that I receive,
And I don't have to walk around with my feelings on my sleeve,
But I do wear on my lapel a replica of my B-17.
"Bottle Baby" was her name and she was a beautiful queen!

We all fight battles every day and there is one we dare not lose.
The devil is at war with God, his offers we must refuse.
Jesus is Commander of our troops and offers us a great reward.
He'll reunite us with our fallen heroes, who are already with the Lord!

Memorial Day

May 28.

Memories On Memorial Day

God knows so well the pain we feel on this Memorial Day.
So those of you who lost a son remember God this way,
He too lost a Son, His Only Son, so we must honor Him today.
For Jesus and all other sons, heroes all, it's for them we pray!

Now Jesus had a family too and they also felt the pain.
For all of you who lost someone the memory will always remain.
Fathers, husbands, brothers, uncles, Moms, daughters and sisters too,
They each fell as they defended well, the Red and White and Blue!

We will never forget those friends we lost who died before their times.
Also Jesus' friends who cried when He died for mankind's crimes,
Disciples, Apostles, close friends all, thousands more who heard his voice
Watched Him die upon the Cross since they had no other choice!

I often wonder why I survived when others nearby were killed.
It wasn't that I was more qualified for we all were very skilled.
I give thanks to Jesus every day that comes for what He did for me,
And I've tried in this earthly life to be what He wanted me to be!

On Memorial Day, two thousand twelve, I've placed another call
To say Thank You and yes, Amen, to Jesus who loves us all,
And also Thanks to those many souls we honor on this day.
I'll make sure before I say "goodnight" to get on my knees and pray!

Love Finds A Way

It isn't strange at all you know that people fall in love.
It comes to some but not to all for some still need a shove.
And for those very lucky few they'll never be the same,
All they know is they're in love don't even know "her" name!

Romance is not a sometime thing it takes a lot of work,
And those who do not do it right are acting like a jerk.
Brush up on all your manners and brush your teeth as well,
You'll want to flash a real big smile with a very refreshing smell!

It doesn't hurt to have a plan to know just what to do,
And that lucky one who falls in love without the slightest clue,
Must find out quickly if "she" is free if he's to have a chance,
And in the meantime do his best to learn about romance!

How do you find a "gorgeous" belle you've barely seen before?
He prays that God will hear his plea and open up a door.
He cruises 'round that neighborhood where he first saw that "dish"
In hopes that "she" will make the scene and he will get his wish!

We know that God does answer prayer and soon it is confirmed,
That "lovely lady" of his dreams has suddenly returned.
Not only that but praise the Lord "she's" with his own Aunt Kate.
Introductions work out well and soon they have a date!

There are some things that really are like that, truly meant to be,
When two folks meet and fall in love that is no mystery.
So if you're having trouble finding the one that's right for you,
There is no doubt the right one's still around, I'm sure she's looking too!

Jesus My Savior, Jesus My Friend

Jesus my Savior, Jesus my Friend,
Jesus the Lord of us all,
How do we show we adore Him?
Will He be there should we fall?

Jesus my Master, Jesus my Lord,
Jesus who sits on the throne,
How do we show we are faithful?
When we are never alone!

Jesus my Teacher, Jesus who leads,
Jesus who brings forth His Word,
How do we show our obedience?
How does He know that we heard?

Jesus my Healer, Jesus who saves,
Jesus who rose from the grave,
How do we show our allegiance?
How do we show we are brave?

Jesus in Heaven, Jesus above,
Jesus forgives all our sins,
How do we show Him we're thankful?
That's when our new life begins!

Jesus the Christian, God's Only Son,
He is the Crucified One.
Now we can show we remember,
Jesus Omnipotent One!

May 31.

Love In Bloom

Love in bloom is in the air, you see it everywhere.
Color is popping out all over, there's lots of it to share.
The beauty of our land surrounds us and all of it is free.
We all must work to keep it clean, it's up to you and me!

There are those who do not care, they're too busy with other things.
They're busy making money so they can buy those diamond rings.
The beautiful flowers that abound are there for all to see,
And nothing beats the beauty of a full bloom dogwood tree!

Last week our area was ablaze with gardens open for view.
Their owners were sharing their treasure with folks like me and you.
People came from far and wide, and let beauty fill their soul.
They left refreshed with natures gifts which was the gardener's goal!

We are fortunate to live in a garden spot and thankful we should be.
We read reports of storms and fires where folks are forced to flee.
The world is full of tragedy and it can happen anywhere.
We must take care of what we have and with others we must share!

This year we've been blessed with beauty and something more.
I feel hopeful that this year our nation will see the end of war.
It's hard to concentrate on beautiful things when gunfire fills the air,
So let's all do our best to help our Nation bring peace everywhere!

Let's don't let world events take the bloom right off our rose,
We here at home must concentrate on good scents for our nose.
Beautiful flowers of every kind bring solace to our eyes.
God bless the good ole' USA where the flag of freedom flies!

Contents *June*

1. Miracles...161

2. Miracles All Around 162

3. Miracles, Luck Or Close Shaves..163

4. Misdirected Love..164

5. More Power To You...165

6. Music Soothes The Soul 166

7. My Friend Herb 167

8. The Therapy of Poetry..168

9. My" Grandfather's Clock..169

10. My Guide and Friend..170

11. My Name Sounds Good To Me...171

12. My Soul Still Follows Where Jesus Leads.............................172

13. Never Give Up 173

14. Never Forget 174

15. Never Give Up Without A Fight 175

16. Father's Day 176

     Father's Day II 177

17. Never Say Goodbye...178

18. Sweet Sixteen..179

19. Observation 181

20. On My Way To Heaven...182

21. One Hundred Days...183

22. One Year Later 184

23. Our Country Can Do Better Than This...............................185

24. Our Greatest Friend..186

25. Out Of The Blue 187

26. Perfection Reigns Only In Heaven..188

27. Place Your Bets..189

28. Planning 190

29. Planning Ahead...191

30. Please Don't Pick On Me...192

June 1.

Miracles

Miracles are a gift from God, they happen every day.
He and Jesus listen in to hear us when we pray.
Sincere prayers don't go astray they answer every one.
They're on the job from early morn until the day is done!

If you have a special need and want them to assist,
Don't worry if it takes awhile, they want you to persist.
So get right down upon your knees and pray to them today.
Each worthy case goes in His Book and it is there to stay!

All the things we see in life don't happen just by chance.
There is another force at work it's not just happenstance.
We don't see all the ins and outs, nor do we know the source.
It is a fact there is no doubt, that nature takes its course!

As we look around each day at all that God provides,
So much of it's a mystery yet wonderful besides.
We know for sure that we cannot, duplicate a rose,
Or any beautiful flower, you see only He can create those!

We often look to God for help when things don't go our way.
If we're sincere then He will hear and listen while we pray.
I'm sure that He discusses all our prayers with Jesus too,
Then they decide what to provide and then they'll talk to you!

All prayers are answered, don't be misled, but some are answered "no."
All others are the "miracles" that God chooses to bestow.
Don't be afraid to seek their aid, ask Jesus to plead for you.
If it's a worthy, sincere case, He'll push it right on through!

June 2.

Miracles All Around

Miracles do happen somewhere every day.
They may be minor, may be small, but miracles in every way.
Don't try to say they didn't happen when you know they did.
It's impossible to prove a lie, you learned that when a kid!

When you see a miracle, you'll know the Lord is near.
Embrace it then and there with all your heart without a bit of fear.
The Lord does not want you to be afraid of Him in any way.
He wants you to know He loves you, you learn that when you pray!

Almost everything we see or touch in life is a miracle of course.
We admit that without God we wouldn't be, there is no other source.
As we move through life each day, miracles pave our way.
When you awake each early morn, be sure to bow and pray!

We're surrounded by miracles everywhere we turn.
We need to daily seek God's help, there's still so much to learn.
We're prone to think that we're the ones who make the world go round,
But without God to lead the way we'd run it into the ground!

We love the beauty of flowers and love to see them grow.
But can you take a flower seed and make the beauty show?
Of course not for it takes a miracle, as almost anything we do
Comes through a shower of miracles from God to me and you!

My wife just came by and said to me, "it certainly is a beautiful day."
I replied, "it truly is, another miracle has come our way!"
So if someone sincerely says to you, "miracles do happen you know!"
Just nod yes and answer, "that's just because God loves us so!"

June 3.

Miracles, Luck Or Close Shaves

Isn't it exciting when things work out just right?
When all the dark clouds drift away and fade into the night?
You're searching for the answer to the problem that's at hand,
And when it drops into your lap you try to understand!

Was that a miracle of some kind that helped you find the key,
Or was it just a lucky guess, or did it drop off a tree?
Miracles are few and far between and all are a gift of God's,
While luck can be really good or bad determined by the odds!

God sheds His blessings on each of us with every passing day.
We need to thank Him for His love in every kind of way.
Many times when things go right, His help may not be in view,
But you can rest assured, my friend He's there with me and you!

"True" miracles are the ones that "Guidepost" writes about.
When you've read the entire story, there's little room for doubt,
And in every case you can be sure, some luck is there as well.
The beneficiary of the miracle has quite a story to tell!

As we each move down the road of life, it becomes routine.
We think in terms of family and friends but not about what it means.
We take too much for granted and we get too satisfied.
We forget the One who gave His life and that cannot be denied!

We're involved with "near" miracles, we call them all close-shaves,
But that's not quite so odd, in fact that's how the world behaves.
The one "true" miracle that blessed us all is that we're still around,
So let's all thank Jesus for this wonderful life which all of us have found!

June 4.

Misdirected Love

The "love of money" is a sin, there's no doubt of it being true.
The more you have the more you want, there's never enough for you.
Don't let your soul be bought and sold, a victim of the greed
That greases the wheels of politics while ignoring people's need!

I'm like most and I realize that the lure of money is strong.
Those without are down and out, those with can do no wrong.
Philanthropy is a virtue and is practiced by a precious few
Who support many worthy causes because it is the proper thing to do!

When money is used to "tip" the scales, then the devil gets involved.
He directs the buying of many votes and that problem must be solved.
Elections should be fair and square and free to one and all,
Not purchased with the highest bid by those who have a lot of gall!

Money on its own is not something that should be despised.
It's the medium of doing business which we all recognize.
Those who buy and sell a product that's to be used,
Use money to seal the deal and it is seldom refused!

The use of money goes back to olden times it's always been the same.
It has its good points and its faults depending on who's playing the game.
We all know that Judas was paid in silver coin to betray our Lord.
Shekels were used by the Hebrews to purchase things they could afford!

Now I'm not saying that money in itself is sinful on its own,
But the "love of money" is surely a sin and that fact is well known.
It's the "love of money" that leads to greed and therein lies the shame.
Some folks will do almost anything if paid enough and money is to blame!

June 5.

More Power To You

It may be close to zero
But the sun is shining bright,
Our power comes from heaven,
So we will be alright!

It always makes me wonder
About those who don't believe.
When earthly power fails us,
From whom will "they" receive?

Our earthly power comes and goes
And it just came on, but then,
Our heavenly power never dies
If we just stay plugged in!

Jesus sends our heavenly power,
And we never get a bill.
There is no need for cords and such,
It flows from His "Good Will!"

But you must open up your heart
To let the power flow in,
And then He turns the power on
To save your soul from sin!

How can one resist this gift?
It's there for all mankind.
This power source gives all a lift
And our sins are left behind!

June 6.

Music Soothes The Soul

Just what is it that makes me so happy today?
Fast tapping Christmas music that I love to play.
As we approach the birthday of the One we love,
I know that He can hear the music up there far above!

Doesn't it seem funny to think of Jesus fast tapping along.
I'm sure He joins the Angel Chorus when they sing a lovely song.
There is no doubt that some of those songs are all about Him,
And we know too that our Bible has songs that are all about them!

How wonderful it is to have lyrical thoughts way down here below.
Can you imagine the Angels singing, "Somewhere Over The Rainbow?"
Just think of them singing a beautiful Christmas song,
With Jesus sitting on the throne with His foot just tapping along!

The Thanksgiving season has passed but our thanks must never end.
Some things that we should all be thankful for will very soon begin.
The birthday of our dear Jesus, our Savior, Lord and King.
To Him we must always give thanks for every single thing!

Jesus inspires the music that will surely soothe our soul.
It's the kind of music that makes the broken hearted whole.
We live in a world today that's filled with sadness and deadly war.
Families are often torn apart when duty calls loved ones from afar!

We all must stand up for our leaders who daily seek the peace.
We must also ask our God to keep us safe until all wars have ceased.
We're fortunate indeed that our God promotes tranquility.
He'll help us overcome the evil force that only provokes hostility!

June 7.

My Friend Herb

It's always hard to lose a friend and see them laid to rest,
But we should not feel sad for them for Jesus knows what's best.
When He died upon the Cross, He paid for all our sins
And when He takes our soul to Heaven our real life with Him begins!

Herb Trost now has a new address, it's beyond the Pearly Gates.
I'm sure it's loaded with lots of tools for him to make things for his mates.
For he was a master craftsman and he knew just what to do
To turn a piece of walnut wood into a beautiful bird or two!

Herb had many interests and they were as varied as they could be.
He loved his work of teaching school and helping the kids to see
Just what they were best suited for and how they should begin.
He loved to counsel and to guide and they all became his friend!

He helped found a chapter of AFA and served as President several years.
He served it well in many ways as a leader of his peers.
He also served in the CAP and rose up through the ranks,
And for all his service to his country he deserved a lot of thanks!

Herb was a devoted family man, with Mickey by his side.
They loved their home on Robin Dale another source of pride.
They could sit in comfort in their sun room and watch the birds at play,
A perfect place to settle down and relax at the end of every day!

Herb knew well the Master of his soul for Jesus was his friend.
He loved to teach and tell others all about the ravages of sin.
You can be sure that Jesus welcomes Herb Trost into the fold.
We know full well he'll be right at home there among the Saints of old!

Dedicated to my friend Herb Trost at his Memorial, February 24, 2011

June 8.

The Therapy of Poetry

I like to write a poem every day.
It helps to pass the time away.
More than that it keeps me fresh
As I search and search for words that mesh!

Right off I know that's not the word.
To use the word "mesh" is quite absurd.
I should have searched a longer time
To find a better word to make it rhyme!

Choosing a subject is the easy part.
The thought always comes right from my heart.
I can't explain what might come next,
It all depends upon the text!

Soon I'm writing and having fun.
The words come easy once I've begun.
Sometimes I write too fast I know,
Have to slow it down so the words will flow!

There is a point to each poem I write.
Don't mean to preach, must keep it light.
I do think words should entertain.
If not, then whose there to explain!

No more need to write today,
I've said all that I had to say.
Once you've read what I've said to you,
Just sit right down and write some too!

My" Grandfather's Clock

I'm almost as old as my grandfather's clock, I just need two more.
"Papa's" clock never slept it just stood there on the floor.
It never missed its tick nor its tock and kept its record too.
2,836,308,000 is very close if you give or take a few!

Ninety years without a nap, that clock got mighty tired.
If there had been a handy outlet he could have had it wired,
But he just pulled the chains each day and wound it up real tight.
He loved to hear it ticking and it sounded good at night!

My grandpa was a hardy soul, an inventor he was by trade.
You should have visited his shop to see all the things he made,
But there was something he could not do, nor did he even try,
To automate that old clock, before his time to die!

Who would pull those chains each day if he was not around?
Of course the clock would stop its ticking, wouldn't make a sound.
He didn't let that bother him he had better things to do.
He couldn't let the ticking of a clock upset his schedule too!

When grandpa died at ninety years the clock began to fade.
There was no one left there to enjoy all the sounds it made,
But it still stood there on the floor, just inside the door,
As if it was waiting just for Papa to pull those chains once more!

That clock was taller than Papa was no one could reach its face.
They couldn't tell that it was crying there in its lonely place,
But it's still there where its always been, lo these many years.
You do not hear the ticking sound but you hear the splashing of the tears!

An adaptation of a very early nursery rhyme I learned as a child!

June 10.

My Guide and Friend

I need to say "I thank You Lord," You've been so good to me.
When I have needed a helping hand You've always let me see
A clear and shining road ahead with signs to mark the way.
That is why I'm still around and standing here today!

As I look back upon my life and things come into view,
If I needed help and called your name You came and pulled me through,
And through it all, the thick and thin, the good as well as bad,
You've provided all my needs the best that could be had!

There have been times I must admit I wondered where to turn.
My life was never a bed of roses, I had a lot to learn,
But with You as my constant guide I learned just how to cope.
I kept on pushing straight ahead You gave me lots of hope!

There were times of troubles too I needed good advice.
I called on You for help and knew that You would treat me nice.
There never was a single time that You have let me down.
It's such a wonderful thought to know that You always are around!

It's been a long and twisting road that's not hard to understand.
No one has it easy every day and those of us who need a hand
Must look to You and ask for help, we all know how to pray.
There is no doubt that help will come and there will be no delay!

Many years have come and gone the road is smoother now.
You've helped me learn I'm not alone and I know just how
To get in touch when I need help, I bow my head to pray.
You've never failed to heed my call, I count on You each day!

June 11.

My Name Sounds Good To Me

When I was just a little tot I loved to write my name,
I think it may have been because my Dad's name was the same.
I know that I was meant to be a junior which was fine.
When I write out my entire name it uses up the line!

When Jesus inscribed my name into His Book so nice,
He didn't use "ditto marks" so had to write it twice.
Dad's name was there already in black and white a very pretty name
The next line had the junior but the rest was just the same!

The Book of Life has many volumes, the entire human race.
Every name is recorded there, for it's the proper place.
You can be sure your name is there, you'll find it easily,
For it will be an important part of your own family tree!

We all start out on even terms for God plants every tree.
In Heaven there is no color bar we're all alike you see,
And when we're born our skin becomes a mix of Mom and Dad.
The color chart that Jesus has does not rank them good or bad!

Our color should play no larger role than are we short or tall,
And also are we fat or bald should have no place at all,
For in the end it is our name that tells folks who we are,
Even if we're President or a well known movie star!

Jacob, Jacob, that's my name and Jesus says it so sweet.
It makes me happy just to think He'll know me when we meet.
To all my loved ones and my friends, your names are in my heart.
Wherever we are, from here on out, we'll never be apart!

My Soul Still Follows Where Jesus Leads

I always loved the Bible stories that my Mother told.
She had a child-like love for Jesus worth its weight in gold.
That's where my faith in God began, at my Mother's knee.
I've never wavered in my faith it's still as strong as it can be!

There were times in my younger days when preaching was my goal.
I always loved to take the stage and relate what I'd been told.
The stories that my Mother told have always served me well.
They formed the basis for my faith and the stories I loved to tell!

World War II was in full swing, I had to change my plans.
The perfect age with a high draft number on whom Uncle made demands.
Stories of 'trench warfare' which <u>my</u> Uncles told had made me want to fly.
I had visions of soaring through the air with Jesus, what better way to die!

I enlisted in the Army Air Corps and became an Aviation Cadet.
It wasn't West Point, which I admired, but was as close as I could get.
I'd never been off the ground before so training was a thrill.
From Piper Cubs to Stearman PT-17 they put us through the mill!

Mr. Hassett who trained me well said he was scared as "hell".
My clumsy attempts to fly the plane were stories I never tell.
After five hours he hopped out and said, "Shepherd, you're on your own."
When he hopped out, Jesus got in, and from then on with me He's flown!

My B-17 named "Bottle Baby" was really my worthy pride and joy.
Twenty-five times I flew it over Germany although I was just a boy.
Jesus was with me and my crew and we never lost our way.
With His help we came back home and that's why I'm here today!

June 13.

Never Give Up

If at first you don't succeed it may not be your day.
Don't give up, try again and things may go your way.
When you take that second chance it's special don't you see,
If you succeed then you will see that it was meant to be!

Success of any kind in life does not come without a price.
So many folks who fail give up, while trying once or twice.
Thank you God for all the patient ones who try and try again.
Perseverance is the word that lets the victor win!

Almost all the inventors that I have read about,
Who were successful in their life, were never lost in doubt.
They might try again and again a thousand times it's true,
But finally found the one that clicks and invented something new!

A person's life has ups and downs, never stays the same.
If one is to succeed they must prepare to play the game.
You try it one way it falls flat, then take your second time at bat.
If that fails don't give up, just remember where you're at!

You're searching hard now, both high and low,
To find that road, the one down which you'll go.
The answer to your quest is there,
So keep on searching everywhere!

It won't be long 'til you succeed, the answer falls in place.
Those forty trials, failures all, are ready to erase.
You package up the new design and take it to the boss.
He pats you on the back and says "Thanks, your design erased our loss!

June 14.

Never Forget

Here's to all those who are known as "Vet."
Been to hell and back but still around here yet.
There were so many of us who gave their all,
We honor them but thank the Lord "we" did not fall!

Not just today but everyday we think of those who went away.
These fine young folks were the cream of the crop they say.
They left their families and their friends to go to Tim-Buk-Too,
When duty called they merely asked, "what do I have to do"?

Our Nation has faced so many trials as we have made our way.
In distant lands and yes here at home, we've had a debt to pay.
We've fought and died in many wars, have never lost one yet.
So every single citizen should say "Thank You" to a vet!

Heroes all, these guys and gals, the ones who took the pledge,
They raised their hand and said "I Will", this put them on the edge.
They joined the forces of our land to fill a vital need.
They all received a number and dogtag that anyone could read!

Regardless what their duty was they all served in harm's way.
Each one was important to the cause they had a part to play.
Whether on the battlefield or not they wanted to survive,
But as with everything in life, not all came home alive!

November 11 across our land is known as "Veteran's Day."
Flags will fly for every force, we'll bow our heads to pray,
"Dear Heavenly Father there on high, the Maker of us all,
Bless everyone of those who served, bring peace to our "terrestrial ball"!

Flag Day

June 15.

Never Give Up Without A Fight

When families begin to disappear the cousins are usually the last to go.
If you have cousins, you have family and that is real good to know.
"First cousins" have a special place, they really are close kin.
They shelter memories of Aunts and Uncles and bygone days again!

My Granddad, William P. was the patriarch of his clan.
He was an inventor, an entrepreneur, a self-educated man.
He became very successful and wealthy, but the big depression arrived.
He lost his fortune and his business, but his inventions and family survived!

"Bill " Hornbuckle was a Christian and a Presbyterian by choice.
He raised a family with lots of kids, four pretty girls and five boys.
All five sons were servicemen and four grandsons as well.
They served in World War I and World War II and all had stories to tell!

Thirteen grandchildren called him "Papa" along with all his kids.
He had a wonderful productive life until his business hit the skids,
But he maintained his expertise and his work became his routine.
He travelled all over the U. S. A. installing his machine!

An early morning hotel fire in Alabama awakened all the guests.
"Papa", always a fastidious man, took the time to get dressed.
No fire escape from the top most floor so he had to build a rope.
All he had was a flag and several sheets, but he was one who never gave up hope!

September 16, '44, in Anniston, the date and scene of the fire.
Alas, the rope was not long enough, not what safety would require.
When he reached the end of his rope, he finally had to let go.
He died in the fall as he had lived, a courageous man who never said "no!"

Written by one of those Grandchildren, Jacob Nathaniel Shepherd
And dedicated to all my cousins both here and beyond!
September 23, 2010
(Sixty-six years and one week after "Papa's" death)

Birthdate of #2 Daughter, Joann Bristol, 1961   **175**

June 16.

Father's Day

When we think of Father's Day we think of our own Dad.
Our greatest thoughts are of his love and fun that we all had.
Dad loved Mom with all his heart and each one of us too.
Their love affair produced us all and made their dreams come true!

God does work in mysterious ways His miracles to perform.
He is the greatest Father of them all, He is the perfect norm.
So we must honor Him on this their day of days.
To our God and my Daddy too we offer up our praise!

Now it's Father's Day again and I'm a father too.
My seven children honor me, the proper thing to do.
I'll be thinking of my love for them as Father's Day is near,
And wishing them happiness and health throughout the coming year!

Days may come and days may go and memories sometimes fade.
It's good to have an album full of pictures that we've made.
I like to look and reminisce at all the days gone by.
Some make me cringe, some make me laugh, and others make me cry!

I see the pictures of my Dad when he was just a lad.
'Twas long before he met my Mom, he looked like me a tad.
It makes me wonder if my boys will ever look like me.
There's Jake and Lewie and John, a really fearsome three!

On Father's Day I also think of Sons-in-law as well.
They all are fathers with sons too and treat my daughters swell.
I offer up my thanks to God, the Father of all mankind.
He's done the most for all of us than all the rest combined!

Father's Day II

Please don't forget to honor God on this dear Father's Day.
The Father of all mankind still has a major part to play.
He stamped His Logo on our Soul and it's still there today.
He gave us all the password to His Heart, we use it when we pray!

On Father's Day we also honor the one we know as Dad.
He taught us how to play and tried to keep us all from being bad.
Many years have come and gone but I still can easily see his face.
He's the one who helped me become a worthy member of the human race!

Father's Day is set aside, a single day it's true,
For you to honor and remember the one who fathered you.
You may not remember all he taught if it was very long ago,
But rest assured they were the kinds of things that you still need to know!

My father taught me how to treat my wife by how he treated Mom.
Things were different way back then before the days of "dot com."
Dad also taught me that respect was more important than apology.
These lessons that my father taught me had a very big influence on me!

My father died and went to Heaven so many years ago.
He taught me to love our Heavenly Father which we all should know.
I've never forgotten what I learned from him, I'll never forget my Dad.
He was just a very simple man but the smartest teacher I ever had!

Another Father's Day is here and there are many thanks we must give.
I know my Heavenly Father will credit my Dad for teaching me to live
The kind of life that he had lived with that help from God above,
So now I welcome this opportunity to honor both of them with my love!

Never Say Goodbye

Say something simple, like ta-ta, but never say goodbye.
The very finality of the thought always makes me cry.
When someone says those words to me, I try to shield my ears,
And then I quickly turn away so they won't see the tears!

For me, goodbye and tears, they always go hand in hand,
Reminds me of a house of cards that was built upon the sand.
Here today and gone tomorrow as sadness fills the air,
'Til happy memories dispel the gloom and the sun shines everywhere!

If you're like most, you've had your share of very sad goodbyes,
But think of all the joy that comes along with a good surprise,
When a long gone someone appears again, after many years,
It quickly brightens up the day and erases all those fears!

A goodbye means that someone is not going to be around.
It doesn't mean that they are leaving for a better place they've found.
They may be forced by circumstance to make that move, it's true.
That doesn't mean they're leaving because they're tired of you!

I like to face life as it comes it's not always what we choose,
But if we accept our fate perhaps, we may not always lose.
When one door closes another opens so be ready for a change.
It may be what you were wishing for, your life to be rearranged!

You may want to say farewell to a part of your life that's passed
And say hello to something new that looks like it will last.
You can embark on a new career you've got time before you die,
But whatever you do and wherever you go, please don't say "goodbye!"

June 18.

Sweet Sixteen

Walker Bristol is my name.
So far I have no claim to fame,
But everyday I'm here on earth,
Makes one more day since my birth!

Today's a special day for me.
I'm sixteen now and fancy free.
I've been waiting for this day.
Now it's safe to "drive" away!

I've got big plans before I rest.
I'm working hard to pass the test.
My Senior year and College too,
Important things that I must do!

I think of all those years gone by,
Which brought me here to Hoggard High.
I will admit it's been quite a trip,
And so far I've made no major slip!

My family have been my biggest fans,
They are helping too with all my plans.
I'll surely miss them when I go away,
But they have trained me well just for that day!

I like to think that I'm a regular guy.
I work real hard and hold my head up high.
My life's been fun with lots of joys,
But I'm still just one of the "Bristol" boys!

I've got one more year before I can gloat,
Got to be careful, can't rock the boat.
Sixteen candles upon my cake,
I'm getting old for goodness sake!
By Grandpa Jake

Birthdate of #2 Grandson, Walker Bristol, 1993

June 19.

Observation

It's fun to sit in waiting rooms and watch the world go by.
You look at every person and wonder, are they in better shape that I?
It's hard to tell the circumstance that each one must abide,
So I just sit and smile at everyone, knowing Jesus is at my side!

The doctor takes one look at me and then begins to grin.
He says "the charts look very good today no changes have there been,
Just keep on doing what you're doing and see me in a year."
Now that was very good news indeed, just what I need to hear!

When I looked around the room, most folks I saw were old.
To them, like me, our Medicare is worth its weight in gold.
Don't know what I'd do without it, I couldn't pay the bill.
They'd just have to take me out, dig a hole, and bury me on the hill!

The health care bill which has been passed is "God sent" to us all.
It provides for everyone, even those who won't play ball.
A certain class of folks in power have "repeal" on their mind,
These same folks who voted to go to war that placed us in a bind!

I didn't intend this poem to be about politics you see,
But today it seems that everything is political, even you and me.
I've got a number, you've got one, most folks don't even know my name,
But given the all-important number they'll know from whence I came!

But folks, please don't let politics determine who you are.
Put your faith in Jesus, you'll be better off by far.
I know for sure that He's the one who will treat us all the same,
And regardless of your lot in life you can bet He'll know your name!

June 20.

On My Way To Heaven

On my way to Heaven I'd like to step upon the moon,
To spend more time than Armstrong did, he had to leave too soon,
To place my feet into his prints will be a pleasant task.
I hope that Jesus doesn't feel that it's too much to ask!

I'm not famous like Armstrong is, nor will I ever be,
For when I step upon the moon it's just for me you see.
The whole wide world saw Armstrong land it was a thrill for all.
That "giant leap for mankind" was in truth a step so very small!

It seems that we think more of the moon than even of our sun,
Since thousands of poems and songs abound, the moon in every one.
The moon suggests romance indeed as it shines throughout the night,
While we forget the basic fact that it's the sun that provides the light!

The sun and moon are just a little part of our vast universe.
Along with earth they form the world, the one that we traverse.
Jesus saw the sun and moon but very little of the globe.
He never travelled far from home but stayed close to His abode!

As we learn a whole lot more about our world today,
We recognize the value of our sun as it comes into play,
To furnish energy of many kinds, to help us all endure,
And to replace some other fuels which now are harder to procure!

For me to land upon the moon is just a "wish" of course.
I'd like to also circle the globe which Lindberg would endorse.
To do these things would be a thrill as I leave the earth behind,
To look "in awe" upon the scene that's been the home of all mankind!

Birthdate of #1 Daughter, Susan S. Sharp, 1958

June 21.

One Hundred Days

One hundred days is not much time,
It quickly comes and goes,
But if you have high walls to climb
You must stay on your toes!

Our new President was placed in quite a spot
When he won the right to lead us all,
The seat he won was still quite hot
Now he must carry the ball!

The pundits all have had their say
And some were not so kind.
Some others sing, "Oh Happy Day"
Still others lag behind.

Barack Obama has built a team,
Good folks they're all first class.
They quickly built a head of steam,
There are tests they all must pass!

Our Congress and our President
Have goals they must combine.
One hundred days were mostly spent
Making plans they must refine!

It's time that they all must buckle down,
There's so much more to do.
If nothing's done we "all" will drown,
<u>Red ink must turn to blue!</u>

June 22.

One Year Later

I can hardly wait to hear the President he makes a speech today,
The traditional State of our Nation speech, he'll have a lot to say.
He's made some progress, not enough, there's still a lot to do.
The health care program is a must, I'm sure he'll push it through!

The opposition he has had has been of the toughest kind.
Turncoats in his own party have really placed him in a bind.
George W. Bush, inept was he, left things in one big mess,
Two wars to fight, big bills to pay, but there has been some success!

The Republican members of our Congress all vote by saying "no".
Their major concern seems to be in keeping their taxes low.
Social Security and Medicare and programs to aid the poor,
Are not the kind of legislative bills that these folks bring to the floor!

We are besieged by "teaparty groups" and talk show hosts who lie.
Their constant drum beat fills the air, rising to the sky.
The Democratic members must move alone their programs to enact,
That's what the President will say tonight, it's time for us to act!

We're slowly ending our war-like stance and peace must be our goal.
Health care and jobs for needy folks are worth their weight in gold.
Let's pass our bills with majority vote and watch our prestige rise.
The effect on our land will be the same as a Limbaugh-Beck demise!

Tomorrow we'll begin a "New Deal" day as F D R would say.
Put people to work and give them hope and for that we need to pray.
Barack Obama's message tonight will provide the spark we need,
To light the torch of liberty and help our Nation to succeed!

June 23.

Our Country Can Do Better Than This

Jesus I know that you're concerned about our land today.
Storm clouds have gathered on the horizon of the good ole USA.
The rich folks in our society are pitching "crumbs" to those in need.
The unemployed are occupying the streets to counter all the greed!

No one knows where this will lead but it cannot be all good.
What these people really need is a job so that they can buy their food.
There is plenty of work that could be done, enough jobs for us all,
But the opposition group will not agree, they only want to stall!

It seems they've all signed a pledge to not raise tax of any kind.
This places our country which depends on taxes in a vise-like bind.
The wealthy people in our midst admit that they should pay more,
But Grover's pledge prevents any action, even that to aid the poor!

I know that when we die we must leave all our wealth behind.
Can those folks who've built up large estates have real peace of mind?
In Heaven they cannot snap their fingers and have their wishes met.
They'll be just like the rest of us who give more than we get!

I'm one of those who fortunately fall somewhere in between.
I have a small amount put aside which is not tax paid but very clean.
A combination of forced withdrawal and social security fills my need.
Once I pay my tax-on-tax to Uncle Sam I feel I've done my good deed!

Bill Gates and Warren Buffett are wealthy but always pay their dues.
Many projects to aid mankind which they fund are often in the news.
They pay their taxes and would pay more but cannot by the rules.
This makes it evident that we're governed by a bunch of silly fools!

June 24.

Our Greatest Friend

Why is it that on a particular day,
Certain thoughts just won't go away?
You wipe those cobwebs from your mind
Seeking the problem you hope to find!

Suddenly there comes a brighter light,
The veil is lifted to clear your sight,
You wipe your eyes the better to see,
And there stands Jesus, yes it is He!

If truth be known, He was there before,
Standing just inside the open door.
You see, it's true, He's always there
Just waiting with His time to share!

Please don't wait for Him to call,
He's been there waiting after all.
It's His desire to help you out.
He's close by, there's no need to shout!

Jesus wants all to be His friend,
Broken hearts He likes to mend,
And all those other problems too,
Just let Him show you what to do!

You can be happy and satisfied,
If you'll keep Jesus by your side.
Please don't wait for we never know,
When it will be time for us to go!

June 25.

Out Of The Blue

I love to see a friendly face as I walk through a crowd.
It keeps me from feeling lonely as I speak to them out loud.
"Hello Frankie", "hello Jack" or "hello you know who"
We stop to chat or chew the fat and always learn something new!

Having friends, a lot of them, can make your life worthwhile.
Just think of all the friends you've made since you were just a child,
But most of them have moved away, leaving you behind.
So keep in touch with the friends you have and go out someplace to dine!

As we go through life, things change, there's always something new.
Never think you know it all, find something that interests you.
You'd be surprised how much you learn if you just lend an ear,
To listen to what others say, you never know what you might hear!

As you are cruising through that crowd, you hear a friendly voice.
The pushing and shoving makes you move, you have no other choice.
You store that voice into your memory, it triggers from "long ago,"
A friend who suddenly disappeared to where you did not know!

You begin a desperate search to find that friend of old.
To make some headway through the crowd you had to be quite bold.
Pushing, shoving, left and right, the crowd begins to thin,
Then when you've almost lost all hope, you hear that voice again!

You begin looking all around that crowd to find a familiar face,
The one you loved who walked away and did not leave a trace.
You realized then that she was near, somewhere in this place.
Suddenly, you were overwhelmed when she fell into your embrace!

Thank You Jesus!

June 26.

Perfection Reigns Only In Heaven

We'll never reach perfection 'til we're in Heaven you see
For only Jesus is perfect, as perfect as He can be.
Everything in Heaven is perfect and we should strive to go.
That wonderful, beautiful garden of Eden is unlike anything here below!

If you should get to Heaven before I do, you won't worry about me.
Not because you're not concerned about me but Heaven is worry free.
No one worries in Heaven for there's nothing to worry about.
Earning a living or buying a house are things we can do without!

Health and happiness are no longer worries once we enter Heavens Gates.
Perfection reigns in all aspects of life unaffected by dates.
Life on earth ends for everyone somewhere along the way.
Life in Heaven lasts forever for in eternity we are there to stay!

No one in Heaven says "I'm sorry, I don't have time."
Since time is not a problem, that fact helps make life sublime.
Can you imagine meeting all the Saints who died so long ago.
I'm sure they'll still be working with the Lord to help those here below!

As we look back into our lives we think of so many who've played a part
In helping us get to where we are today, it's known as "having a heart."
No one makes it on their own no matter how hard they try.
Everyone needs a helping hand to get to Heaven when they die!

All those who've helped us make it there will greet us at the Gate.
While we don't know everything lying ahead they seem to know the date,
And since the restraints of time mean nothing to them they'll be there
To let us know they're glad to see us and our old friendship again to share!

June 27.

Place Your Bets

Everyone wants to be a winner we always hate to lose,
But you can't be a winner if you don't pay your dues.
You cannot take the easy route and expect to land on top.
If you don't mind your "p's and q's" you will surely be a flop!

It's true that once you know the ropes you have a better chance.
That way you can show everyone just who wears the pants.
That doesn't mean that you will win you still must place your bet,
But you can always be assured that you have your best chance yet!

If you love and believe in Jesus you're a winner that's for sure.
Those folks who say there is no God are losers and insecure.
They have no knowledge of what's in store once they're dead and gone,
But without Jesus to show them the way they'll be left there all alone!

I wouldn't want to face the devil's hordes without someone on my side.
Wherever I'd be going it sure would be a very lonely ride.
It's never too late, you know, to ask Jesus to save your soul.
Just ask Him to come into your heart and He'll play a vital role!

We all are given our "free will", we make our choice in life.
We are free to choose our daily needs and that includes a wife.
How to make a living is an important choice of course.
If you continue to play the "odds" you might wind up with a horse!

I know that I'm a winner, but there are things that I could lose.
I guard my reputation for it's awfully easy to bruise.
I call on Jesus every morning and ask Him to be my guide.
There is no way that I can lose with Jesus by my side!

June 28.

Planning

Jesus loves always to hear us pray.
Our words can help to make His day.
He'll make a note of all our cares,
So don't forget to say your prayers!

As we all look back into our past,
We made big plans that didn't last.
We started out with so much pride,
We then let down, our big plans died!

Too often we forget we're never all alone.
We shouldn't try to do it all or do it on our own.
The plans we make with Jesus' help are written in His Book.
They'll last at least a thousand years so take a real good look!

Get right down upon your knees, tell Jesus that you care.
Ask Him to lead you on the way and help you to prepare,
To guide you to the future and make a forward plan.
He'll put you on the straightest road toward the "Promised Land!"

Think long and hard before you take the lonely "solo" route.
Jesus wants to go along, He wants to help you out.
He has with Him the Golden Book He keeps on me and you.
In that Book you'll find the plan that tells what you must do!

As I have said so much before, He loves for you to pray.
He's always listening for your voice, I'm sure He's there today.
So don't delay and do not wait to make your wishes known.
He'll be right there to help you so you won't be alone!

June 29.

Planning Ahead

Are there some things you want to do while you are still alive?
I suppose we all have lists but how long will we survive?
Can we accomplish all those things that we had hoped to do?
Unless we start to work right now we never will get through!

First of all let's check that list, are you sure that it's complete?
Are there things on that list that you could easily delete?
Don't even think about the cost, that's not important now.
Spend all your wealth, you can't take it with you anyhow!

My list is short, just a few things that I truly want to do.
In fact, some of them I've done before, there's really nothing new.
My problem is that I don't have time, I'm busy don't you see,
Doing all those things I like to do, my daily activity!

If I have too long a list, that means I've missed a lot,
And I suppose it's all true but there are some things I forgot.
I don't want to jump from planes or climb to mountain tops,
But I do want someday to follow a rainbow, that is until it stops!

I'd like to write a lovely song that everyone will sing.
That would mean a lot to me, it would mean everything.
I've done most everything I set out in life to do,
So I'm winding down by writing some poems just for you!

I'm sure there are some things I still must do, my list is not too long.
I'm going to spend some time I know, writing that lovely song.
I made my first list long ago, finished it last year,
So I think I'll just coast along and play everything by ear!

June 30.

Please Don't Pick On Me

Is there someone picking on you while you stand idly by?
Do they keep on picking and picking until they make you cry?
You must develop a good defense or it will ruin your day,
And the best defense is a good offense, just merely walk away!

That someone who was picking on you will take offense you see.
They'll be offended that you defended and did it easily.
You didn't try to pick on them and they missed the chance to say,
"Why don't you quit picking on me, does it make your day?"

If no one's picking on anyone else then peace begins to reign.
We all look for something else to do and hope to cause no pain.
We could skip a rope if there were three or "hop scotch" by ourself,
Or we could even play a game of "Jacks" which is sitting on the shelf!

You know, Nations would be much better off to act like kids, it's plain.
Quit picking on one another, you'll have much more to gain.
Find another Nation that needs some help and offer to be a friend.
If no one else then picked on you, well warfare would reach an end!

How much better off this world would be with everyone at peace.
We wouldn't be afraid to travel and tourism would increase.
Airplanes flying overhead would have no bombs but be enroute instead
To some exotic foreign land while happy thoughts danced in their head!

I know this sounds too simple and will never come to pass.
Nations will continue to fight over who has the most oil and gas,
Or they'll even "pick on" their neighbors who have no real defense.
This is what brings on a war, my friend, and doesn't make much sense!

Music
Interlude

Hymns by Jacob N. Shepherd

All are copyrighted and
permission to use in any
setting will be granted by
the Author.

Jshepherd5@ec.rr.com

Hymns About Jesus

196
I Love Thee Lord Jesus
Tune: Beneath The Cross of Jesus
197
I Have A Friend In Heaven
Tune: Original by Tom Solley
195
You'll Never Be Lonely Again
Tune: In The Garden
199
Dear Jesus Is My Hero
Tune: O Jesus I Have Promised
198
Do You Feel A Need For Jesus
Tune: What A Friend We Have In Jesus

You'll Never Be Lonely Again

Words by Jacob N. Shepherd

Music pre-existing "In The Garden" by C. Austin Miles
1912

Slowly, solemnly ♩. = 52

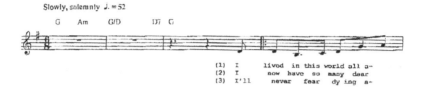

(1) I lived in this world all a-
(2) I now have so many dear
(3) I'll never fear dy ing a-

lone,---- 'til Je sus took me as His friend   Then the love   He gave   made me
friends   and Je sus looks out for us all   He is there to behold all the needs
gain----   for Je sus will be by my side   He will take   me home   never

strong and brave, His love is such a   treasure   Then He said   it's true, I really do
of our soul He's sure to answer all our calls
more to roam with Him   forever to reside

love you   you're mine and for ever will be   So rejoice and sing   to Him

1.2.   3.

Who   is King   You'll never be lonely   again!

I Love Thee Lord Jesus

Words
Jacob N. Shepherd 2011

Music
Frederick C. Maker 1881

1. I love Thee Lord Je - sus, please come and take my hand
2. What won - ders You've blessed me with while I've been here on earth
3. My life has not been per - fect, I know that I have sinned
4. Please let me know dear Je - sus, just what I have to do

Please take me home to live with Thee, there in the Promised land
I've never wavered in my faith, I've loved You since my birth
But You have been forgiving and You've always been my friend
To place my soul upon the Cross and come to live with You.

I ask for-give-ness for my sins and mercy on my soul
I loved to hear dear Jesus name in stor-ies my mother told
I've worn a breast-plate of the cross and it has served me well
Just check my record in Your Book and tell me where I stand

Just place Your Hand upon my brow and that will make me whole!
Those stories still are in my heart and never will grow old!
It has been my shield from mortal sin and it has never failed!
So I don't miss the flight that's going to the Promised Land! A-MEN

I Have A Friend In Heaven

Words Jacob N. Shepherd

Music Tom Solley

(1) I have a friend in heaven, the one that we all know,
(2) I have a friend in heaven, He died that we might know,
(3) I have a friend in heaven, He gave His life for me.

(1) I talk with Him and He with me, I know He loves me so!
(2) The path that we must follow, as home to heaven we go!
(3) Not just for me but one and all, and soon in heaven we'll be!

(1) I have a friend in heaven, His earthly days were spent,
(2) I have a friend in heaven, He rose and lives today,
(3) Jesus, our friend in heaven, requires not much from me,

(1) To teach us all that God is love we learned just what that meant!
(2) He's always there if I should call, He always makes my day!
(3) Our friendship is alive and well, His faithful steward I'll be!

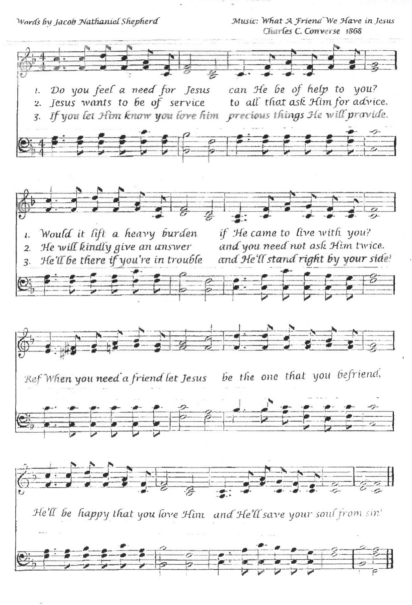

Do You Feel A Need For Jesus

Words by Jacob Nathaniel Shepherd

Music: What A Friend We Have in Jesus
Charles C. Converse 1868

1. Do you feel a need for Jesus   can He be of help to you?
2. Jesus wants to be of service   to all that ask Him for advice.
3. If you let Him know you love him   precious things He will provide.

1. Would it lift a heavy burden   if He came to live with you?
2. He will kindly give an answer   and you need not ask Him twice.
3. He'll be there if you're in trouble   and He'll stand right by your side!

Ref. When you need a friend let Jesus   be the one that you befriend,

He'll be happy that you love Him   and He'll save your soul from sin!

Dear Jesus Is My Hero

Words: Jacob Nathaniel Shepherd

Music: Pre-existing O Jesus I Have Promised/Angel's Story
Arthur H. Mann 1881

(1)Dear Jesus is my hero my savior and my friend
(2)Oh Jesus help and guide me in all I do today,
(3)Oh Jesus bring me someone who needs my help today,
(4)Oh Jesus let me listen as you speak to me again,

(1)He's guided me through all my days and forgiven all my sin.
(2)Don't let me faint nor falter and please don't let me stray.
(3)I'll work to solve their problems and send them on their way.
(4)You grant me strength and courage that keeps me free of sin.

(1)I place my trust in Jesus each morn when I awake,
(2)The world is full of pitfalls don't let me fall therein,
(3)So many folks are needy and have no place to go.
(4)I love to hear your whisper falling softly on my ear,

(1)I know that He will lead me on the paths that I must take.
(2)Just keep me on the straightest path that leads away from sin.
(3)Take all I have and share it with lots of love also.
(4)It will provide me comfort throughout the coming year.

Contents July

1. Poetry...201

2. Pray For Peace...202

3. Promises May Be Broken...................................203

4. Americas Birthday..204

5. Put On Your Happy Face...................................205

6. Raindrops Are Falling...206

7. Realities Of Life...207

8. Recruits Wanted..208

9. Rejoice...209

10. Reminiscing..210

11. If You Don't Believe, What Then.......................211

12. Should We Begin To Worry?.............................212

13. Smart, Dumb Or Stupid...................................213

14. So True..214

15. Something To Crow About................................215

16. Sometimes A Push Is What I Need....................216

17. Sometimes Right and Sometimes Wrong...........217

18. Just Smile..218

19. Spend Your Day With Jesus...............................219

20. The War That We Must Win..............................220

21. Stay On The Alert...221

22. Struggling...222

23. Sudoku...223

24. Sunrise..224

25. The War Zone...225

26. No Threat To Microsoft....................................226

27. Tears Of Sorrow Become Tears Of Joy...............227

28. Tears Of Sorrow Born Of Guilt.........................228

29. Thank God Who Leads The Way.......................229

30. Get Ready For The Battle..................................230

31. Thank You Jesus For Your Gifts........................231

July 1.

Poetry

There doesn't seem to be a set format for writing poetry,
So why not put your thoughts on paper so everyone can see.
It's fun to share your thoughts with others and hope that it will rhyme.
It will keep you busy for awhile, a good way to spend some time!

When I first started I thought, my gosh, that doesn't sound so good,
But when I had changed it several times, that fixed it so it would.
You see there is no absolute, everything is fair game.
No two folks will each write a poem and make them sound the same!

Some folks write in "open" form, there is no rhyme in those.
For me that's not "pure" poetry, I prefer to call it prose.
That's okay for lots of folks, for me it's touch and go.
I like to write my poems a la Edgar Allen Poe!

When I'm writing the wheels are turning, my mind's an open book.
I try to find the proper words that rhyme, no matter how they look.
I twist and turn the words around to keep my train of thought,
And when I finally write it down, it sounds just like it ought!

Another thing that's important, at least it is for me,
And that's the meter of each verse that makes good poetry.
When I'm reading poetry I like to get myself in gear.
If I get it all just right it's very pleasant to the ear!

Sometimes it's hard to say just what you mean and you must improvise,
And yes sometimes it's necessary for you to compromise,
But whatever you write, make sure it comes right from your heart.
You never know what you can do, so why not make a start?

July 2.

Pray For Peace

Where would we be without the Lord to guide us every day?
Most of us there is no doubt would surely go astray.
We are by nature sinful souls needing help from above.
When we get down upon our knees to pray Jesus sends His love!

Precious Jesus be our guide and help us see the light.
Without your help and loving care we don't know what is right.
If you're not in our thoughts each day the devil plants a seed.
Don't let us overlook your love for us for that's just what we need!

Jesus, sweet Jesus, we praise your Holy Name.
If we don't pray and call on You, we have ourselves to blame.
There is no one but You dear Lord who loves us as we are,
And let's us know that You'll be waiting when we cross the bar!

Dear Lord I pray you'll hear me now and forgive me of my sin.
There are so many faults I have I know I must begin,
To seek your help in every way and keep You by my side.
I know You love us one and all and for our sins You died!

It's not too late to ask the Lord for mercy on our soul.
If we're sincere do not fear, He will make us whole.
We can't save ourselves alone, let Jesus lead the way.
Get busy now and praise the Lord, He'll hear us when we pray!

The greatest need we have today is peace for all mankind.
So many of our young have died with loved ones left behind.
Let's all pray for peace on earth and God will surely hear.
He's the one who can save us all, we'll have no more to fear!

July 3.

Promises May Be Broken

It's awfully hard for me to understand why some folks don't believe.
That Jesus Christ can save their soul, they just cannot conceive,
That this One solitary Man can save the entire human race.
Our belief is built on Faith alone, until we die and meet Him face to face!

Some folks really are afraid of death I think they're afraid of Him.
I am not afraid to die and I know it's only "because" of Him.
If I did not know and yes, believe, then I'd be afraid to die.
They would have to bury me real deep so they couldn't hear me cry!

On another hand when Jesus takes my soul at death and looks me in the eye
I think He'll ask me then and there are you ready to live here in the sky?
I can answer loud and clear, Yes Lord, my Faith has made me whole.
I see my friends and family who've gone before who welcome this old soul!

Oh Lord, please help me to convince those folks who don't believe
To accept your offer of salvation, it's the one thing they "must" achieve.
We all have many offers of beliefs, but most won't satisfy
That longing put into our hearts by God to reach our homeland in the sky!

Is it really possible to believe that there is no life after we die?
That all the stories of God and Jesus are nothing but one big lie?
The devil is a master showman and he has a powerful pitch.
His major weapon is a promise, "Follow me and you'll be rich!"

Promises, promises, sincere indeed, no truer words were ever spoken.
We all hear promises every day, but most of them are broken.
God, the only God, sent His Only Son Jesus, down to earth to die,
And to save every single one of us who believe in God's Heaven in the sky!

July 4.

Americas Birthday

America is the land of the "brave and the free."
'Twas founded by Patriots to wipe out tyranny.
Their worthy efforts have passed the test 'lo these many years,
Protected by many others who have given blood, sweat and tears!

Oh yes, I went to war, along with many of you,
Just to preserve the freedom of the red, white and blue,
And today when I salute or place my hand upon my heart,
It says to everyone around that I've tried to do my part!

What do these actions say to folks around the world?
As they watch in silent awe as our flag becomes unfurled?
America, America, the greatest nation of them all,
Where people sing, "Let Freedom Ring" o'er this terrestrial ball!

The beauty of our country attracts folks from everywhere.
They look at us and say "Americans have so much to share."
They pack their bags with all they own and then they say "goodbye."
They're heading for the "promised land" and good old apple pie!

The freedoms that we all enjoy are abused by a lunatic fringe.
The air waves all across our land echo things that make us cringe.
The drum beat from these "prophets of doom" go on night and day.
We must accept the bad with the good, for it's the American way!

This year as we celebrate the founding of our beloved land,
Let's remember again and never forget those Patriots who had a hand,
In building for everyone of us, a country where we could be,
Proud to be an American in the land of the brave and the free!

Independence Day

July 5.

Put On Your Happy Face

Are you content with your life as it is today,
Or do you wish things were different in some fantastic way?
Not too sure what you'd change if you just had the chance?
Before you make a drastic move evaluate your circumstance!

You may be overlooking the most important things of all.
They may seem insignificant but they could cause you to fall.
Sometimes we let a very simple thing disrupt a tranquil scene.
If you would just take a bit more time then things could be serene!

Helter-skelter is a term I'm sure you've heard before.
It's a game the devil plays as he tries to get in your door.
The smoothest moments of your life can easily become a dread.
You must resist the devil's pitch before you wind up dead!

Now this is no idle threat the devil makes as he interferes.
He isn't content when you're smiling for he likes to see your tears.
A happy family life is something that he just cannot condone,
So don't let him back you into a corner where you'd be all alone!

The very darkest moments of our life come when the devil is nearby.
Jesus sees that trouble is brewing as he watches o'er us from the sky.
If we just look to Him day by day and let Him take us by the hand,
We can overcome the work of the devil and head for the "Promised Land!"

There's nothing else that can compare with the joy of a happy family life.
The man is fortunate indeed who finds a real helpmate for a wife.
The devil will try to stick his nose in where it truly does not belong,
But you must be content and yes, beware and smile and sing a happy song!

July 6.

Raindrops Are Falling

It seems the rain will never stop,
It keeps on raining drop by drop.
We should be happy that it's free.
Imagine what the bill would be!

We should be glad that it doesn't stop.
It would be bad if we got not a drop.
The trees would die and so would we.
It's better to be wet than not to be!

Feel sorry for those who rarely see,
A nice rainfall to water their tree.
They scan the sky and search in vain,
Hoping that there will soon be rain!

Folks, rest assured, God Himself is well aware,
Where rain is needed, He'll send it there.
He doesn't charge for what we receive,
Asking only of us that we believe!

When you see storm clouds form above,
Think of them as expressions of His love,
And then when the raindrops begin to fall,
Thank Him for the "showers" upon us all!

Beautiful sunshine follows the rain.
Each one can now be happy again.
Happy of course that the rain "did" fall,
Happier still that God loves us all!

July 7.

Realities Of Life

Life and death are but a breath apart.
They both connect right to the heart.
A whole lifetime flows in between,
With us at the center of every scene!

We are all just actors on the stage of life.
One of the greatest roles is that of wife.
Of course the husband has a great role too.
God picks the cast and I'm glad He picked you!

The stories of life are all written by God.
We start life in heaven as babies like peas in a pod.
When the full cast is chosen and life's underway,
The curtain goes up and the band starts to play!

We know how different life is for us all.
We're surrounded by players to whom God gave a call.
The success of our story will depend on the cast.
Each one must follow the script 'til their whole life is past!

Your play may be one act, two acts, or more.
Some sagas carry the story for three acts or four.
God in His wisdom gives us the script act by act.
We won't know our life story until it's after the fact!

When my story is over and the curtain comes down at last,
I'd like God's Academy to award an Oscar to the entire cast.
To all my family and friends, players and all extras too,
It's been wonderful and a pleasure to know every one of you!

July 8.

Recruits Wanted

The solitude was broken by the rustling of the trees.
There was something about that lovely sound that put me on my knees.
I closed my eyes and listened as the wind moved through the leaves.
'Twas then I heard the voice of God, I'm one who truly believes!

This early morning interlude helped me to start my day,
For when I heard Him speak to me I knew I had to pray.
"Dear Lord please tell me what I can do, how can I serve you best?
But first I ask You to please forgive those sins I have confessed!"

"Thank You Lord for wiping those black deeds from my heart,
I'm ready now to serve as best I can I'm ready to do my part.
I'll be listening daily Lord to hear your next command.
Please tell me Lord what I can do to help my fellow man!"

Lord our world today as You well know is in a terrible mess,
And all those sinners who led us there aren't likely to confess.
We're fortunate to have You in our midst and have You in full charge,
As we fight the forces of the devil to save the world at large!

I'm ready Lord to join the fray and ready to enlist.
I see the need and want to help, how could anyone resist?
The enemy we face have formed a very "cunning" crowd,
They seek to overcome our efforts by shouting out real loud!

Lord You use the "soft" approach, wind blowing in the trees.
It drowns out all of those who shout and then the devil flees.
We all must join together in the fight and do everything we can.
The Lord will direct our winning cause to save our fellow man!

July 9.

Rejoice

Dedicated to Mike and Donna Baynai, 4/27/2009

My soul is waiting for the Lord.
Waiting to hear Him say the words,
The words that make us all take heart,
And remind us all "how great Thou art!"

There is so much that we don't know.
One thing for sure, He loves us so.
Those words we learned when we were young.
How much we've loved that song we sung!

Each day we pray and thank the Lord,
For all the things that we've enjoyed,
He's taken care of all our needs.
We must repay with our "good deeds!"

The greatest thing that we possess,
Is Jesus' love and righteousness.
It comes to me, it comes to you,
There's nothing special we must do!

I love You Jesus, I love You Lord.
Say these words often, you won't get bored.
Don't let big words lead you astray.
Keep it simple, that's God's way!

I'm thinking now of that elusive phrase,
And waiting to hear those words of praise,
Ringing out from God's precious voice,
He says, "Come back home and we'll rejoice!"

July 10.

Reminiscing

I'm going to sit right down and write myself a letter.
I'll tell myself that everything I say to me is true.
I won't need to question if I'm lying,
For I'm the one that everything I've said has happened to!

It won't bother me if some folks think I'm bragging,
For I have always been inclined to be quite proud.
In all the years I've been around it's true I've done a lot.
Most things are good, others not, my best achievement I'll shout out loud!

My life began so long ago, 'twas really way back when.
Our country was in a terrible mess, we didn't know how bad then.
Depression fears sure took a toll, no-one escaped scott-free.
Everyone of us pitched in to do our part and that included me!

I wore a lot of "hand-me downs," I felt I was well dressed.
But some good friends "in overalls" were not that well impressed.
I couldn't pay my school book-fees, my teacher made me feel so bad.
I knew how bad things were at home, but I did not fault my Dad!

Many years have passed since then, much waters flowed 'neath the bridge.
Our country's again in a terrible mess, but different from before.
Different strokes from different folks have brought much blood and gore.
Our greatest hope is our new President and he's doing more and more!

Those many years ago when things were hard, we placed our faith in God.
He sent to lead us at that time one known as F D R.
That raised our hopes, gave all a lift for he was a real ram-rod.
He led us through some terrible times, including the great world war!

And now we find ourselves in tough times once again.
Our country's in a terrible war, the economy's down the drain.
But I am sure that with God's help, each of us on board as well,
Our country will survive the test, there's no way we can fail!

July 11.

If You Don't Believe, What Then

What can I do to help mankind increase their faith in God?
I wish that all of us could walk the path, the one that Jesus trod.
So many folks don't read the Bible to them it's just a book.
They don't believe what they have heard so they won't take a look!

Out Creator gave us humans a brain and the power of free will.
My early training was by my Mom and Dad and it is with me still.
The basis for my love for Jesus was learned at Mother's knee,
And all she taught me in those early days still means so much to me!

Many years have come and gone since my heart began to beat.
God planted my soul in my chest and said, "Now you are complete."
It was then that I was born and my life on earth began.
What I learned as a little boy has been my salvation as a man!

When I look back into my life I can see the ups and downs.
It's been a wonderful passage of time full of smiles and frowns.
So much has happened to me and mine, the story would fill a book.
It's hard for me to believe sometimes all the twists and turns it took!

Even if it were possible today I wouldn't turn back the clock.
Through it all, the ups and downs, I've been standing on solid "rock."
That "rock" that we all know as Jesus has led me by the hand,
And He still leads me every day as I approach the "Promised Land!"

I love to tell folks of my love for Jesus and how He died for me.
I wish everyone would get the "Spirit" and dear Jesus see
For Who He is and what He's done and what He can do for us all.
Mankind is standing on a precipice but Jesus won' t let us fall!

July 12.

Should We Begin To Worry?

You cannot get so deep in trouble that God can't get you out,
But when you reach the tipping point, don't just sit and pout.
Bow your head and ask for help and things will start to change.
Do not despair, God will hear you, He's never out of range!

We think we're smart down here on earth just look at all our stuff.
God don't need our fancy things, to Him it's just so much fluff.
Out leaders cannot get along, they each know best you see,
And so our country just muddles along as if they're lost at sea!

Sometime soon the dam will break and we'll be in the flood.
It won't be water that does us in but red ink mixed with blood.
Our people are so obsessed with greed they're buying up lots of gold,
While many folks without a job or home are left out in the cold!

We're really at a place right now when it's close to sink or swim.
Our leaders are squabbling over what to do, but do not call on Him.
I'm speaking of the Master of the Universe who could solve our ills today,
But they're too proud and would be mortified to get on their knees to pray!

Mark my words our country is failing its people day after day.
The devils forces are all around and they have too much to say.
The gullibility of us all leads us to buy what they have to sell,
And so much of it is purpose prone to lead us straight to hell!

We are already deep in trouble and God should be allowed to speak.
Our leaders must ask for His advice, that doesn't mean they're weak.
God's interest is in everyone, not just those who have the gold.
Our leaders can overcome our problems if they will do what they are told!

July 13.

Smart, Dumb Or Stupid

It's okay to be somewhat dumb but stupid is something more.
You can be quite dumb in fact but know what something's for.
Stupid people draw a blank when they try to use their brain.
The saying goes that they don't know when to come in out of the rain!

The main thing wrong with stupid people is they're too stupid to know
That when they do those stupid things their stupidity begins to show.
There is a tendency for most of us to laugh at stupid things we see,
But we should realize right off that stupid things cause catastrophe!

Now I don't want you to overlook smart people who do stupid things.
Somehow these smart people get into power and start to pull the strings.
We read about the stupid things they do in our local "rag."
The outrageous nature of their acts makes one want to gag!

Smart people with power think everyone but they are stupid.
They are so determined to have their way they start to playing cupid,
To "woo" us all, the rank and file to seeing things their way.
Before you know it we have no choice, it seems they're there to stay!

I believe it's when smart people are scared they do some stupid things.
Scare tactics work on many folks and chaos is what it brings.
It's hard for us to overcome these forces who have no shame,
But if we give up without a fight we'll surely go down in flame!

So, what to do, what CAN we do, we've been through this before.
Be sure to vote on election day and kick them out the door.
Smart people who do stupid things are the ones I speak of here.
I may be dumb, but I am not stupid so I have naught to fear!

July 14.

So True

A house is not a home without a "miss."
A home without a "miss" won't long exist.
So take the necessary steps to rectify the void.
It wouldn't hurt to find a "miss" who's gainfully employed!

You can travel far and wide while searching for a bride,
Around the world and back again 'til you are satisfied.
That beautiful "chick" that you have picked is just the one for you.
That house will now become a home, a place just meant for two!

Don't wait too late, just set the date, let nature take its course.
Soon you'll be the bride and groom with family there in force,
Listening to the vows you take before you say "I do."
There is no greater thrill than this and God is there with you!

That house has now become a home, the "miss" will settle down.
It won't be long 'til she begins to move things all around.
She's going to place her "stamp" on things which is well and good,
For she is now the one in charge and that is as it should!

Though love and harmony will abound, there'll be adjustments made.
There'll be some "give and take" involved, as feelings are displayed.
You'll soon find that kisses for the "misses" will keep things in check.
Don't be surprised too when you will get, a hug around the neck!

Well I'm not here to tell a "fib," all that I've said is true.
Throughout the days ahead you'll find, it all depends on you,
To set the pace and keep the peace, and do it without a fight,
And never, ever forget, that you must kiss that "miss" goodnight!

July 15.

Something To Crow About

There's always been a mystery about the chicken and the egg.
Without the egg there'd be no chicken and then of course no egg.
To find the answer I asked my Rooster when I was in the yard.
He says to me, "Why Daddyo that answers not so very hard!"

"When God created the Garden, the one that we all know,
He also created the Rooster and taught him how to crow.
He created Eve to be Adam's bride and after that He then
Created a beautiful mate for me and called that gal a hen!"

Eve did not come from an egg but sprang from Adams rib.
I suppose we could say that's why we now have "women's lib."
She was formed by God with a full supply of eggs in place,
From those eggs she bore Cain and Abel, this mother of the human race!

"Back in the Garden, my bride the hen, was created with eggs as well,
One important difference though her eggs were covered with a shell.
Mankind discovered that the egg was very good to eat,
And not only that but if left alone to hatch, became a source of meat!"

I suppose it would be correct to say, the chicken did come first,
Albeit with a full supply of eggs from which little "biddies" burst,
But since they were all created as one, who's to say?
I guess it's not that important since they both are here to stay!

Let's not forget our friend the Rooster, he's been here all along.
He crows to announce the sun is rising and it's not a pretty song.
He was also crowing when Peter was busy denying,
And mankind learned to crow as well, without even trying!

July 16.

Sometimes A Push Is What I Need

God gave me a push this morning to help me start my day.
A gentle push I must admit but it got me on my way.
So here I am with vigor galore and with pep to spare.
I have some tasks I must perform, with others I must share!

I want the whole wide world to know of Jesus our dear Friend.
He takes the heavy load from our back, not once but again and again.
He lets us know that He is there and never far away,
And when you need His loving help just bow your head and pray!

We all have problems we can't solve that's just the way it is.
We may not share these cares with others it's really no one's biz,
But when we're overwhelmed and don't know what to do,
Just lay your head in Jesus' lap and He'll take care of you!

I look back into my early years and wonder why I was blind.
I was doing quite well I thought and wasn't in a bind.
I wish I had known then what I know now, Jesus was right there.
He saved my life more than once it was not luck but care!

I hope that you will heed my voice and call on Jesus now.
He sent you here as a tiny baby and with your birth His Vow
To love you 'til your dying day and help you live life as you planned,
And to always be nearby if you needed a helping hand!

So let's not forget that Jesus is the bedrock of our soul.
He is the only One who truly can make us whole.
Never fail to say your prayers and thank Him for His love.
When we reach the end of life, He'll take us to our Home above.

July 17.

Sometimes Right and Sometimes Wrong

Things may not be as they seem so check and double check.
Make decisions when you're sure but don't stick out your neck.
"Haste makes waste" the old saying goes, makes a lot of sense.
Make sure you're right then make your move, cut down on the expense!

No one of us will live a perfect life, it was not meant to be.
We'll make mistakes there is no doubt, maybe two or three.
Accept the fact that you are wrong and correct it right away.
A big mistake, if left "as-is," can really ruin your day!

That's why we must always be on guard and make the proper moves,
For what we do must mesh with others and fit into the grooves.
None of us act completely alone, for others are involved.
Our mistakes affect the others until the problem's solved!

Don't dwell upon the faults of others and overlook your own.
"Do unto others as you'd like them to do" is surely very well known.
All members of the team must pull together to reach the common goal.
"One for all and all for one," can make success unfold!

If you're like me you'll find your life is always give and take.
You'll find that people that you meet are friends that you should make.
From among those many folks you meet be sure to pick and choose,
Some of those new friends you make will be the ones you never lose!

I'd like to tell you here and now that I have made mistakes.
Perfection has always been a goal I've tried for goodness sakes.
Without the help of friends and others I'd not be where I am.
I'm also thankful for the help I got from dear old Uncle Sam!

July 18.

Just Smile

There is no need to worry when there is nothing to worry about,
And yet there are those without a problem and all they do is pout.
This would be a better world if we would just begin
To smile at everyone we meet, or if not smile then just grin!

It's true that smiling is contagious like the yawn we know about.
There are those who will see you smile who now are down and out,
The contagious nature of the smiling virus will cause those folks to grin,
And before you know it big smiles break out, they couldn't keep them in!

You might say "oh well, ho-hum" please tell me something new,
It takes an effort to smile all day there is so much else to do,
But then I say again, "oh well, why not," and I put on a "happy face,"
And as I go about my business now there are smiles all over the place!

It's a fact that life's too short for us to fill our day with gloom.
We need to smile and others will too when we walk into the room.
When I see people smiling I know that life is good,
Those folks who smile will do no harm even if they could!

I feel that people pay me a compliment when they smile at me.
It lets me feel that I'm okay and that's the way I want to be,
And that fact too makes me smile again and starts the ball to roll.
Before you know it there will be smiles on the face of every single soul!

Let us make this a special day, let's begin it with a smile.
Lots of things will happen which I'm sure will be worthwhile.
We can brighten up the entire world by just having a smiling face.
So simple a thing to do a lot of good for the entire human race!

July 19.

Spend Your Day With Jesus

Someone has said and I guess it's true
Our life on earth depends on you.
We're given all the things we need
To make our way as we proceed!

It's not too late to start anew.
After all that we've been through,
We all should know by now what's right
And move along without a fight!

When we get ready to begin
We need to contact our dear Friend,
For Jesus always wants to know,
Just what we're doing down here below!

We must spend time down on our knees
Let Jesus tell us just what He sees,
Ask for His blessing on us too
As we learn what we must do!

When Jesus says His sweet "Amen"
We'll get to work on our task again.
This time we will have good plans
For they have come from the "Masters" hands!

When we wrap up our work today,
Jesus will join us as we pray.
Thanks abound for jobs well done,
We've spent all day with God's own Son!

July 20.

The War That We Must Win

There is but one thing that we must do in order to save our soul.
Just believe in Jesus Christ and He will make us whole.
We cannot make it all alone without the help he gives.
We are so happy and blessed too, to know that He still lives!

God has enemies of many kinds and He wrestles with the devil.
He fights for every human soul each day to save us all from evil.
When Jesus was alive on earth the devil made his pitch,
He promised Jesus everything and said he'd make Him rich!

Throughout the past two thousand years the devil too has thrived.
We're fortunate indeed that until now Christianity has survived.
Some wars we fight in foreign lands against the force so evil,
The remnants of the Mongol hordes with instructions from the devil!

Even in our beloved country we must always be on our toes.
So many are willing to sell us out and we have a lot of foes.
While fighting wars around the world we must stay strong at home,
Where we believe in Religious Freedom which allows our foes to roam!

The Anti-Christ who roam our land are trying to succeed.
They are on the warpath every day and they're motivated by greed.
Our country has had tremendous growth the past five hundred years,
Propelled by Christian faith and philosophy which takes away our fears!

We must all continue to do our part to protect the way we live.
We all must talk with Jesus every day and ask that He will give
Each one of us the help we need to keep our Nation strong,
Christians know Jesus loves every soul not just those who to Him belong!

July 21.

Stay On The Alert

The devil is stalking me today I must be well aware.
He wants to do me so much harm and he is everywhere.
He's battling Jesus for my soul I must not let him win.
I pray that Jesus will take my hand and save me from my sin!

The devil has a "bill of goods" which he always has for sale,
But all of them are the kinds that lead one straight to hell.
Forbidden fruit is all around, attractive as can be.
He's doing business in the open where everyone can see!

I pray to Jesus every day and ask Him to be my guide.
The devil is always listening in, from him I cannot hide.
He'll try to offer me a special deal and wrap it up in gold,
The lure of which is very strong, you know he's mighty bold!

I know that Jesus wants to help He wants to save my soul.
I'll do my best to follow Him and He will make me whole,
But meantime I must be alert and tell the devil to go away,
And let him know that I am not interested in his wares today!

I have a very happy life because Jesus makes it so.
He's been my Master many years and loves me this I know.
The devil keeps on stalking me just hoping that I will cave,
But I know that Jesus is always near, my soul He wants to save!

What can I do about today the devil will not give in.
I must be diligent and trust the Lord to save me from my sin.
I'll be walking hand in hand with Jesus, I know He'll win the fight.
The battle for my soul may go on, but I'll sleep good tonight!

July 22.

Struggling

Have you ever had the kind of day
When it seemed that nothing ever went your way,
Couldn't get anything to turn out right,
Although you tried with all your might?

There's usually a cause for those kind of days
Which calls for us to change our ways.
Have we lived up to what's required
To get the results that we desired?

Sometimes it's hard to find a reason.
Could be as simple as a change of season,
As our beautiful summer moves into fall,
We pick up "sniffles" with aches and all!

There are plenty of things that we must do.
We have to get busy and follow through,
Getting ourselves ready for all the days ahead,
When we can't play golf for there's work instead!

We'll get more accomplished if we have a plan,
So make out a check list if you can.
Mark those jobs off as you proceed.
There's no better way for you to succeed!

When all the work is over and done
You'll be quite proud of "number one."
You've got things off to a running start.
You can relax, for you've done your part!

Sudoku

I love puzzles but they sure will drive you wild.
I've been doing puzzles of all kind since I was just a child.
What puzzles me is how does the puzzle writer know
That a four will go in a certain box but a five will not go?

It isn't common sense of course for we all have lots of that.
If that was all it took I'd have it done in 30 seconds flat,
But it sometimes takes much more time that I can really spare,
Yet I hate to quit before it's done and all is fair and square!

Now there are eighty-one boxes in the frame, nine on every line,
And nine in every column which must "all " be from one to nine.
You can't repeat on any line nor in any column, see,
It's not as simple as you might think, not like one, two, three!

The puzzle master gives a hint by filling a box or two.
Several hours down the road you may wish that you were through,
But by now you've worn out three erasers and pulled out lots of hair,
And you find that in that last empty box a seven can't go there!

What to do, it's getting late and you've got lots of things to do,
But you can't quit, it's in your blood, you've got to follow through.
Try to find that errant number that's out of place somewhere.
You may even have to start all over, so start it with a prayer!

Divine help is what you need, just as in everything we do.
When you think you've got it made please look out for "you know who."
The devil will whisper in your ear, "that's a number six."
That doesn't work at all of course it's just one more of his tricks!

July 24.

Sunrise

There is nothing much more beautiful than the rising of the sun,
Especially if there are fleecy clouds then it becomes a lovely one.
The redness signals danger for those who sail the sea,
But it adds to all the beauty which is there for all to see!

Some folks never see the sun rise for they are still in bed.
They don't know what they are missing by being a sleepy head.
The beauty of the sunrise is fleeting and doesn't last too long.
When the sun completes its rising then it becomes real strong!

You cannot look directly at the sun, into that roaring flame,
Except while it is rising and yes while setting it's the same,
Its power is in the rays that shine upon the earthly scene.
It begins at dawn and ends at dusk but shines brightly in between!

The junior partner of the sun is Mister Moon, who's quite a sight.
A full moon rising is quite beautiful and brightens up the night.
For some it's quite romantic, especially if it's in the month of June,
And then it becomes a treasure of the heart on someone's honeymoon!

It's true that moon light is subdued but it helps a lot at night.
Its rays are but reflections of the sun but they give a welcome light,
And it magnifies the power of the sun in a very special way,
As it extends the brightness of the night until the break of day!

The sun sits at the center of "our" solar system, in the universe.
It shines on all our stars as well and that light comes to us in reverse,
So let's all hail the glory of the awesome power of the sun,
But let's always thank dear Jesus bringing power from God's only Son!

July 25.

The War Zone

The devil is afraid of Jesus and wants to do Him in.
He wants to show us all his wares and engage us all in sin,
But Jesus counters his attacks and guards us "tooth and nail."
"Get thee behind me Satan" He says, and "go on back to hell!"

Yes Jesus is the guardian of our soul it's precious in His sight.
We can be sure He's always near He's with us day and night,
But still the devil lurks nearby, just hoping for a sale.
His wares are very tempting but they do lead straight to hell!

When we look around the world today the devil is in plain sight.
He plies his trade around the world, yes even in broad daylight.
He'll tempt you with his line of goods but don't let him wear you down.
It's best to avoid him at all costs so don't go near his playground!

No one could escape the devils snare if they were on their own.
We all are sinful and would be lost if it was up to us alone.
God recognized the frailties we all had and sent Jesus to save our soul.
Jesus died and rose again through Him we can reach our goal!

The devil will not give up his quest for our soul until our dying day.
We can't relax and let down our guard for he'll lead us all astray.
If we will truly believe that Jesus died for us, we have no need to fear,
But we must still resist the devil for he'll try to get our ear!

This world is a constant battlefield, not just for wars and such,
But always battling between good and evil and it doesn't change too much.
We all must join God's mighty army as Christian soldiers born again.
We'll follow Jesus Christ our Leader in the fight to overcome sin!

July 26.

No Threat To Microsoft

Our entire life is governed by all the choices we make.
Almost everything we do is based on choices, which one do I take?
So life is just a giant multiple choice test, much like we had in school.
We get some right, we get some wrong, by using our only tool!

The tool which we all use is our own brain, without it we are dead.
You often hear folks refer thereto, "Why don't you use your head?"
The more you use that brain of course, the better it reacts.
It helps you get your choices right by having all the facts!

Our brain is our body's computer, the best one ever known.
It's always working it won't shut down until we're dead and gone.
Those dreams that you have at night are from your brains own data base.
You must keep your "hard drive" clean by deciding what to erase!

I'm sitting here right now at ease my brain is still in gear.
You see it never completely stops, has not for many a year.
We continue to learn every day no matter how old we are,
And we don't want to close that door, please leave it slightly ajar!

God made our bodies durable and they're good for many years.
Some parts wear out and are replaced but the brain is still in gear.
The older we get the more knowledge we have, our hard disk overflows.
Don't let that slow you down, just relax, reload and reset the dominos!

You may not agree with my concept here, but that's okay with me,
For I have found that "different strokes" have helped to set me free.
I can think of unusual things and I dream of others too,
While my computer keeps on spinning I have lots of things to do!

226

July 27.

Tears Of Sorrow Become Tears Of Joy

People cry when a loved one dies, that certainly isn't rare.
The bond is broken between the two for it's no longer there.
But think again, it's just delayed, they'll be together again.
Just like you and me when we both go 'round the bend!

We never forget those departed souls, they're finally at rest.
We pray for every one of them and hope they passed the test.
It's hard to think about but is true, some souls don't make the grade.
They spend eternity being punished for all the mistakes they made!

I've made mistakes and I'm sure you have for it's a fact of life.
God sacrificed His Only Son to help us overcome that strife.
We must place our trust in Him since it's the only way.
Don't hesitate to call on Jesus, just bow your head and pray!

There are many different ways to pray, there's no single protocol.
The important thing is to show respect for Jesus who will hear them all.
As for myself I always pray whenever I feel the need.
He's always there when I call and I don't hesitate to plead!

There is but one Judge who will hear our case and Jesus is His Name.
He knows us well and He loves us all, He treats us all the same.
Don't be afraid to talk with Him and tell Him of your love.
He'll forgive you of your sins and welcome you up there above!

So never be ashamed to cry when a loved one dies.
It's expected and for no one is it a big surprise.
But let your tears of sorrow turn into tears of joy.
Your loved one will be with Jesus, a meeting they will enjoy!

July 28.

Tears Of Sorrow Born Of Guilt

You never get too old to cry if something really bothers you.
Old memories reside within your heart and sometimes make you blue.
If crying helps in any way then let the tears begin.
Jesus cried we know for sure and He was free from sin!

We need to cry from time to time to purge our soul from guilt.
It helps relieve the stress and strain that years of sin have built.
Jesus will forgive those sins and take away those tears,
For it was He who died for us and helps relieve the fears!

When you think about your life are there things you'd like to change?
It's much too late, the windows closed, no way can you arrange
To undo things or take back words but Jesus can save the day.
He's always ready to hear your plea it's time for you to pray!

Let Jesus know where you went wrong, He's heard it all before.
He'll help you get things back on track and even up the score.
No matter what is troubling you He can ease your pain.
Just place your trust in Jesus' Hands He'll make you whole again!

Our world is full of troubled souls some don't know where to go.
It's not just in the U.S.A. it's all around the world you know.
Troubled times are upon us and we need help from above.
Jesus is waiting for us to ask, He'll shower us with His love!

There's nothing wrong that He can't fix but we must ask of course.
He has the answers to our plight, He is the major source.
What we need is lots of prayer and faith that He will hear.
If we just put our trust in Him, we'll have a happy year!

July 29.

Thank God Who Leads The Way

I feel sorry for my friends whose wives have passed away.
God knows how much they miss their love every single day.
It's true that men are not inclined to live the lonely life,
So God with His superior wisdom sends someone to be their wife!

However, some men live without a mate and get along just fine.
They have their pets and hobbies and computers to get on line.
They spend their day as they see fit, always a lot to do.
When five o'clock in evening comes they have a drink or two!

And way down deep these fellows keep a flame that burns so bright.
It's somewhat like that beacon on the shore that's always giving light.
The more these fellows loved their mate the more they feel the loss.
They miss her saying everyday I'm the brains, you can be the boss!

Let's not forget the other half, those gals whose dudes have gone.
They are no less inclined than men to want to live alone.
It's true that they are better equipped to live without a mate,
And when they find some time to waste it's easy to get a date!

These situations are not rare they are a fact of life.
Women lose their husbands dear and men, they lose their wife.
This set-up is tailor-made for matches made in heaven.
While some folks had no kids at all, some guys like me had seven!

Down this lonesome road of life so many folks have trod.
I've walked down that road twice and both times heard from God.
In each case He saved my life by providing me a mate.
If you're a lonesome guy or gal let God decide your fate!

July 30.

Get Ready For The Battle

The devil is alive and well we need to be aware.
It's easy to forget that he always wants his share.
The battle for our very soul is one we must not lose.
Those rosy offers the devil makes are ones we must refuse!

The devil comes in many forms a master of disguise.
We have to be real careful for we'll like his merchandise.
The major thing that we can't do is let him take us in.
He'll be fighting tooth and nail to wrap us up in sin!

When we awake each morning you can bet the devil's near.
He wants to catch us early before Jesus gets our "ear."
He'll open up his bag of tricks and show us something new.
If we should weaken and take the bait he'll have his hooks in too!

The best defense is a good offense we've often heard it said,
So we must be ready for a fight when we roll out of bed.
We'll call on Jesus right away He's been there through the night.
He'll arm us with a "devil spray" and join us in the fight!

The battle for our soul goes on the world's a battlefield.
The devil's forces don't give up to them we must not yield.
Jesus uses different means to train us for the fight.
He overwhelms us with His love and helps us do what's right!

The devil is a crafty foe but God won't let him win.
He sent Jesus into the world to save us all from sin.
With Jesus fighting for our soul the devil to repel,
We'll follow Jesus everywhere and we won't go to hell!

July 31.

Thank You Jesus For Your Gifts

Every day that we're alive is a gift from God.
To find us on our knees while thanking Him should not be so odd.
We have no other source of life it all comes straight from Him.
Jesus and the Saints gave us the Bible, this story comes from them!

God created Heaven and Earth and all that is there-in.
Heaven is "perfection personified" while the Earth is filled with sin.
When God created the human race, He also created some rules.
He knew the nature of the humans who sometimes act like fools!

During the Old Testament days God depended largely on the Saints.
They did well with what they had but there were many complaints.
So God sent Jesus, His Only Son, to Earth to rectify the mess.
Jesus taught His motley crew and the masses their sins they must confess!

The human race did not accept the Savior, they murdered Him instead,
But God was watching all the while and raised Him from the dead.
This "sacrifice" which God allowed placed Jesus back in Heaven,
From whence He guides us every day away from being heathen!

So where are you today, my friend, can He depend on you?
Do you talk with Him each day and ask what you should do?
Or do you go about your daily tasks alone and self-satisfied,
Not worried at all about your after-life but feeling justified!

The greatest mistake that we all make is feeling justified,
In not believing in the story of Jesus who gave His life and died.
What we must do is change our tune and ask for "mercy" instead.
Jesus will accept our plea and save us from the dead!

This poem is dedicated to my friend Dr. Malcolm Chester McIver, Jr.
who was buried November 8, 2011

Contents August

1. Good Morning Dear Jesus...233
2. We Love You Lord..234
3. How Soon Will We See Jesus? 235
4. At The Foot Of The Stair..236
5. August 5, 2009...237
6. Another Year Gone By..238
7. Be Happy..239
8. The Trustee Of My Soul 240
9. Are You Greedy?..241
10. Three Cheers For Jesus 242
11. Will You Be Ready? 243
12. Just For Today 244
13. How Much Do You Love Jesus.................................245
14. Let Us Pray..246
15. "Fear Not" Said He 247
16. God Loves Us...248
17. Thank You Mother 249
18. Holy Spirit Be My Guide 250
19. Join The Army..251
20. Jesus Lover Of Every Soul 252
21. Lend A Hand 253
22. "Son" Shine...254
23. Spread The Word..255
24. Carrying The Message 256
25. My Friend Jesus...257
26. Happy Birthday To James.......................................258
27. We All Must Face The Music...................................259
28. Thank You Jesus 260
29. A Vision Of Jesus 261
30. Trouble In Our Time..262
31. Sweet Jesus 263

Good Morning Dear Jesus

Good morning dear Jesus, thanks for another day.
I bow my head in silent prayer and search for words to say.
How wonderful is the life You give to us a chosen few.
You ask our help to tell the world that they must come to You!

We're not disciples like Saint Mark, or Matthew, Luke or John,
But we have talents You can use today, tomorrow and beyond.
To spread the word of Your love for us, a love that will not die.
The world is at our doorstep and we can't let it pass us by!

I look forward everyday to saying "Hi" to You,
To tell You of my plans each day and ask what I can do,
To pass the word of Jesus' love for each and everyone,
And hear His voice say to me, "Thanks for a job well done!"

It's not hard for me to talk with Jesus, He's my friend.
I know He writes about me in His book and will until the end,
Keep track of everything I do and everything I say.
It's wonderful when I think as each day ends, I heard His voice today!

I hope that you've contacted Him and feel His presence near.
Just open up your heart and pray, there's not a thing to fear.
For Jesus wants each one of us to get in touch each day.
This world would be a better place if everyone would pray!

I'm writing poems for this little book, one for every day.
When you read the daily poem please don't forget to pray.
I have a feeling and it is strong that Jesus lives here-in.
So let Him know that you're on board, He'll be your beloved friend!

August 2.

We Love You Lord

There'll never be a better time to say "We love You Lord!"
Our world's a mess, we need His help, to wait we can't afford.
There is so much that He can do that we should not delay.
Each of us must do our part, get on our knees and pray!

Jesus loves for us to call, He wants to help us out,
But we must tell Him of our need, He'll help without a doubt.
Too often we don't think of Him when we are in real need.
Because He gave us our "free will" we hesitate to plead!

God did give us our "free will" but put some limits on it too.
Our guide is called "Ten Commandments" and they are tried and true.
Moses got these rules up on the mount, they were cast in stone.
It's up to us to spread these rules around they're not for us alone!

I'm sure that He must wonder why we fear to seek His aid.
Our founding fathers called on Him, He helped with plans they made.
We must not let our Nation fail, we must defeat our foes.
The Lord will help us in our fight He'll keep us on our toes!

O'er all our battles when we fight, God's flag must fly on high.
It tells our enemies what we all know, we're not afraid to die.
In all the wars we've ever fought, God's been there on our side.
With Him watching over us we won them all, it is a source of pride!

Let us pray now with all our hearts to God in Heaven above.
"Dear Lord, look down upon us all, protect us with your love.
Please bring peace to all mankind, bless those who seek relief,
From sickness, hunger, victims all and save us all from grief!"

August 3.

How Soon Will We See Jesus?

How soon will we see Jesus, when we have met our fate?
Will Peter lead us to Him, when he meets us at the gate?
We watch in awesome wonder, while Peter takes our hand,
and leads us from the "pearly gates toward the Promised Land."

Angels in all their glory, watch o'er our growing throng,
They fill the air with music, and we join them in the song.
Matthew and Mark, and Luke and John, and others, well known too,
Lead groups of other pilgrims, for they know what to do.

And soon we reach that Holy Place, with Jesus on His Throne,
Surrounding us on bended knee His Heavenly light He shone.
When Jesus spoke, 'twas loud and clear, and this is what He said,
"My Father did this once for me, I've raised "you" from the dead."

"Now go My children, seek your place, your souls are white as snow,
I washed them clean with My own Blood, two thousand years ago."
We know how Jesus loves us all, the Bible said it's true,
And now our fears are gone for good, for Jesus said it too!

August 4.

At The Foot Of The Stair

The Lord was waiting when I arrived.
I am so happy that my Mom survived.
Jesus held on to my Mother's hand,
And she lived to do the things she planned!

Mom told me, "Son, your birth I feared,
But your Dad was so happy when you appeared,
And the Good Lord helped me to weather the pain,
And Dad never had to go through that again!"

There were so many stories she told.
Especially of Heaven and it's streets of gold,
Of Jesus love for all mankind,
And the most wonderful place we'll ever find!

She taught me how to say my prayers.
She enjoyed talking to the "Man Upstairs."
My love for Jesus was born right there.
I like to call it "the foot of the stair!"

The things I learned there have served me well.
The stories of Jesus I love to tell.
My life would have never been the same,
Had I not been taught Dear Jesus' name!

Well I'm still around at eighty-eight.
Tomorrow is my real birth date,
And one thing I can say with lots of pride,
I've always had Jesus by my side!

Birthdate of my #3 Grandson, Simon Opitz, 1993

August 5, 2009

Today's a special day for me,
My birthday anniversary.
I'm eighty-nine and going strong.
At this age you can't do much wrong!

Wonderful years have come and gone,
Happy days go on and on.
I feel so blessed to be around,
No better life could I have found!

All my family have paid their dues.
They've been in touch with much good news.
Just what it takes to make my day
I say again "I'm blessed" in every way!

I've got girls and I've got boys,
All of them bring lots of joys.
I've got lots of grand kids too.
A precious gift from you know who!

Yes, God's been good to "number one."
Without His help not much was done.
He's been my guide through thick and thin,
And He has cleansed me from my sin!

Now as you grow old in terms of years,
Let me save you from a lot of fears.
If you will just take my advice,
Put all your trust in God, He'll treat you nice!

Birthdate of the Author, Jacob Nathaniel Shepherd, 1923

August 6.

Another Year Gone By

Eighty-eight years ago my Mom was trying to get some rest.
I'm sure it was hot in that little house but she was doing her best
To hold off birth of her second child for three more days and then
The two of them could celebrate on August 6 like a set of twins!

My sister Kathryn was born in 1921 on August 6 you see.
Two years later I was in the works and headed for delivery.
They didn't know it would be a boy but Daddy hoped it would.
Hoping the baby would come on August 6 they did everything they could!

It was hot in that little house on Bernau Street on Sunday August five.
Daddy called Doctor Sharpe late that day as the baby was about to arrive.
I couldn't wait to make my entrance on Kathryn's birthday 2 hours away.
At ten PM on Sunday evening August 5, 1923, I was here to stay!

My Mother didn't feel so good she was suffering from the heat.
The terrible pains of childbirth too hit hard she really did feel beat.
My Dad was tending Kathryn when he heard the Doctor say "it's a boy."
When Dad went in to see Mom and the baby both were filled with joy!

I missed my sister's birthday by a bit but I had one of my own.
We always celebrated separately, that is until we both were grown.
We grew up during the roaring twenties and remember the '29 crash.
Hard times hit everyone, recycling helped us get by, using others trash!

It's been a long eventful road, to tell it would fill several books.
Some good times, some not so good, you can't always go by looks.
The Good Lord has been so good to me I never will complain.
It amazes me, I'm still around at eighty-eight, it's August 5 again!

August 7.

Be Happy

The world's so full of doom and gloom we need some happiness,
So why not fill our paper with views of sunshine and success!
They're all around us every day, some things are doing well.
They're pushed aside by greedy ones who've got some stock to sell!

We must start by calling on the One who made us all.
He's never very far away and waiting for your call.
Don't be too proud or feel ashamed, get on your knees to pray.
God awaits with open arms to talk with you today!

When you woke up this morning were you feeling good,
Or did you feel queasy-like and were in a terrible mood?
Then when the headline in the paper said that things are getting worse.
Did this begin a terrible day and make you want to curse?

No matter what friend, don't forget, that you are not alone.
Many more are down and out, so you must not sit and moan.
There are many things we all can do to help our nation out.
First and foremost we all must learn not to cry and pout!

Get all your ducks lined up, put them in a row.
Then put on a "Happy Face" so that your smile will show.
Folks who see you walk with pride will join with you as their guide.
They'll learn that song that's in your heart, it will be magnified!

Smile and the world smiles with you, sing a song.
Don't be weary just be cheery all day long.
Whenever your trials, your troubles and your cares,
Seem to be more than you can really bear,
Smile and the world smiles with you, sing a song!

August 8.

The Trustee Of My Soul

My heart belongs to God, the Trustee of my soul,
When all my dreams are shattered, He quickly makes me whole.
He binds up all my wounds, and takes away the pain,
And when all else is said and done, I feel like new again!

Thank You God for all Your love, it makes my spirit sing.
Thank Him too, for life itself, He gives us everything.
When I need help and tender care, for troubles large and small,
I only need to kneel and pray, He quickly cures them all!

Mankind works to solve our ills, our system has no end,
They even help to pay the bills, there is no dearer friend!
Physicians search to find the cause, the cure's a pill each day,
When experts fail and all is lost, God's there to show the way!

So never lose your faith in God, He's always there you know.
And should mankind have failed, no cure could they bestow,
You only need to say a prayer, He'll take you by the hand,
God will take you by His side, into the "Promised Land!"

August 9.

Are You Greedy?

God's been too good to most of us,
He's spoiled us quite a bit.
We've let greed become our goal
And we just can't seem to quit!

There are millions everyday who have no food to eat,
No clothes to wear, no place to live, no hope for they are poor.
It's sad among the rest of us, we overlook their plight,
We pile up things that we can't use and still we want much more!

Everything that mankind has comes from God of course.
Our health, our wealth, our daily bread, there is no other source.
We need to be more thankful for all that He provides.
Get on our knees and say a prayer, He gives us love besides!

Most of us will not be rich, that is not God's intent.
Even if we don't have much at least we are content,
But He expects us all to share with those who are in need,
So we should open up our hearts and do our own good deed!

We find among mankind today an awful lot of greed.
Some don't obey the "Golden Rule", dismiss their neighbor's need.
Others even bend the rules and take more than their share,
And when it comes to helping out, they do not seem to care!

Beware, for God is watching us to see what we will do.
He knows all our faults and all our good points too.
When Jesus came He taught us all that greed's a deadly sin.
Everyone must learn to share, so let us all begin!

August 10.

Three Cheers For Jesus

Stand up and cheer for Jesus if you are on His side.
Someday He'll take you up to heaven where with Him you'll abide.
Let everyone around you know that Jesus is your friend.
He will welcome all your love and save your soul from sin!

So many folks are shy and cannot open up their heart.
They don't wish to join the group and so they stand apart.
I'm sure that Jesus would be glad to have them for a friend.
It would mean so much to Him if they would just join in!

There are so many avenues that one can take today.
You don't have to be the one who's always asked to pray.
But just remember Jesus and let Him be your guide.
You'll find that life is always better when He is at your side!

The Christian life is awfully good, it brings contentment too.
You'll find you like the choice you made when Jesus chooses you,
To be the one to stand up tall and lead the cheering throng.
That's when the Hallelujah Chorus begins to sing their song!

There are so many songs that tell of Jesus and His love.
They're all sincere and do not fear, they all come from above.
So open up your voice and sing the one that you like best.
Pretty soon they'll all join in and you can get some rest!

Today is just another day, but God has made them all,
So we must honor every day and help Jesus carry the ball.
We'll join the crowd and stand and cheer when Jesus makes a score.
He's rescued one more soul today and looks around for more!

Will You Be Ready?

When God comes knocking at your door
Will you be scared and hide?
Would you be too afraid of Him
To let Him come inside?

Don't be afraid of Him my friend,
He loves us one and all.
Take Him now into your heart
And He won't have to call!

When you love Jesus, you love God
And Spirit makes it three.
Never fear that you're alone,
They all watch over thee!

Open up your heart right now
And God will step inside.
There'll be no need to fear again
With you He will abide!

If we love God and Jesus,
And the Spirit, WHAT A THRILL,
From this day forward, never doubt,
For we've received God's Will!

August 12.

Just For Today

Do you make time for Jesus
Sometime within each day?
You don't have to be in church
To bow your head and pray!

Jesus loves to hear from you,
He always books your call.
He listens to your every need
And fills them one and all!

When Jesus talked while here on earth
And thousands came to hear,
It must've been a joy to be there,
He spoke so loud and clear!

The mountainside was filled with folks,
They came from far and wide,
To hear His message, free of jokes,
'Twas useful as their guide!

Though Jesus is not here with us
He's not so far away,
And though He's busy as can be,
He loves to hear us pray!

So bow your head, RIGHT NOW,
And close your eyes in prayer.
Without any doubt, He'll hear you,
For He is everywhere!

Birthdate of my #1 Son, Jacob N. Shepherd, III, 1956

How Much Do You Love Jesus

How much do you love Jesus?
Is He your dearest friend?
Are you in touch with Him each day,
To hear what he might say?

You won't need a telephone,
The sky's an open line,
Just lift your eyes and say "Hello,"
And then you'll do just fine!

Jesus loves to hear from you,
Don't wait to place your call.
He always answers His own line,
And doesn' t charge at all!

Just talk with Him like you with me,
He has no protocol,
He'll save your message in His Book,
The one He keeps for all!

Don't neglect your love for Him,
He'll fill your every need,
He'll write up facts about your call,
Jesus, your friend indeed!

Let Us Pray

When you bow to say a prayer
Can you feel Jesus standing there?
He's by your side and listens in.
That's how He saves us all from sin!

Just say aloud, "Hi Lord, it's me again.
I need your help so I won't sin.
I'm trying hard to do what's right.
Please come and join me in that fight!"

Tell Jesus then, what's on your mind.
He listens well, and you will find
He'll give you answers 'bout what to do.
He wants to help, for He loves you!

You may not think that He's nearby,
But think again, He fills the sky!
He's there to help all those in need,
And no one has to shout and plead!

Do not worry, do not fret,
Just call on Jesus lest you forget,
God sent Him to die for all.
He stays close by so we don't fall!

So when you pray, please have no doubt,
Jesus is near to help you out.
Always thank Him when you're through,
Your love for Him is surely true!

"Fear Not" Said He

Jesus loves to share our joy,
Our pain and sorrow too.
In truth, He wants to be a part
Of everything we do!

He loves to spend each day with you,
For travels far and wide,
We're not afraid in all we do,
While He is by our side!

He's always there when we awake,
He watches while we sleep.
So do not fear for Heaven's sake,
Our soul is in His keep!

He will guide us through our day,
He'll help our spirit sing.
And if perchance we go astray,
He'll take care of everything!

What a gift, how blessed are we,
To have Him always near.
We only need to bend our knee,
He'll take away the fear!

So listen all, and listen well,
He's there for young and old.
He loves to visit where we dwell,
Jesus the guardian of our soul!

August 16.

God Loves Us

How does God protect us all?
He doesn't want a soul to fall.
He gathers us all 'neath Golden Wings,
And points us toward eternal things!

Have you said your prayers today?
If not, you must stop and pray.
Don't miss the chance to talk with God.
He'll touch your head with His divining rod!

What do you ask for when you pray?
Is there something special you need today?
Always thank Him when you're through.
That's the Christian thing to do!

God is waiting to take your hand,
To train you for entering the "Promised Land."
He's got with Him His Book of Deeds.
To know about you, that's all He needs!

Do you feel you can pass His test?
In your life 'til now, have you done your best?
It's not too late to improve your score.
Don't wait 'til you're at Heavens Door!

God knows we're human after all.
He also knows that some might fall.
Thank Him, right now, and to Him say,
"Thank You for Jesus, He showed me the way!"

August 17.

Thank You Mother

There is no one but Jesus who can truly save your soul.
Stop looking for that easy "fix" that somehow becomes your goal.
Your Mother teaches you right from wrong and helps you do your best,
But you lose that precious, saintly guide when she is laid to rest!

I remember those early days, they seemed so long ago.
It wasn't hard for me to believe for Mama said 'twas so.
I carried Jesus in my heart it wasn't hard at all,
And when I needed Him to help I didn't have to call!

As time moved on and years went by the devil came to call.
Golden promises could be mine if I'd agree to just play ball.
Looking back it seemed so easy there wasn't much I had to do.
The devil moved into my heart, told Jesus "there's no room for you!"

The bulging bank account and fancy clothes belied the truth you see.
Somehow I made it work by thinking "this was meant to be."
While I was happy, Mom was sad, she saw the changes too.
Throwing caution to the wind she said "There's something you must do!"

"Get off that "road to riches" that the devil led you to.
Get on your knees and ask the Lord to tell you what to do,
I'm going soon to be with Him but I'll keep my eyes on you.
I'll be waiting to welcome you when Jesus pulls you through!"

When Mother died, I cried and cried, I lost my dearest friend.
I turned to Jesus once again and He said "Where have you been?"
I hung my head in shame for sure but now I felt real good.
Jesus occupies my heart again just as I knew He would!

Holy Spirit Be My Guide

Have you ever had the feeling that you were not alone,
No one else was present but there really was someone.
The Holy Spirit of the Lord, precious and so near
Just stopped by to say hello, so there's no need to fear!

Next time you have that feeling, you'll know that He is there.
You'll find that He is real nearby, in fact He's everywhere.
He'll take away your problems your troubles are fair game.
He'll lift the load that's on your back and that is why He came!

We human folk are oh, so proud and we think we need no help.
We feel so high and mighty that we're never out of step.
That's why we're oft alone, our friends we've left behind.
The Holy Spirit sees our need as He watches o'er mankind!

As the Holy Spirit watches, you can be sure He's near.
He tunes in to our thoughts to be sure that we're sincere.
If from the narrow path we stray, can't find our way back home,
Just call on Him, call His Name, He'll be sure to come!

So never fear if you're alone, just open up your heart.
Say a prayer to Jesus, always do your part.
He loves to come and help us out, to lend a helping hand.
We'll join the Holy Spirit on the road to the "Promised Land!"

August 19.

Join The Army

If Jesus shows up at your door, be kind and let Him in.
He's there to pay a visit, and save your soul from sin.
How better could you spend your day, than showing Him around?
You'll find that He's a regular guy, best friend you've ever found!

Jesus wants us all to know, that He is always near.
Although He may not ring your bell, He's ready to appear.
For any problems you can't solve, ask Him to come aboard.
He'll join right in to help you out, our friend, our precious Lord!

So many people on this earth, have never met our Lord.
They've never felt His loving touch, have never heard His word,
But Jesus loves them every one, as well as you and me.
When they learn to seek His help, from sin they'll be set free!

Our world is such a lovely place, beauty for all to see,
But war and perils cloud our skies, so fearful we should be.
We all need to call on Jesus, let Him know we truly care.
There is no doubt He'll come to help, our problems He will share!

All mankind must turn to Jesus, God's only beloved Son.
Who can save us now, all nations under the sun,
There is no one else around, nor has there ever been,
For sheer destruction always comes, when we're overcome by sin!

Are you, as one of Jesus' friends, willing to do your part?
Will you join this mighty battle and work with all your heart?
For it will take all mankind, under our God's command,
To follow Jesus in a fight for peace, and to save our "Promised Land!"

August 20.

Jesus Lover Of Every Soul

Jesus lives in every heart no matter who you are.
In every land around the world the language is no bar.
The color of a person's skin means not a thing at all,
For Jesus is the "soul" of man, just waiting for the call!

When we die our "soul" lives on, it will never disappear.
It rises up all on its own, there's not a thing to fear.
It's on its way to Heaven for that's where Jesus lives,
And there the "soul" of man will rest in the abode which Jesus gives!

Don't try to hide from Jesus for it just cannot be done,
As He is in your very "soul" and that's true of everyone.
If you will let Him, He will lead you, every single day.
If you open up your heart and bare your"soul" He will hear you pray!

Since Jesus rests in every "soul", He wants us all to thrive.
He does His best to cure our ills and keep us all alive.
He needs us all to tell the story of what He's done for us,
For there are still so many who don't know about dear Jesus!

Regardless of your religious choice, Jesus occupies your "soul."
God emphasized "My Only Son" I send to help you reach the goal.
As Christians we need to do our best to keep things on the level.
We fight against those misled hordes, the forces of the devil!

What about those evil ones, do they not have a "soul?"
Of course they do as does everyone for Jesus is real bold.
He died but lives in every "soul", even those who stray.
He'll bring us all together again on that wonderful Judgment Day!

August 21.

Lend A Hand

God is looking after me I feel his healing touch.
It's not rare to have his help for me He's done so much.
When I'm in need and can't seem to find my way,
I lift my eyes and call on Him then get on my knees and pray!

So many folks go through their life without a helping hand.
They aren't aware that God's at work throughout our cherished land.
I think that it is up to us, known as the favored few,
To reach out to these needy ones and help to pull them through!

Are you willing to follow God into that fertile field?
Where broken hearts and broken dreams were once the only deal,
To seek out those who hunger for an answer to their plight.
There are so many who need aid you'll work from morn 'til night!

The world is full of "shysters" who are out to make a buck.
Those "shysters" sell a bill of goods to those down on their luck.
It's up to us to root them out to keep them from their prey,
To help these poor downtrodden folk to see a brighter day!

If you're one of those who are well off can God depend on you?
The needs are great in many ways there is so much to do.
Don't hold back but step right up, be sure to raise your hand.
Let's all pitch in to help our friends head for the "promised land!"

Our world would be a better place if we all just did our part.
If we reached out a helping hand and prayed with all our heart,
For God to bless us everyone no matter who we are,
And lead us home to Jesus when we have crossed the bar!

August 22.

"Son" Shine

Do not despair the Lord will save you.
He will be your constant guide.
Reach out your hand and call His Name.
He'll lead you to the other side!

There are none who can resist Him,
If the honest truth were known.
If you look into His Face,
You're gone for good, you are His own!

Don't be afraid and don't hold back.
Lift up your eyes and look on high.
Our Lord , our friend, will take your hand.
His love for all He'll not deny!

If you feel unworthy of His Love,
Remember this, "He died for you."
If you've been bad and full of sin,
He's always there to pull you through!

On those days when you're down and out,
Open your heart let the "Son" shine in.
Jesus will save you, there is no doubt.
He'll set you free from all your sin!

August 23.

Spread The Word

Jesus died upon the cross,
'Twas there for all to see.
His death a gift for all mankind,
A precious gift for you and me!

When Jesus died so long ago
Our world was smaller then.
His word was spread by word of mouth
By those who were His friend!

Friends of His, the disciples band,
Were at His beck and call.
They gathered 'round Him close at hand,
And became Apostles all!

Peter, Andrew, James and John, Matthew to name a few,
Philip, Simon, Bartholomew, Thaddeus and Thomas too,
Another James, and Judas, the one who turned Him in,
When Judas fell, Matthias joined what was a motley crew!

Jesus taught these Saints of old
God's words of wisdom, strong and bold,
Then sent them out both far and wide
Where they could preach what God foretold!

John the Baptist played his hand.
He preached of Jesus and baptized too.
Along came Paul a traveling man.
God's team was set with work to do!

Birthdate of my #3 Daughter, Rebecca S. Opitz, 1963

Carrying The Message

What does Jesus mean to you, is He really your best friend?
Have you already accepted Him, to follow to the end?
When you find yourself in need do you always seek His aid?
You must know He wants to help those are the vows He made!

We often hear the name of Jesus there are no sweeter sounds,
And when we show our love for Him there really are no bounds.
When God sent Jesus to planet earth to save our souls from sin,
It was the greatest gift for all that there has ever been!

Since Jesus came to save mankind two thousand years have passed.
Millions of souls have come and gone it doesn't happen fast.
Each and everyone of them were just like you and me.
They had to make a choice in life, where to spend eternity!

There still are folks around the world who don't know Jesus' name.
It's up to all the rest of us to teach why Jesus came.
Everyone should have the chance to share in Jesus' love.
If we will do our part to help He'll send more from above!

The need for saving people's souls exists both far and wide.
Everyone should look around there's need right at our side.
Yes the need exists in foreign lands, it occupies the news,
But there's work to do right here at home we have to pay our dues!

Today is not too soon my friend for us to get on board.
We all must dedicate our lives to working for the Lord.
Sit down, right now, and make a list of things that you can do.
Jesus Himself will bless your list and add a thing or two!

August 25.

My Friend Jesus

I have a friend in Heaven,
The one that we all know,
I talk with Him and He with me,
I know he loves me so!

I have a friend in Heaven,
His earthly days were spent,
To teach us all that "GOD IS LOVE",
We learned just what that meant!

I have a friend in Heaven,
He died that we might know,
The path that we must follow,
As home to Heaven we go!

I have a friend in Heaven,
He rose and lives today,
He's always there if I should call,
He always makes my day!

I have a friend in Heaven,
He gave His life for me,
Not just for me, but one and all,
And soon in Heaven we'll be!

JESUS, our friend in Heaven,
Requires not much from me,
Our friendship is alive and well,
His faithful Steward I'll be!

This is the very first poem the Author wrote!

August 26.

Happy Birthday To James

This poem was written on demand, it just had to be
To keep my record going, a poem each day you see.
I've never made seven for seven this just might be the one.
Irene the hurricane is bearing down and just might spoil the fun!

Oh well, what the heck, I've set lots of records before.
I might as well keep it going although I'm not keeping score.
Today may turn out to be number six but there's still one more to go.
I'm sure there'll be something to write about when Irene begins to blow!

Today is August 26, my oldest grandson's date of birth.
I remember well that magic day when Jake IV came to earth.
An Army hospital in Fort Ord, CA, his Mom suffered through the night.
Grandma and I consoled his Dad, assured him 'twould be alright!

With forceps marks all over his head that baby looked good to me.
I held him and kissed him, he was as beautiful as he could be.
I knew he would be a star and that's how things turned out.
There're twenty-two candles on his cake today and for that we can shout!

He's number one of six grandsons and every one of them is a star.
They're setting records in all they do I'm sure they'll all go far.
That makes old Granddad mighty proud as he contemplates the past.
Happiness is always mixed with sadness as the years roll by too fast!

As I said above so what and what the heck, life is mighty fine.
The ageing of our souls is like the ageing of good wine.
What goes around comes around so we must stay on our toes.
Where our jolly "merry go round" will stop, I'm sure that no one knows!

Birthdate of my #1 Grandson, Jacob N. Shepherd IV, 1989

August 27.

We All Must Face The Music

We must not cry for those who've died and gone on ahead.
They've passed the test of death itself and no longer have to dread,
Those final moments when all must face that sad and last goodbye,
It's true we should not mourn for them for they're in Heaven in the sky!

Of course we're sad when a loved one dies, leaving us behind.
If we just rely upon our faith in Jesus we'll have peace of mind,
For it was He who died upon the Cross and rose to show the way,
And let us know we need not fear but please thank Him when we pray!

With so much turmoil in this world we know, can Jesus save the day?
The devil is busy stirring the pot in Egypt and leading folks astray.
As long as he can get recruits then wars will never cease,
And there is no way that we can expect to see a lasting peace!

Even in our beloved Nation our leaders cannot agree.
You see, the devil won't leave them alone, he won't let them be.
The devil is allowed to spread his influence all around,
But if you mention your religion you're quickly run out of town!

I'm sure that Jesus loves everyone but some people hate His Name.
They bow down to other Gods which helps to fan the flame.
The troubles which engulf the world have religion at the core.
When the devil adds his influence why it's Katy "bar the door"!

I am a Christian, born and bred, but I respect what others think.
I follow footsteps of Jefferson, Madison and Franklin who were the link
That formed the chain of our Democracy and made it truly great.
Jesus always loved the USA and He will determine our ultimate fate!

August 28.

Thank You Jesus

The Good Lord's blessings fall upon us every single day.
He never forgets so why should we, it's time for us to pray.
Okay, we're busy, and so is He, but He still lets us know
That we can always count on Him because He loves us so!

We must never let it appear that Jesus died in vain.
There is so much we could lose but there's much more for us to gain.
Don't get too busy to count your blessings and offer thanks for them.
Remembering all the while that they all do come from Him!

It doesn't have to be Thanksgiving Day for us to give thanks you know.
We receive these bounties every day and it's proper for us to show
The grateful nature of our hearts and always say our prayers,
And never forget that all our needs come from that "Man Upstairs!"

We're all born as sinners and we develop a lot of pride,
Which within itself can be a sin for which dear Jesus died,
But you can be proud of Jesus and let your love for Him show through,
Then He will open up new pathways for things you want to do!

Oh what a thrill to know that Jesus loves us all,
And if we find ourselves in trouble, He's there to take our call.
You don't need a telephone to talk to Him you know.
The air waves serve just fine you see, you just have to say "hello!"

Jesus' helpers, there in Heaven are folks like you and me.
They lived a life down here on earth 'til Jesus set them free.
Now they are a part of the Almighty Chorus giving a helping hand
As He prepares a place for all of us, there in the "Promised Land!"

August 29.

A Vision Of Jesus

I had a vision yesterday,
It all started when I knelt to pray.
I saw Lord Jesus standing there,
That's not so strange He's everywhere!

This vision was so bright and clear,
To me it seemed He was so near.
His voice too was sweet and strong,
And He was singing my favorite song!

"Great is thy faithfulness" is what I heard.
I knew the next line, knew every word.
He motioned for me to join right in,
He raised His hand for me to begin!

Try as hard as I might, not a sound could I make.
His sweet voice continued, there was no mistake,
These words were written about Him and His love.
His solo of course came straight from above!

My voice would not function, I could not assist.
He knew I was trying but did not insist.
"Strength for today and bright hope for tomorrow,"
Healing words for our nation and all those who sorrow!

"All I have needed, thy Hand hath provided,"
What better words for a world so divided.
The Lord ended His song, a strong melody,
"Great is thy faithfulness, Lord unto me!"

August 30.

Trouble In Our Time

Praise to the Lord on High, your Savior and your friend.
You needn't ask Him more than once and He will take you in.
Where would you really be without someone like Him
To guide you in your daily lives and meet your slightest whim?

Now don't sit back and wait for Him, reach out and take His Hand.
He's always waiting there for you right in the "Promised Land."
He's watching very carefully everything you do,
Helping you to stay on track, He'll watch until you're through!

He will forgive your greatest sin if you'll just be sincere.
Don't ever think He doesn't know, you cannot hide the fear.
For all of those who've gone astray and lost their way in life,
He'd love to hold you in His arms and take away the strife!

The entire world right at this time is in a tragic mess.
We haven't placed our trust in Him, we haven't done our best.
It's time that we all recognized the serious spot we're in,
And pray that He will help us out and save us all from sin!

There's not a single one of us who haven't played their part,
But if you really feel you're free from sin, look deep within your heart.
Pray to the Lord your sin to take, you'll never be the same,
For He's our Precious Lord on High and Jesus is His name!

August 31.

Sweet Jesus

Sweet Jesus, you're my everything,
I speak your Name and Angels sing.
What would I do if you weren't there?
My life would be so fraught with care!

You are my heart, 'tis not my own,
It beats for you, not me alone.
I feel its beat I know you're there,
That's not so strange you're everywhere!

I think of you, you're on my mind,
You came to save all of mankind.
So blessed are we, you know us well,
You'll take us home with you to dwell!

When heart beats stop, my mind goes blank,
You're right there for me to thank.
You've given me a precious soul,
And when I die, you'll make me whole!

Sweet Jesus you're my friend indeed,
You've filled me with my every need.
Yes, when I die, with you I'll go.
JESUS LOVES ME, THIS I KNOW!

Contents *September*

1. Tick Tock 265

2. It's Labor Day Across The Land 266

3. Time Won't Wait 267

4. L O V E 268

5. To Rosemary With Love 269

6. Today 270

7. Today Is A Good Day 271

8. Tragedy 272

9. Travel Plans 273

10. Heavenly Music 274

11. Trust In Jesus 275

12. Tweet Tweet 276

13. Visions of Heaven 277

14. Wake Up And Smell The Roses 278

15. Walking With Jesus 279

16. We All Get To Play In The Game Of Life 280

17. What You Don't Know May Be A Blessing 281

18. What's In Store 282

19. We Always Have A Choice 283

20. We Are All Christian Soldiers 284

21. We Can't Do It Alone 285

22. We Know What Jesus Would Do 286

23. The Super Bowl Of Life 287

24. We Must Keep Trying 288

25. We Need Jesus' Help To Stay The Course 289

26. Wealth Has No Place In Heaven 290

27. What Day Is It? 291

28. What Next 292

29. What Shall I Say? 293

30. What Would The Founders Do? 294

September 1.

Tick Tock

Time has a way of just slowly slipping away.
Before you hardly know it it's a spanking brand new day.
You find yourself wondering where was I yesterday,
Then you remember all the fun and realize that it's okay!

One never knows just how much time is left upon the clock.
When we are young we hear the tick but seldom hear the tock.
So time moves slowly then and is of no real concern.
We burn the candle at both ends until we finally learn!

It finally dawns upon us one bright and shining day.
Oh yes we only have a finite time and it is slipping away,
But we still refuse to accept the fact and waste a lot of time,
So busy doing nothing much we miss the bells that chime!

Sometimes we sit and wonder what do we need to do today.
We often even make a list to follow, no matter come what may.
Tomorrow we find that crumpled list showing things we haven't done.
It seems we spend a lot of time just carousing and having fun!

Amidst the hustle and bustle of every day, do we ever think of Him?
I mean that One who loves us all and meets our every whim?
He gives us all the time we need to live the life we choose,
So why not say "Thank You Lord" right now, there is no time to lose!

After all is said and done and much time has slipped away,
We may reflect and cogitate and think "what did I do today"?
There is no better use of time than saying "Thank You" once again,
And with that happy thought in mind, we'll sing a new refrain!

September 2.

It's Labor Day Across The Land

When you think you can't go on just stop and say "Amen."
That's when Jesus will lift your load for He's your Dearest Friend.
You'll learn that you were not alone there are many in that boat.
Jesus loves to hear us call He wants to keep us all afloat!

When I was born in twenty-three, I didn't have a dime.
What Jesus gave me at my birth was lots of love mixed with lots of time.
I've tried to use my eighty-eight years to repay Him for His gift,
And every time I've been in need He's given me a lift!

What's happening today is nothing new we've been in trouble before.
The devil loves to stir things up he's knocking at our door.
He'd love to see our Nation fail, that is his biggest goal.
The merchants of doom are riding high and they are peddling gold!

I watch in fascination as our fortunes ebb and flow with the tide.
The devil is orchestrating all the ups and downs he's in it for the ride.
Most of us must go along there's not much else that we can do.
I place all my faith and trust in Jesus for I know that He'll pull us through!

While we have problems our Nation is well off we really must give thanks,
There are others in the world who are starving as their nation "tanks."
To see children starving breaks my heart I wish I could do more.
Everyone should do their very best and help to feed the poor!

Our leaders must do everything they can to keep our Nation strong.
We're known as a Christian Nation but even our leaders can't get along.
That shows the influence of the devil as he battles for the power.
We can defeat him as we've done before, it will be our finest hour!

September 3.

Time Won't Wait

It seems that life just rushes by it's gone before you know.
You put off some things that you should do and say I'll do it tomorrow.
The fact remains as we well know when midnight dies it's now today,
So no matter how we try to dodge it tomorrow gives way to yesterday!

Somehow we never have the time to sit and "ponder" things.
The hours fly right on by as if they really did have wings.
Left without sufficient time to "ponder," we do the best we can,
And usually find no peace of mind in "service on demand"!

The good Lord gives to everyone of us, enough time in each day.
It's true that some folks schedule well and then have time to play.
They are the ones who "ponder" in advance and allocate their time,
In fact I'm "pondering" with this verse to find some words that rhyme!

Another month is almost gone and I am lost at sea.
I can't see that I've accomplished much at least it seems that way to me.
Holidays are approaching fast, in fact Thanksgiving is next week.
I'll have to "ponder" long and hard to reach the goals I seek!

Big family plans have all been made, they're all set up to start.
There still are some things that I must do, I have to do my part.
I've tried to leave some extra time in case things should go awry.
Things can happen to upset the plans, no matter how hard we try!

We'll ask the Lord to join us, when we sit down to eat.
We must thank Him for everything that made our plans complete.
He's given us all the time we need to "ponder" some at least,
And with all the "pondering" that's been done, we'll have a fancy feast!

September 4.

$\mathcal{L} \ O \ \mathcal{V} \ \mathcal{E}$

"LOVE" is just a word but "my, how good it sounds."
When it's used in proper time and place its influence knows no bounds.
Say the words, "I love you" and launch them from your heart.
There is no force in all the world could tear that thought apart!

"Je vous aime" is precious too, if you speak French at all.
Follow that with red roses soon, that's proper protocol.
It's awfully strange, but it is true, resistance melts away,
When two hearts meet and bond in love, romance is underway!

Everybody knows the words but some can't find a way.
To put that lovely simple phrase to work for them each day.
Our world would be a better place if "love" could replace "war".
Rose gardens abound instead of battlefields and peace reigns evermore!

It sounds farfetched I know and some will quickly say "what next?"
To think that those three simple words could have some good effects.
Just over two thousand years ago "love" came to all of us.
God sent "love" to all mankind, His beloved Son dear Jesus!

Who would stall and try to block a wonderful thing like "love?"
There's plenty more of it in God's store, up there in Heaven above.
Just think how wonderful it would be if love came down like rain.
The sins of all would wash away and peace would thrive again!

Let's not let the ugly face of war destroy the beauty of our land.
The devil's war lords from afar are a destructive unholy band.
"We can win" should be our battle cry, for "love" is on our side.
Let's all enlist and join the quest for "love" and peace can then abide!

September 5.

To Rosemary With Love

Springtime is like heaven on earth
Or that is what they say.
All around, we see new birth
As April turns into May!

We wake up early every morn,
Can't wait to get outside,
We watch entranced as day is born
The sun's a crimson tide!

If you love flowers springs for you
As winter fades away,
You find that there's a lot to do
And start at break of day!

You never let a day pass by
That you don't stand in awe,
And count your blessings, my oh my,
As you spread out the straw!

The flowers bloom dispel the gloom
And clothe our entire plot.
We beam with pride as we abide
Our beautiful garden spot!

Thank You Lord for giving us
This land where we can be
Happy and healthy without much fuss
And live in harmony!

September 6.

Today

Today is not a "special" day but then let's think again.
If you think that it's not special, think about a friend.
To them it could be special, in fact more than any other day,
So let's agree that every day is special to someone in a special way!

Let's take the word "today" and ask what's so special about that?
Often , we don't give things much thought and dismiss it off the bat!
But "today" is just as special as all other days you see,
While it may be true that it's just not so special to you or me!

There is a list of "special" days that mean so much to all.
There's Christmas day and Easter day, holidays when we have a ball.
They are certainly special to everyone, but let's not forget "today."
There are millions of folks out there for whom today is their birthday!

"Day" is just a three letter word until it's modified.
It's useful and can stand alone, but is better when magnified.
We make "day" special by the very words we use,
And it can be most any "day" by the modifier we choose!

So when I say "today" is special it's because it's modified.
I could just as well say "yesterday" but would not be satisfied,
For "yester" is gone and in the past while "to" of course means now,
And that's what makes "today" special so we will take a bow!

Another thing that makes a day special is that God made them all.
He sends them to us, one by one, in winter, spring and fall.
For that gift I think it's right that we should bow to pray
And thank the Lord for that special gift, the one we call "today!"

Today Is A Good Day

I hope today will never end I'm having so much fun,
I woke up feeling very good the day had just begun.
Things went well, soon was noon the sun was shining bright.
If afternoon goes just as planned I'll hate to say goodnight!

It's a fact we all know, in every life some rain must fall.
Perfect days they come and go, not every day but almost all,
We need to ask the Lord above to help us, come what may,
For it is He who thinks of us and brings a glorious day!

When things go well for us, no problems on our plate,
Do we feel that it's our due, that it is just our fate?
Or do we truly recognize that Jesus had a hand
In bringing all those good things, subject to our command?

Precious Jesus knows our needs and wants to hear our plan.
If He doesn't hear from us He does the best He can,
And while this may not be exact, the same as we would do,
It still reflects His love for us and proves His love is true!

It's up to us to stay in touch with Jesus every day.
It's just not difficult at all to get on our knees to pray.
Tell Him all about your plans and thank Him for His love.
Even if we fail to tell Him of our needs, He'll send them from above!

If you've had a perfect day don't think that you're so smart,
But rather you must thank the Lord and pray with all your heart.
For without Him there is no doubt, your day would've been a mess,
So bring Him in on all your plans, He'll see you at your best!

September 8.

Tragedy

I said a prayer for Jesus today I know He's sad indeed.
I know He must feel overwhelmed with all the folks in need.
The Pearly Gates swung open wide when the Japanese arrived,
Thousands more are in dire straits but fortunately survived!

I watched in horror as I saw the tragedy unfold on my TV,
The likes of which I've never seen and hope never again to see.
For thousands of folks their life was ended in the twinkling of an eye.
Thousands more are in harm's way and many of them will die!

These terrible tragedies should wake us up and teach us to beware.
We never know what might come next, be sure that you prepare.
Be sure that you're ready to meet the Lord, tell Him of your love,
It may come sooner than we expect when He'll take us home above!

I don't mean to frighten anyone, please don't be afraid to die.
Be ready to ask forgiveness for your sins, to Jesus you cannot lie.
Say a prayer for our Japanese friends, so many died today.
It happened so quickly that I'm sure they didn't have time to pray!

This tsunami reminds me somewhat of the flood in Noah's day.
Noah followed the Lord's directions and also took the time to pray.
Perhaps we don't do enough to prepare for a catastrophic event,
For Jesus said "always be ready", and we know just what He meant!

I like to think that I'm prepared if my time should come today,
If Jesus said "Come home dear friend" and the trumpets began to play.
I pray that I can walk the walk when He takes me by the hand,
And we then can walk together into the sunshine of the Promised Land!

September 9.

Travel Plans

Jesus waits for us in Heaven, it's called the "Promised Land."
We'll spend our eternity with Him and all the Christian band.
There are some things that we must do to reach that lofty goal.
The first thing is we must admit we're members of the fold!

Sunday is a hallowed day, we all should go to church.
It's there we join with Christian friends to do some more research.
There is so much that we don't know we need to stay abreast,
So that we don't veer from our goal and get sidetracked from our quest!

We must start out every day with Jesus on our mind.
He has the key to Heaven and works to save mankind.
We need to pause and pray each morn, let Jesus be our guide.
If we wander off the course, He'll help us turn the tide!

There is no way we can survive if we start out alone.
Don't be afraid to call on Him, He's watching from His throne.
You can put your trust in Him He's never let us down.
He'll lead us to those "Pearly Gates" in Heaven where we're bound!

In the meantime here on earth we each must do our part,
To help our Lord and Savior we must fight with all our heart,
Resisting all the evils that would lead us all astray,
And when we find we need His help, get on our knees and pray!

You'd be surprised but I surmise that Jesus gets a kick,
When watching us and sees our need He gets there extra quick.
It's then we know He's always there waiting for our call,
And inviting us to join the Christian band, He loves us one and all!

September 10.

Heavenly Music

When I hear those Heavenly bells, I'll know my time has come,
While Peter guards the gate with Jesus on the throne,
The invitation comes not just to me, but to everyone.
I won't resist, I can't resist, for Jesus wants me home!

We don't know how or even when, those bells will ring with pride,
Moving 'round the world and back again, cross every land and sea,
They represent that story, how Jesus died for me!
I will not hide, I cannot hide, my ears are opened wide!

I am listening patiently, for bells to start to ring,
While I wait with faithful joy, I bend my knee to pray,
"COME ON HOME CHILD", that's what I hear Him say.
Angel Gabriel blows his horn and the others start to sing.

Angel voices all ring out, this message I must heed,
We're here for you and you must know, that Jesus bids you come,
We'll bear you there on Golden Wings, no carriage do we need,
When Jesus calls, the die is cast, and you are welcomed home!

Thank You JESUS, Thank You GOD, and Thank You SPIRIT too,
And thanks to all those earthly saints, a very precious few,
Who taught me well that GOD is LOVE, that JESUS came to save,
The SPIRIT guided me through life, and saved me from the grave!

September 11.

Trust In Jesus

If you're feeling lonely, never fear, you are not alone.
There's always someone you can reach and you won't need a phone.
Jesus keeps an open line just waiting for you to call.
You see, Jesus loves us, everyone, with our warts and all!

I like to think of Jesus when He was just a little boy.
His parents knew that He was special and He gave them so much joy.
He was so wise beyond His years, His elders were amazed.
They asked Him many questions but He was never fazed!

We all know the story well, of Jesus and His love.
He lived and died right here on earth, now lives in Heaven above.
He watches over us day by day and provides us with our needs.
We must follow in His footsteps by performing our good deeds!

We need to spread the word around that Jesus is our friend,
Show people by the life we lead that He keeps us free from sin.
We'll be blessed with happiness and other signs of Jesus' love,
And when our earthly journey ends, we'll rest in Heaven above!

Our world today, right here on earth, is full of sin and shame.
Too often we do things we shouldn't do and try to shift the blame,
But Jesus knows our every move and is waiting for us to ask
For His forgiveness for our sins…it's not too big a task!

I'm sure the world would be a better place if our faith was cast in stone.
As mere mortals we're born and raised in sin, and made of flesh and bone.
It's time we changed our way of life so just ask Jesus to save our soul.
There is no doubt if we're sincere that He'll take us into the fold!

Patriot Day

Tweet Tweet

I hear the twitter of a bird.
A prettier sound I've never heard.
A mocking bird it is, I'm sure.
So many calls and all are pure!

A pair of birds flew into view.
They are a "couple" just those two.
Their beautiful song says "we're in love."
Such lovely sounds come from above!

Jesus loves all birds like these.
Let's them build nests in all the trees.
It's there they raise their family,
And broadcast songs to you and me!

It's often said, "I sometimes feel as free as a bird."
It's a very nice thought we all have heard,
But with that freedom that the birds enjoy,
There are many chores they must employ!

When you see them digging in the ground,
That's where most of their food is found.
They also need a good water source.
Not just for drinking but to bathe of course!

God loves for birds to be everywhere.
That's why they fill the skies out there.
He provides for them just like He does for us,
And it's in Him that we all trust!

Visions of Heaven

There is a place called Heaven I believe with all my heart.
That's where Jesus lives, that's where He got His start.
He came to earth a tiny babe just like you and me,
Wrapped up in his mother's womb awaiting delivery!

It's always been a mystery and it's still unknown today,
The exact location of Heaven, there's no address and no highway.
Jesus as the Son of God knew whence He came and the way back,
He spent His entire life to help us stay on the right track!

Our major task while here on earth is to ensure that final ride.
While we don't know the time nor place it won't happen 'til we've died,
And that my friend is why we must be ready every day.
We came into this world with naught we'll leave the very same way!

Jesus gave us insight into Heaven and what our role would be.
He described a wonderful place it's one I want to see.
I try to live my life on earth as Jesus said we should,
So I can take my place in Heaven just like He said we would!

Jesus wants each one of us to join with Him some day.
If we are ready when our time has come we'll soon be on our way.
But there are some who still have doubts, don't know which way to turn
And if they can't accept God's gift to us, they may just have to burn!

When I reach those "Pearly Gates", St. Peter's there with the key,
Those Angels bearing me aloft approach him holding me.
He looks into that big book of life and soon he finds my name.
"Turn him loose and let him fly" he says, we're really glad he came!

September 14.

Wake Up And Smell The Roses

It's a beautiful day in our "neck of the woods," it's truly Heaven sent.
You couldn't buy one half as nice no matter how much you spent.
There's one thing that man has never mastered that's the weather of course.
Good days come and go "at will", we rarely know the source!

If you get outside our atmosphere our weather does not exist.
If you rise above our stratosphere there are no clouds or mist.
Our moon has never had a cloudy day it's dusty as can be.
Neil Armstrong's footprints remain I'm sure, waiting for us to see!

Our spacestation is a masterpiece, it proves what can be done.
As time goes on, it won't be soon, some folks may live on one.
Trips for folks to visit the moon may one day be in store.
A man may one day get to Mars, but I cannot guess what for!

God created the entire Universe for mankind that we know is true.
He also gave us brains and "free will" so we'd know how and what to do.
Mankind has occupied the earth now for over seven thousand years.
All Nations must begin to cooperate and erase all our built up fears!

I'm an old man now and I won't be here long so I'm going to miss a lot,
But I'll be keeping touch from Heaven and I'll give it all I've got,
To help the Heavenly Council and all the Saints of old,
Prepare this old worn out world for the end and that will be the goal!

Nothing ever happens fast when we're planning "eternal" things.
I know that you may think I'm nuts, and I certainly don't have wings,
But I take Jesus at His Word, and I want to lend a hand.
I hope that He will give me a good job to do, there in the "Promised Land"!

September 15.

Walking With Jesus

I walked through the shadow of death
With Jesus right by my side.
When He reached for my hand I took a deep breath,
Knowing He'd take me when I died!

Since then there's been nothing to fear.
It's comforting to know that He's near.
I try mighty hard to please Him each day
By being thankful and kneeling to pray!

I love Jesus and try hard not to sin.
I always tell Him where I've been.
I always accept His advice which is exceedingly nice,
And is straight to the point and concise!

It's true Jesus has not let me down.
He keeps me from just fooling around.
I stay busy each day in the usual way,
Doing things that I should have done yesterday!

I'm thankful that He's always nearby,
In case I should break down and cry.
When I need Him, He's there since He's everywhere,
And I can reach Him real quickly through prayer!

Jesus has long been my best friend.
When it's my time to go I know He will send
His Angels who'll give me a hand,
Our destination, the Lord's own dear Promised Land!

September 16.

We All Get To Play In The Game Of Life

There's no one here but Jesus so I have no need to fear.
I always have companionship for He is always near.
He's the Rock on which I stand, there is no firmer ground,
And He'll be with me here as long as I'm still around!

Better still is the fact that we never have to say "goodbye,"
For when my time on earth is done I'll join Him in the sky.
I'll never be able to thank Him enough for what He's done for me,
And joy of joys to know that my time in Heaven will be for eternity!

We're in training here on earth for the latter days above.
Our coach's name is Jesus and He brings us all His love.
Who better to lead us as we prepare for our demise.
He wants us to pass His final test, the one on which He relies!

I've lived a long and fruitful life with help from all my friends,
But most of all I've followed Jesus who taught me to make amends.
When I sit quietly and reflect upon the past, I see mistakes I've made.
Most of them would not have happened if I had just obeyed!

Thanks to God for sending Jesus to save us all from sin.
With His help we've fought the devil who has tried to lure us in
To all the sinful traps he sets that entice us one and all,
But Jesus is always real nearby just waiting to take our call!

We're always in a hurry here on earth, our days pass quickly by.
It seems that I rarely have the time to call up and just say "Hi,"
To all those friends of mine who have helped me to make the grade.
To them I now say, "thanks dear friends for the part that you played!"

September 17.

What You Don't Know May Be A Blessing

The future is a mystery and that's how it should be.
Our life would be so different if the future we could see.
Planning for our tomorrows is what our life is all about.
To live each day as it unfolds is something we couldn't do without!

All our friends would disappear for they'd have so much else to do.
They'd be so busy fulfilling their schedule they'd have no time for you.
In such a world we'd lose so much like the element of surprise,
Since everybody knows everything which I don't think is wise!

No one could have a secret for how could you hide the fact
In a world where everybody knows everything there'd be no need to act.
Life would become so cut and dried, much like robots on parade,
And life itself would seem to us like one more, great big charade!

There's just one thing in our future that is no mystery at all,
The fact that when we die we go to Heaven requires no crystal ball.
The Bible tells us all about it, that is, all we need to know.
That's where we learn that we'll be saved because Jesus loves us so!

Everybody loves a mystery and many books are sold
Where we don't know how they will end until there-in we're told.
Once we know the ending we close the book, it's all over then,
But at our death it's not the end for our Eternal Life will then begin!

Jesus knows us, everyone, it was He who sent us to the earth.
He sent us to our Mom and Dad as a present at our birth.
He has all our records in His Book, our sins and good points too.
Whether we can pass His final test, it's really up to me and you!

Constitution Day

September 18.

What's In Store

When we get to Heaven will we still look the same?
Will we be identified by the same earthly name?
Will we each have a job to do as in the here and now?
Things will surely be unique but I'm sure I don't know how!

God doesn't reveal His plan to us until it's time for us to go.
If we're accepted into the Promised Land He'll put us in the know.
The devil keeps on fighting for our soul we must not let him win.
We must put all our faith in Jesus to save us from our sin!

The Universe is God's creation as well as you and me.
We know He also made the rose, its beauty for us to see.
Everything we've seen mankind produce came from Gods own Hand.
I think we all will be surprised at the wonders of the Promised Land!

My imagination is running wild, Hollywood could never compete.
Magnificent vistas we see on earth will never be more complete.
Once we enter the Promised Land we'll never want to leave.
That's what Jesus meant when He said "In Me you must believe"!

Can you envision a lovely setting where you know everyone,
Where there are no language barriers and no one even has a phone.
No one is a stranger there and there are no family ties.
Eternity is forever and there's no sickness so no one dies!

Competition goes by the boards equality exists for all.
Perfection is the norm for everyone, that's proper protocol,
When Jesus ordains us in our Heavenly home,
And we'll be there with Him forever, never more to roam!

Birthdate of the Authors Sister, Christine S. Stephens, 1915

We Always Have A Choice

Have you said your prayers today, what are you waiting for?
Jesus wants to hear from you and you know He's keeping score.
He has your record in His Books, He checks it every day.
He makes an entry by your name when He hears you pray!

Jesus sent us all to earth as gifts to Mom and Dad.
Sometimes a girl, sometimes a boy and sometimes both were had.
Sweet little babies all were we, just like He had been.
Unlike Jesus, every one of us, conceived and born in sin!

It's true that each one has a brain and something known as free will.
We train from birth to use our brain and put parents through the mill.
Yes, free will means we have a choice in everything we do,
With good advice and moral courage, you do what's good for you!

Now some folks think they know it all, they never seek advice.
They just go merrily along each day pretending to be nice.
The choices that they make in life most often are all wrong,
And they wind up many times in places where they don't belong!

We have plenty of help with our choices, just bow your head and pray.
You will always get good advice, the kind that will make your day.
Each request you make of Him is recorded in His Books.
The empty pages disturb the Lord, do they belong to crooks?

Throughout the world are problem spots, the devil leads the way.
The people there must make a choice but they won't stop to pray.
They will gang up in the streets and disobey all the rules.
I'm glad that we in the USA are free will and do not act as fools!

September 20.

We Are All Christian Soldiers

Don't be afraid to die my friend, death comes to everyone.
Let Jesus come into your heart, He'll help you overcome
All the fears that you might have, you see, He knows the way.
He died for us and rose again on that glorious Easter Day!

Don't be misled, you must believe in Jesus to be saved.
The devil is always lurking real nearby in case you haven't behaved.
Don't let temptation lead you astray, let Jesus take your hand.
He's always ready to take you with Him to the "Promised Land!"

Our world today is in danger as the devil's forces abide.
Their influence on the human race reaches far and wide.
They are a greedy, lying, cheating group, who follow the devil's creed.
The world is at a crossroads and Jesus must intercede!

All those folks who are on Jesus' side speak up with a prayer.
With Jesus helping we must push the devil back into his lair.
If we just stand our ground and fight, we can save the world,
But we must be sure that we get the Christian flag unfurled!

There is no need for you to fear, to run and hide today.
If you feel threatened in anyway, just bow your head and pray.
Jesus Himself will hear your prayer, and rush to your defense.
He's always happy when he finds folks with some common sense!

That's just the way it is today my friend, we have to be on guard.
Be sure the devil is not hiding out, right in your own backyard.
He is crafty, more than most, recruiting gives him a thrill.
He can't save your soul at all, but I'm sure that Jesus will!

September 21.

We Can't Do It Alone

It seems the world is so uptight we're squeaking when we walk.
With all the troubles throughout the world it's a wonder we can talk.
Sometimes it seems that we forget that we are not alone.
The only one who holds the key cannot be reached by phone!

Meanwhile we are busy as can be, at least it seems that way.
Running here and running there, are we trying to run away?
We can't abandon this old world we have no place to go,
But Jesus says "now don't give up, just tell Me your tales of woe!

There is no problem too hard to solve if we just seek His aid.
It's when we think we know it all and think we've got it made,
That's when we hit the roadblocks that fall into our path.
The answers to these knotty problems demand a brand new kind of math!

Science is a wonderful field but we need Einstein on our team.
The answers to our major problems requires more than someone's dream.
Yes, with that extra help from up above there's nothing we can't do!
I'll be very glad to do my part and hope that you will too!

When I look around my neighborhood my heart sometimes skips a beat.
Beautiful flowers are blooming everywhere, it truly is real neat.
I'm reminded once again of Him who makes those flowers grow.
He'll also help us solve other problems if we'll just let Him know!

I can't tell you what to do you know your needs, not me.
Just ask Jesus what you should do, all His advice is free.
I know that I must stay in touch with Him so I don't lose my way.
That Friend I have in Heaven will surely hear from me today!

We Know What Jesus Would Do

Holidays are lots of fun but they just come and go.
Today is July 5th and the day is starting out real slow.
I'm sure that it will soon begin to speedily move along
And we can brighten up the day by singing our favorite song!

"Great Is Thy Faithfulness" is the song I like to sing.
That song says that God loves me and to me that's everything.
I put my trust in Jesus so many long years ago.
He has fulfilled my every need and He makes the roses grow!

I'm sure that Jesus looks down from Heaven with tears in His eyes,
As He observes the current turmoil brought about by all the lies.
Our government used to help those in need but now it favors the rich.
The billionaires are riding high while the poor folks are in the ditch!

It would not be so bad if everyone "fairly" shared the load,
But the burden falls heavy on the middle class, they're losing their abode.
Foreclosures and the Nation's debt climb higher by the minute,
But those who have the most pay the least there is no equality in it!

The folks who vote must turn the tide, it's time to see the light.
We must reverse the present course, it's time to do what's right.
Warren Buffett and Bill Gates know what's wrong they should pay more,
But others sit upon their hoard and use it to open up the door!

Every able bodied man and woman must be given a job to do.
Our Nation, the envy of the world, must provide that job for you.
Let's bring our factories back on shore and give our folks a chance.
It's time to let Uncle Sam show all the world, just who wears the pants!

The Super Bowl Of Life

Persistence is the name of the game, it will pull you through.
Always try to do your best that is the thing to do.
Perfection is a lofty goal but it's not everything you see.
Someone must be in second place and that could be you or me!

Contests of any kind are fun you don't always have to win.
If you finish in the pack you know to lose is not a sin.
You'll always have another chance to show what you can do.
Persistence brings you back again and again and it's also good for you!

The losers of any race that's run are the most important of all.
Without them pushing the winner there would have been no race to call.
Oh yes, the winner will get the glory but it's the loser who made the race
And it is the loser who again tomorrow the winner will have to face!

Some folks are afraid to lose and because of that they never try.
Life itself is like a game that we all must play until we die.
We became a member of a team when we joined the human race.
Whether we win or lose will be determined by problems that we face!

The Super Bowl of life is the one we engage in every day.
This is truly a wonderful game because everyone gets to play.
The "Team of Light" is coached by Jesus who has never lost a game.
The "Team of Dark" is coached by Satan who is wrapped in flame!

You can join the "Team of Light" and Jesus will sign you in,
Or you can join the "Team of Dark" and Satan will help you sin.
We all know who the winners will be and we want to be with them.
The "Team of Dark" never gives up and starts much more mayhem!

September 24.

We Must Keep Trying

I know I don't please everyone but I do the best I can.
I look at problems from all sides, I respect my fellowman.
I never fault a different "point of view", that's okay with me.
It's possible that we may both be right, on that we can agree!

I like to think that I've helped someone with something that I've said.
I try to be uplifting but there are some who just can't be led.
If there is no proof there is no belief, then there is no faith at all
And those who tell us 'there is no God" have got a lot of gall!

I pity those who fail to see that God is all around.
There was a time when folks didn't believe that the world was round.
I pray for them and know that Jesus wants to save their soul.
He battles the devil every day for our salvation is His goal!

When I look back into my life I know that I have sinned.
Jesus is the only One who can forgive, on Him I must depend.
The richest person in the world can't buy what He can give
To those of us who believe in Him and get to go to Heaven to live!

If you don't believe in God that's entirely up to you,
I merely ask respectfully what do you have to look forward to?
Your soul will live eternally, it doesn't disappear at death.
I know for sure I'll go to Heaven when I draw my last breath!

Education comes from books that try to teach us what to do.
We all have read lots of books and we've learned a thing or two.
God Himself inspired the Bible which was written by the Saints.
It should be on our reading list for the beautiful picture it paints!

September 25.

We Need Jesus' Help To Stay The Course

When I think that Jesus knows my name it gives me quite a thrill.
He's watched o'er me since I was born, I know He always will.
Just having Him to lead the way has made my life worthwhile.
I still remember the Bible verses my Mother taught me when I was just a child!

Jesus' life when He was on the earth was much different from today.
However, the basic things He talked about are still done the same old way.
We bow our heads to say our prayers and often get down on our knees.
We know He's listening to our voice since we get answers to our pleas!

I've had a long and fruitful life and must give credit where it's due.
I wouldn't be where I am today if Jesus hadn't pulled me through.
There were times when I was lost and could not find my way.
At times like that I was extremely glad that my Mother taught me to pray!

The world we live in, here and now, is similar to that of old.
While we have much more knowledge now, we continue to worship gold.
Hunger exists around the world and sickness takes its toll.
We continue to rely on human means whereas God could make us whole!

I don't mean to imply here nor advocate reliance in faith "on call".
However our vast knowledge of the human body should be available to all.
Some folks even dare to say that Christianity is taboo for Jesus was socialist.
If that be true then "hallelujah, sign me up and put me on His list"!

Let's face it folks our whole world is in a state of sharp decline.
It's gotten to be a "dog eat dog" society, "screw you, I've got mine".
Mankind is spread across many nations and each one wants to lead.
There is no nation strong enough to force all others to listen and to heed!

There is a reality at work in the world which we have got to face.
Evil forces are doing their best to control the entire human race.
We as Christians must stand up strong and ask God to intervene,
For the whole world is His domain and only He can make it clean!

September 26.

Wealth Has No Place In Heaven

Here on earth we show our age in many ways you know,
But we cannot hide the truth, our wrinkles always show.
We must accept the way we are and do the best we can,
Until the Good Lord calls us home into the "Promised Land!"

Our life here on earth is measured by what we know as wealth.
We spend our life accumulating to the detriment of our health.
No matter how much wealth we have we must leave it all behind.
It's better not to have so much, but to have more peace of mind!

It's hard for us to think of eternity when we are worried about the years.
We don't like to think about our death it's one of our greatest fears,
And yet we all know we won't be judged until we've crossed the bar,
For Jesus has our record in His Book and He knows just how we are!

As human beings we all have plans and goals we hope to reach.
We learn most everything in school but we must practice what we preach.
We won't be judged on our A's and B's but on our do's and don'ts,
And on how we've helped our fellow man with his needs and wants!

"What we have to fear is fear itself" I've often heard it said.
If we will put our trust in Jesus then we won't be misled.
He'll wrap those fears that we all have in precious bonds of love,
And give us all a short preview of the life we'll have above!

So please don't worry, my good friend, Jesus is standing by.
He's watching everything we do from His Home there in the sky.
If we should falter or start to stray, He'll take us by the hand,
And lead us back to the "Glory Road" that leads to the "Promised Land!"

September 27.

What Day Is It?

Father's Day has come and gone, all Dads have had their "day."
All the kids have honored him and had a lot to say.
Every "day" is a special "day" to honor this or that.
There's even a "day" that everyone must go without a hat!

Each "day" of the week is special and has its special name.
Today is Mon "day," tomorrow Tues "day, none can be the same.
Don't know how Wednes "day" got to be, with Thurs "day" right behind.
There's Fri "day" and Satur "day" of course all days of a different kind!

There's one more "day" in every week we haven't talked about.
It's the most important "day" of all we cannot leave it out.
Sun "day" is the Sabbath Day a special "day" indeed.
We couldn't do without that "day" it's one that we all need!

You may not all agree with me but I think there's been a mistake.
The spelling of the word Sun, it's one that we all make.
I'm sure that God would spell it Son, a really special "day"
To honor His own Beloved Son, a time for homage and to pray!

Every one of us is given a special and unique "day."
That's the "day" that we were born, which is our very own birth "day."
We usually refer to it in calendar terms, don't use the "day" of the week.
You should never neglect the name of the "day" it's the one we seek!

I was born on Son "day," August 5, in nineteen-twenty-three.
That "day" is very special for it's the day I came to be.
You see, I am my Father's only son and born on Son "day" too.
I must get busy for to "day" has arrived and I've got things to do!

September 28.

What Next

It seems our country's in a mess of late,
And many of Satan's pals are out in order to spread the hate.
We find that our new President is trying hard to cope
With new progressive plans and programs which offer a ray of hope!

We have the finest form of government in the world you can be sure.
It has served our country well and has kept us quite secure.
Two houses of elected peers meet regularly to set the course.
Each citizen of every state vote for their peers to form this ruling force!

Internal to each group of peers, other clubs are formed as well.
The party system is the main divide, but some have their votes for sale.
Lobbyists of special interests are paid big sums and form a marketplace.
Influence is the merchandise, some peers fall and show their second face!

The Majority Leader of the Senate and the Speaker of the House,
Are both elected by their peers to lead members while they joust.
They're charged with passing all the laws that govern our sweet land,
And presenting them for the Presidents Seal inscribed himself by hand!

Our governing system is quite complex and requires a lot of votes.
Majority rules in every case but sometimes a group revolts.
They're influenced by untrue tales and spread by messengers of hate,
The people's will is trampled in the dust, yet they must pay the freight!

So where do we stand now at this extremely important date?
Can we expect our congressmen to overrule the hate
And get themselves in gear to pass, the most progressive plan,
The one prepared by our new President for us and our fellow man?

September 29.

What Shall I Say?

Something keeps on calling for me to say a word or two.
I don't know where this is going, it's just like Sudoku.
I pick and choose a word that seems to be the one,
But then I find that it doesn't rhyme, that radical son of a gun!

Ideas keep floating throughout my brain right now.
There are things I want to say, don't really know just how.
The words I choose don't always fit, I have to start anew
And pick another, then another, and so on until I'm through!

I really love to write a poem, one that makes some sense.
I like to read them over and over to be sure I have used the right tense.
It's somewhat akin to crossword puzzles, searching to find a word.
Sometimes the answer that's correct is the dumbest I've ever heard!

Once you get started with an idea, you can't just up and quit.
You twist and turn the words around until you make it fit.
It may take a lot of time and sometimes you must admit,
Those who are prone to quit will never win, a winner will never quit!

It gives me satisfaction when I get a point across,
By being careful what I say, I don't like to boss.
People do not like to be pushed, but they are easily led,
So be up front with everything, be happy with what you've said!

I know when you read this you'll think I've lost a screw.
I'm really not just treading water to have something better to do.
There is a message in here somewhere, find it if you can.
It's all about not giving up and leaving "footprints in the sand!"

September 30.

What Would The Founders Do?

What would Thomas Jefferson do if he were in our shoes?
Would he be happy with the "status quo" or would he want to choose
A different path that put the people ahead of corporate greed,
And make sure that the plans they made would take care of our need!

Now "T.J." was not a common man he came from better stock.
He built his home upon a hill from whence he watched his flock.
He loved to stand upon his porch to survey his great domain.
Monticello and UVa are unsurpassed and long may they remain!

There is no doubt that "T.J." was as smart as a man could be.
He helped to draft our country's plans as part of the first big three.
He joined with Washington and Adams to set our nation on its course,
And later met with Madison across the fields upon his horse!

"T.J." wrote the Declaration which freed us from the King.
The war with England had surely proved that we should do our thing.
Benjamin from Philly joined in and played an important part,
And when these fellows signed their name it was our Nation's start!

George and John, Tom and James, and Ben were quite a motley crew.
There were many others who joined in too, more than just a few.
There were no Roosevelts, no Kennedys, no Bushes at work here,
But there was one more hero in the game, his name was Paul Revere!

These men and many, many more, all met in Constitution Hall.
They were not politicians as we know, they played a better game of ball.
They learned to leave their politics at home, were "patriots" to the bone.
The greatest of these men of course was Thomas Jefferson alone!

Contents October

1. Who 296
2. Who Can It Be? 297
3. Who Gets Your Vote 298
4. Why We Need Him 299
5. Will The Christmas Season Lift Our Spirits? 300
6. Will We Follow Jesus 301
7. Will We Let The Devil Make Us Do It 302
8. Will You Be My Friend 303
9. Thank You Lord For All Your Help 304
10. Writing Poetry Helps My Disposition 305
11. X Is No Sub For Christ 306
12. Yawn Away 307
13. Yes We Do Have Options 308
14. You CAN Believe This 309
15. You Can Count On Jesus 310
16. You Cannot Hide From Jesus 311
17. You Can't Go Wrong 312
18. Your Soul Is Everlasting 313
19. This Is How I See It 314
20. Your Soul Will Never Die 315
21. You've Still Got Time 316
22. That's What Friends Are For 317
23. The Battle 318
24. The Bee And The Butterfly 319
25. The Bible Is Our Source 320
     The Book 321
26. The Earth In All Its Grandeur Is Not Like Heaven 322
27. The Holy Trinity Is At Work 323
28. The Man Upstairs 324
29. The Master Of The Universe 325
30. The Old And The New 326
31. All Saints Day 327

October 1.

Who

Who are these people we all call "they", do they have a name?
Can you identify the "they" you mean or are "they" all the same?
What I mean is, can we all share this one called "they"?
Or would we have to question them to see what "they" would say?

Okay do I have you muddled up and wondering what would "people" say?
Are these "people" to whom I refer are they the same as "they"?
I mean, are "they" and "people" just the same do you know both of them?
Can you identify either one enough so we can call them "her" or "him"?

You know, I would like to do a lot of things but what would "people" say?
"They" say this or that is good or bad and we echo "that's what they say."
Why can't we just use proper names and call people by who they are?
It seems to me that we'd be better off, much better off by far!

If we always knew who said this or that, would it mean the same?
Do we give more credence to a stated fact if we know from whom it came?
Everyone becomes expert when they are talking about what "they" said.
It's easy to say why "they" said this or that if you quote them instead!

I know I'm guilty as is everyone in quoting what someone said.
It makes idle conversation interesting when it isn't over our head.
You don't solve many problems during this chatter, that's for sure,
But it helps to pass the time of day and enables you to endure!

"They" say that men don't make passes at ladies who wear glasses.
That's like trying to prove something is "honey" that's obviously molasses.
Now I'm beginning to get "facetious" and you know what "they" will say.
So I must say "so long" to one and all and "have a wonderful day"!

October 2.

Who Can It Be?

Who's that knocking at my front door?
It's early morning, not yet four.
If it's Jesus, let Him come in.
He can save our souls from sin!

If it's the devil please send him away.
I don't want to see him at all today.
He only wants to do all of us harm,
And take us to his place where it is warm!

Maybe it's someone who we don't even know,
In need of assistance because of the snow.
When you open the door, don't open it wide,
But invite the stranger to come inside!

It could be Jesus, but who's to say.
I sure would hate to turn Him away.
This may be a test and we can't hide,
Now that we've let the stranger inside!

If he was the devil we soon could tell,
For he would love to have us all on the road to hell,
But the stranger spoke up with a comforting voice
And we knew then that we'd made the right choice!

Relieved we listened as the stranger said,
"I'm sorry friends that I roused you from bed,
But for me tonight you granted me a big favor."
It was then we knew that this was indeed our Savior!

October 3.

Who Gets Your Vote

Today is a bright and cheerful day.
It's kinda' cool but that's okay.
The sun is shining, the temperature's rising.
My spirits are high and that's not surprising!

I'm thinking now about all my friends.
I hope none of them are at "loose ends."
It's days like this that makes folks cheerful,
Drives away those thoughts that make one fearful!

We're in the midst of real seasonal change.
Let's hope things move along in a reasonable range.
We need lots of sunshine to dry things out,
It'll make things grow as well, there is no doubt!

We must give credit where credit is due.
The beautiful weather comes from "you know who?"
Jesus Christ who watches over us from above.
Along with all His gifts, He sends undying love!

It's true, I place all my faith in Him,
And He doesn't leave me to "sink or swim."
What ever I have needed, He has always provided.
I'm sure that He'll help me survive in this world that's so divided!

I'm reaching out to all my friends, they're really everywhere.
Please join me in giving thanks by saying a sincere prayer,
That Jesus will be watching over the important coming election,
And will lead us all to do what's right in making our selection!

Why We Need Him

Happy is my soul when all is right with God.
I've had my talk with Jesus and got his welcome nod.
I'm ready now to begin my day and see what comes my way.
I know that there are lots of folks that I can help today!

I feel someone is calling me from somewhere real nearby.
It may be that I can be some help at least I want to try.
God works through us and helps us take the call.
He doesn't seem to mind a bit if we get credit for it all!

But first of all I must identify the needy one.
All lines are open now as I listen for the phone.
I pray the Lord will lead them to my door,
Or lead me to a place where I'm needed even more!

I keep thinking how good the Lord has been to me.
When I count my blessings I'm as rich as I can be.
My greatest wealth comes from all the folks I know.
I wouldn't trade a single friend for Warren Buffett's dough!

Our nation finds itself today in one big unwelcome bind.
Our leaders can't see eye to eye, it's as if they're flying blind.
Each one has a different view, they've all become real flighty.
So many have deserted our Leader Supreme, the Lord God Almighty!

Now most people will admit that the one God in Heaven started it all.
He's still the Father of all mankind and would never let us fall,
But He must be included when we're making our future plans,
That's what makes our nation different from all the other lands!

Will The Christmas Season Lift Our Spirits?

Our country is going through hard times, but Christmas brings some cheer.
There are some in government who care less and make it very clear,
That they don't care who suffers most as long as they get theirs,
And that's why I am praying hard for help from that Man I know upstairs!

We take great pride in keeping our faith and politics very much apart,
But it's very sad that when we push aside our faith we push aside the heart,
And politics becomes a bitter battleground where souls are put on sale.
The needy can't afford to buy those tickets on the "gravy train" to hell!

What can you say to these folks who say that they are on your side.
I've lost a lot of respect for those whose record shows they've lied.
It doesn't seem to bother them as they are bought and sold,
They like to play the game of "gotcha" since they have all the gold!

Now I do have firm beliefs especially of right and wrong.
I think that everyone should have a chance to sing a happy song.
We all are part of what is truly the greatest land on earth,
And we have been a favored group since our Savior's birth!

How do we let Jesus know that we have that special need?
I'm sure that He is well aware that so many are driven by greed.
Although we are quite equal in that Jesus loves us all,
He is saddened when He finds that so many just won't play ball!

It's sad to see our country have troubles such as these,
Where one side favors only those who they would like to please,
While there are some who work all day and get their pay in crumbs,
Makes me think that those who are so well off are just a bunch of bums!

October 6.

Will We Follow Jesus

I feel compelled to call on Jesus to help those folks in need.
They're like the hungry birds who starve when there is no feed.
We who have more than our fair share must help our fellow man.
Jesus will smile and bless us all who lend a helping hand!

There are many wealthy folks today who will not spare a dime.
They are so tight they squeak if walking and won't tell you the time.
Somehow I think they feel they're smart and they look down on you.
They can't help feel that you are poor and they are the chosen few!

If Jesus was here on earth today he might be homeless like some,
Looking for a warm place to sleep, not like our Heavenly Home.
We see them every day as they migrate about our town,
Looking for a place to lay their precious few possessions down!

All of us must do our part to help our Nation out.
We must join hands and share the load and let there be no doubt,
Rich or poor, we all must help we all can surely see the need,
But some will merely sit idly by as they're overcome with greed!

The only way that we can survive is for all to do our part.
We must be willing to pitch right in and work with all our heart.
Americans have always had the will to defeat our many foes.
Let's all show that we're up to the task as our economy grows!

As I've said so many times and in so many different ways,
We'll never go anywhere unless Jesus is leading the way.
I know full well that there are many with a very different view.
Are you going to turn your back on Jesus, the OneWho does love you!

Birthdate of my #2 Son, Andrew Lewis Shepherd, 1959

Will We Let The Devil Make Us Do It

We have the finest country in the world but something is amiss.
We kick Jesus out of schools but let the devil rant and hiss.
Jesus resisted the devil at every turn, but we don't seem to care.
Too many people buy the devil's wares, you can find them everywhere!

It seems our leaders feel that they can't mention Jesus' name.
This Man who gave His life for all of us is forced to share the blame,
While anything the devil touts is ablaze in neon lights
And you can find your choice of "sin" dressed in scanty tights!

We all must face this paradox but there is something we can do.
We must resist the devils pitch it's not for me and you.
We must let everybody know that Jesus is our friend
For He is the only one who can help us help our country mend!

The problems that we face today are no different than those of yore.
Though our country is awash in wealth there's poverty outside the door.
Some folks are living on the street and have no place to go,
And yet those folks who've got it made, they like the status-quo!

When our government helps the poor, it's known as the welfare state.
When the wealthy agree to share their wealth they rule the "ship of state"!
Opinions differ on every side of just what the government role should be.
If truth be known we'd be much better off if left up to you and me!

We must be sure that those we elect know that Jesus is their friend.
Democracy demands an open door so that everyone can come in,
But we must always be aware of the devil and his plan,
He wants to rule the entire world and he's started in Iran!

October 8.

Will You Be My Friend

Someone somewhere needs a friend do you think you could be the one?
Are you the one who fills that need or are you also all alone,
Just waiting for that someone to come along and help to fill that need,
And prove once more the old adage that a friend in need is a friend indeed!

Everybody needs someone who will listen to their complaint.
It could be another lonesome soul, doesn't have to be a saint.
When two lonesome souls become a pair, friendship has begun.
No longer can that friend in need be called the lonesome one!

Too many people in our world have no one on their side.
They exist by talking to themselves their lives are a lonely ride.
When they can't find the answer to their prayer they don't know where to turn.
They turn inward to escape with no further chance to learn!

It's hard to be a lonesome dove a nest is built for two.
When God created the human race He knew what He must do.
He knew that everyone needs someone to be their constant mate,
So He fashioned Adam from the dust and Eve to be his date!

Now I don't mean to be facetious but that's the way it all began.
The entire human race evolved from that lonesome man.
This means that all of us are "kin" and should be glad to be,
A cousin and a friend indeed to everyone else we see!

We all must help our fellowman to be the best he can,
For by helping him we help ourselves and that is just God's plan.
Don't fail to act, but do your part to help the world endure.
You see, we all share Adam's DNA and it is absolutely pure!

October 9.

Thank You Lord For All Your Help

Most big problems in my life were not really meant to be.
They occurred because my decisions were mostly made by me.
Too often I failed to ask the Lord to give me His advice.
Those self made plans of mine did not always turn out nice!

God gave to each of us the power of self will,
But He has helped me my entire life and He helps me still.
It's up to us to ask for help, we do that when we pray.
If you have important decisions to make get on your knees today!

God likes for us to talk with Him and that's one thing we must obey.
He likes to know how we are doing and that everything's okay.
Take every opportunity that you have to let Him hear from you.
Just get down on your knees and pray, it's the proper thing to do!

The greatest role model we could have is Jesus Christ, our friend.
He likes for us to be like Him and follow Him 'til the end.
The transition to our heavenly life will not be so hard to do,
If we have lived the kind of life that Jesus wants us to!

Throughout our lifetime here on earth we're hard at work each day.
Too often we don't take the time to hear what Jesus has to say.
We're so busy on our own just doing what we think is best.
What "we" think is best may not be good enough to pass His final test!

We don't hesitate to contact "Google" when we're seeking some advice,
And there's certainly nothing wrong with that, but it may not suffice.
So why not deal directly with the greatest source of all?
Your password is simply "Jesus" and He will always answer your call!

October 10.

Writing Poetry Helps My Disposition

I'm never at a loss for words my mind is never blank.
I know that I owe someone and it's Jesus that I thank.
I pray to Him each morning, He helps me start my day
And when I call on Him He tells me what to say!

I think my poems are precious for they are not mine alone.
When I am writing I hear His voice and it's not on the phone.
That's how I know that He's nearby I even feel His touch.
I can see Him standing there, for me He's done so much!

I love to read my poetry to others, to tell them how I feel,
And to let them know that God loves them, that His love is real.
He helps me think of the words to use to get my point across.
Although I sign my name below I know that He's the Boss!

I hark back into the golden days when I was just a kid.
Jesus watched over me even then, He knew just what I did.
When I said my prayers at night He let me understand
That anytime when I felt alone He would take my hand!

I do not apologize for being Christian through and through,
But other people get involved and try to tell us what to do.
That's what's known as politics and it should play no part.
Just put politics aside and let Jesus guide your heart!

I love Jesus with all my heart and I love my country too.
They are both important to my wellbeing and to each I must be true.
We must never mix them up, that's not the thing to do.
A knee bent at the foot of the Cross I salute the red, white and blue!

X Is No Sub For Christ

Christ died upon a cross, that much we know is true,
So don't use the cross in Christmas no matter what you do.
That word you see spelled Xmas eliminates Christ you know.
That X is nothing but a cross and we shouldn't use it so!

The name of Christ in Christmas is there to honor Him.
It's not there by happenstance and certainly not a whim.
When you meet Christ in person, please don't call Him X.
Just call Him Jesus, that's His name, so he won't be perplexed!

There are those in our world today who don't honor Christ as King.
You'll find that they use the X for Christ in almost everything.
Don't be surprised, it's nationwide, you'll see it everywhere.
Xmas gifts on Xmas trees on Xmas Eve, even Xmas day it's there!

A real big X took Christ away two thousand years ago.
But God our Father brought Him back because He loved us so.
We must never again let the X erase Christ without a fight.
Christmas gifts on Christmas trees on Christmas Day that's what's right!

Wonder who started that X in Christmas thing anyway.
Was there not enough time to write out Christmas on Christmas day?
Whoever it was who suggested it should really be ashamed,
And since we don't know who that who was they'll have to go unnamed!

Let's all let folks know our feelings about X in our Christmas day.
Christmas season is near and we'll be seeing the X used Xmas way.
With all the schooling that we've had, we certainly know how to spell.
Please join me now in a worldwide move to send that X to hell!

October 12.

Yawn Away

Never yawn in someone's face it's not the proper thing to do.
Boredom is so hard to mask they'll think much less of you.
Don't be surprised that if you yawn then they will do the same.
It is catching, that's for sure, it's really not a game!

It you're talking to a friend and they yawn right in your face,
Just yawn yourself, it won't be thought of as a big disgrace.
One yawn triggers another it's so hard to hold them back.
Right away you're yawning again so please try to use some tact!

Yawning is so catching that you can easily bring one on.
Just think, right now, about a yawn….I hope you are alone.
You'll be yawning before you know it, and it helps to also sigh,
For sighing helps you to take in air and you can do it if you try!

There's just something about yawning that's an impulse to us all.
Human nature being what it is, we all have too much gall.
Some folks yawn to show contempt and then just walk away.
They're the kind who wouldn't bother to give you even the time of day!

I think you'll be yawning even before you finish reading this,
The impulse should be working now it's sometimes hard to miss.
A good yawn will help you clear the cobwebs from your brain you see,
And if I happen to be talking to you, it won't bother me!

I've been yawned upon by almost everyone I know.
Some of them do open wide and put on quite a show.
Most of the times I just yawn right back since that's okay to do,
And after all is said and done a great big yawn is always good for you!

October 13.

Yes We Do Have Options

Do you know what each pill is for, those that you take each day?
I'm happy that someone knows the score and knows that I'm okay.
My doctor tells me what to take, how many and even when.
If it wasn't for his good advice I wouldn't know where to begin!

We're all victims of our own neglect, beset with many ills.
That's why it's necessary for us now to take a lot of pills.
Right now our nation's in a fight, to set a steady course.
Medical care for everyone, with government as the source!

We hear opinions from everyone, there is a great debate.
Let's trust that all can come to terms, and right the "ship of state."
There are too many, though, who do not see the need,
And many more who want their share, motivated by greed!

There have been so many unfair tales, no truth to them at all.
It's sometimes hard to know what to think, or even who to call,
To get the full unvarnished truth right from the horse's mouth,
That will prove good for everyone, from east to west or north to south!

There is One I'm sure who's listening, that we don't hear about.
It's ironic that He who made us all is left completely out.
I'm not ashamed and will hereby ask, what's best for me and you,
But here's the question we "all" should ask, "What would Jesus do?"

October 14.

You **_CAN_** *Believe This*

Today is the day we're supposed to die, I'm going to sit and wait.
The question I have heard no answer for is "How did they know the date?"
There are 525,600 minutes in each year, so "How did they know the time?"
These calculations are so ridiculous it's hard to make them rhyme!

There is a reason that we're not told the date that we will die.
God created the entire universe including us, I mean you and I.
To let us know how we should live He gave us a set of rules.
Should we choose not to follow Him then we're a bunch of fools!

Before Jesus was born on earth, God's people followed the Old Testament.
Those Saints who sat at Jesus' feet and then wrote the New Testament
Were privileged to know God as a man and learned what they must do
To tell the story of God's Love, to all the world as Jesus asked them to!

They were not told so did not record the date when the world would end.
The Bible tells us chapter and verse how to live and worship our Dearest Friend.
It's up to each of us to follow His teachings and not to look for clues
That tell us when our time on earth is up and it's time to pay our dues!

Mankind has had its share of brilliant people in all aspects of life here below.
They have unlocked almost all the secrets that God wants us to know,
But nowhere has anyone been able to calculate when the world would end,
And those folks who claim they know the date are whistling in the wind!

Although we will not know the date we can prepare in advance.
Just be sure that Jesus knows that you believe in Him, so why take a chance.
Let Him know each passing day that you'll be ready when your time comes,
To join the streams of Christian believers travelling to our Heavenly Homes!

Columbus Day

October 15.

You Can Count On Jesus

Jesus died a horrible death to save me from my sin.
I think of that each time I pray, it helps me to begin.
No one could save Him from that fate, that's truly why He was born.
Imagine the joy His followers felt on that glorious Easter morn!

The moment Jesus died upon the Cross His Soul arrived in Heaven.
His followers didn't know it then, but their sins would be forgiven.
When He reappeared outside the tomb they all were filled with joy.
They gathered around to worship Him, His presence to enjoy!

Jesus wants us all to follow Him to Heaven when we die.
That's why God established it, that rest home in the sky.
When we go we'll go to stay not just a lifetime or a day,
But for all eternity which we ask of Jesus when we pray!

We must not be afraid to die for it's true we all must go.
We should spend our life preparing on earth down here below,
But we are too busy with other things, no time to say our prayers.
We all must bow and call on Jesus to help us climb those stairs!

To think that I might not go to Heaven is something I can't abide.
I try to do my best each day knowing Jesus is by my side.
With His help and with His Love, I know I'll make it there.
Jesus wants to save us all, He has so much Love to share!

Satan comes to see me every day he surely will never give in.
He wants to win my very soul, and urges me to sin,
But Jesus has a better choice and drives the devil away.
I'm glad that I did not forget to say my prayers today!

You Cannot Hide From Jesus

You cannot hide from Jesus He's with you night and day.
He may not make his presence known but He'll hear you when you pray.
He comes to visit here on earth to check on you and me
To be sure we're getting prepared and know the way to eternity!

Why would you want to hide from Him, He wants to be your friend.
He wants us all to have the tools to overcome our tendency to sin.
There's nothing new about the worldly sins, but we are weak you know,
And sometimes let the devil's forces lead us where we should not go!

Our Moms and Dads thought we were perfect and often told us so,
But there were things we hid from them, they didn't need to know.
Now they're gone and we're alone and we must bear the blame.
Those things that we were hiding come into view, we must bear the shame!

Jesus never hides from us when we are seeking Him.
He wants us to stay afloat if it's a case of sink or swim.
He spends a lot of time and effort to help the poor and needy,
And that's where He comes in contact with the rich who are so greedy!

Jesus wants us all to be happy here and so He lends a helping hand.
He wants us all to get proper credit for leading our precious land,
But we must never forget our daily thanks for blessings that we share,
To let Jesus know that we're among those many folks who care!

This world of ours is not perfect we all know that for sure.
God created it that way so the human race could help to make it pure.
We've learned a lot and made some gains but there is still a way to go.
It's obvious that we'll never know it all and some things we'll never know!

You Can't Go Wrong

Don't be disappointed when things don't go your way.
God may have a better plan for you to use today.
You never know what lies ahead so always be prepared.
You can bet you'll ne'er forget those moments that you've shared!

As you move through life each day let Jesus be your guide.
Let Him tell you where to go and what to do beside.
He will lead you to the places He feels that you should go.
You'll be glad you followed Him for He'll be there also!

As your life unfolds before your very eyes,
Many of the things you see will be a big surprise.
You'll see a lot of things you'd miss if you didn't follow Him.
If there's a place you'd like to go, He'll grant your slightest whim!

Jesus wants each one of us to have a happy life.
That's why He spends so much time protecting us from strife.
And it's true that for all the time He spends He does not set a fee.
He'd be glad to spend His entire day and it would be for free!

If today you're in a bind and cannot find your way,
Stop what you're doing, hold the fort, bet you forgot to pray.
Ask Jesus to come and lead the way, to tell you where to go.
He'll be there before you know then you can start the show!

Find some way you can be assured that Jesus is at hand,
For He knows the way so well into the "Promised Land."
Just keep Him always in your heart He'll always be nearby,
And you can be quite sure that He will never say goodbye!

October 18.

Your Soul Is Everlasting

It's hard for us to see the light and so many don't believe.
We may need a wake-up call, our reluctance to relieve.
There's nothing that will get your attention like seeing someone die,
Then you begin to see the light as you look up to the sky!

If you're one of those who don't believe, I pray for you today.
I hope that somewhere down the road you'll have the yen to pray.
When you make contact with the Lord, He'll open up your eyes.
When you meet Him face to face it will be a wonderful surprise!

I feel so sorry for those who don't believe, I pray for them each day.
I know that Jesus has them on His list and wants to hear them pray,
But if you don't believe you don't pray for you think they're empty words.
Who do you think created beautiful flowers and the singing of the birds?

Believe it or not but every human has a soul and it belongs to God.
That soul of yours will never die, to do so would be quite odd.
When you die your soul returns to Him and He decides your case.
This might be the very first time that you meet Him face to face!

The Heavenly Court is full of wandering souls who are in a daze.
They didn't believe there was a God and so never offered praise.
God hates to lose a single soul for He created all of them.
He will give every soul, every chance, to finally believe in Him!

Don't make it hard for God to save your soul, for He can you know.
He'd like for you to believe in Him while you are still down here below.
Just look around and see what He has done to make our life worthwhile.
He'd love for everyone to accept Him, just like a little child!

October 19.

This Is How I See It

America, I regret, is no longer the land where we are free.
Our freedom died in Washington yesterday, we're in for misery.
A group of men, racists all, who sit in their Senate seat,
Let proposals by our President, yes, he's black, go down in sad defeat!

They've rigged the system so it's unfair, not as it's supposed to be.
There's no one up in Washington now who represents you and me.
When two and two no longer equal four but now it equals five.
There is no way that such a system will let the USA survive!

I yearn for the olden days of yore when stalwarts were the norm.
Men of integrity who had a conscience, from them both parties formed.
They didn't vote according to "who paid me the most,"
But "what can I do to help my people" was no idle boast!

I know there are many among you who will cheer what's going on.
I hope that we never see the day when our "right to vote" is gone.
I was flying a bomber in combat before I was old enough to vote.
The chances of me ever being denied that right, I hope are very remote!

There are moves afoot right now that would take away some rights
From people who have voted for many years who may now have to fight.
We're regressing, not progressing, as a country where once we were free,
If you don't have the money to pay your way then you may cease to be!

It's not like it used to be when we could trust the "powers that be."
They have agendas all their own with no interest in you and me.
As long as they can do just as they please, it won't be long "pray tell."
They will favor those who pay while the rest of us can just go to hell!

Your Soul Will Never Die

No one ever dies alone for Jesus will be there too.
He exists in every soul it doesn't matter who.
Throughout our lives He's watching over our precious soul,
When Jesus died upon the cross that was His lofty goal!

God loves every soul He makes and Jesus moves there-in,
Everybody has a "heart" and "soul," it's there when we begin.
The "heart" provides the power and the "soul" provides the glory,
These two when working together weave a wonderful true story!

We're very conscious of our heart we feel its constant beat.
We must think more about our soul, it's what makes us complete.
I like to look at it this way and I think about it every day,
At each heart beat our soul says Amen, a wonderful way to pray!

The "heart" and "soul" could not exist without the "body" too.
There are some folks who live and love for "body" and "soul", those two,
It seems these folks just cast their "heart" aside and let the devil in.
While he's there he'll be promoting every kind of sin!

We know the devil was smiling while he watched Jesus on the cross,
But watching too from Heaven above was God who's still the boss.
The "souls" in hell are there by choice, they let their "body" rule.
Their "body" overruled their "heart" and became the devil's tool!

The war to control our very "soul" is fought in every way.
We're all involved and must do our part to help Jesus every day.
Put on the armor that God provides to shield yourself from sin,
Fight with all your "heart" and "body," your "soul" will shout "Amen!"

October 21.

You've Still Got Time

When you look back into your life do you feel satisfied?
Have you done all the things you hoped to do before you died?
If not, don't give up hope, you've still got time you know
To do a lot of things you missed before you have to go!

Sit down right now and make a list of things you want to do.
The list may be longer than you thought but that is up to you.
To have some goals you want to reach will keep you occupied.
You'll be proud not only of the things you did but of all that you tried!

Too many folks retire too early to their "golden rocking chair."
They quit thinking of things to do and just sit and rock and stare.
They're content to dream of the past with no plans for what's ahead.
Many have no cause for living and keep wishing they were dead!

Wake up my friend today is the start of the rest of your life on earth.
Think of it in positive terms just like it's your second birth.
Your brain is full of expertise in all those things you've stored away.
Just wipe away the cobwebs and start a new career today!

In my life there were times when I thought that I was through.
I had the feeling that I was too old to think of something new,
But then I found out how wrong I was, your age is not the key,
That unlocks the door that leads to success and victory!

Don't look at the life that you have left in terms of what to do.
Get busy working on that list, you know, the one that's up to you.
Don't ever give up, don't ever quit, you're nowhere near the end.
Look forward to tomorrow and start out fresh my friend!

That's What Friends Are For

If you could contact all your friends and talk to them today,
What would you want to tell them, what do you think you'd say?
Would it be about how much you love them, how much you care,
And how much you hope to see them soon since there's so much to share!

What would you do without your friends, would life be the same?
If you lost your address book, could you remember their name?
As we age we may sometimes forget so it's always better to stay in touch.
That way we'll always remember those friends, the ones we love so much!

Tom Edison and Alex Bell helped put our voice on line.
I can talk with my friends around the world and hear them all just fine.
Bill Gates and Steve Jobs brought us a means to store our valued brain.
E-mail helps us spread our intellect so that it may long remain!

I put my thoughts out on the air they're picked up by my friends.
My inbox often gets overloaded with junk the spammer sends.
I try to be judicious and send things they like to hear.
My poems all have a meaning and I think are pleasing to the ear!

I've learned a lot from all my friends and that's why I'm so smart.
They've nurtured me all these years and loved me with all their heart.
Had I not had all those good friends, I'd still be in second grade.
You see it's true that I'm a product of all those friends I've made!

I think that most folks will agree that what you see is what you get.
In life that's true to some extent, but you can change it yet.
To make things better for you today, just call and say hello.
Tell your friend that you love them and just wanted them to know!

October 23.

The Battle

I gave my heart to Jesus for He's my dearest friend.
I know that He will keep me from getting lost in sin.
There are temptations still of course everywhere I look,
But I ne'er forget He's there to help, my name is in His book!

If you are wondering what to do, have choices you must make,
There's someone there to help you decide which road you ought to take.
Just place your case in Jesus' hands and leave it up to Him.
Get on your knees and pray or even sing your favorite hymn!

Some folks find it hard to believe that Jesus came to save.
They continually seek proof even tho' it was His life He gave.
Their faith isn't strong enough to think He died for them.
Lord please help me to help them to place their faith in Him!

In our world today it should be obvious for all to see,
There are forces at work in order to destroy Christianity.
Led by the devil himself who openly promises treasures
And sweetens his rewards with visions of virgins for pleasures!

These servants of satan are obsessed with sadistic acts of terror.
Any grievous havoc they can wreak on Christians is what they are for.
These agents of pending doom are giving their lives in vain.
Their suicide acts are tickets to hell with nothing at all to gain!

Don't be afraid or ashamed to place your faith in Jesus.
He's the one who sacrificed His life and died on the cross for us,
And he's the one who at our death will lead us all to glory.
Because of Him and who He is servants of satan will continue to worry!

October 24.

The Bee And The Butterfly

The butterfly was floating on the breeze and heard a buzzing sound.
He had no idea where it came from so began to look around.
As he was "flitting" all about he passed right by a hive.
That's where the buzzing sound came from, it really seemed alive!

The butterfly now headed for a rose bush that he saw nearby.
The roses on that bush were so beautiful it made him want to cry.
He moved around from rose to rose gathering pollen with his feet.
Never had he found a bush where the petals were so sweet!

As he moved from rose to rose he heard that buzzing sound again.
He started looking all around and then thought, could it be the wind?
It wasn't long before he found the source, it was a beautiful sight.
It was a magnificent, well built, female bee out on an early morning flight.

Bro' butterfly got all excited by her sexy look and almost lost his cool.
His beautiful patterned wings were flapping like he was some kind of fool.
He was balanced atop a beautiful rose when she lit on one nearby.
Now he became so overcome that he couldn't even fly!

Well, lady bee was young and sweet and had some work to do.
Gathering nectar was easy work, but for her was quite new.
She became aware however that bro' butterfly had given her the eye,
And soon he worked up courage enough for him to tell her "Hi"!

Bro' butterfly was smart enough to know that someday she might be queen.
He also knew that their blood lines did not match they had a different gene.
Now put all differences aside, as love won out, it was a sight to see,
When bro' butterfly to lady bee said, "Would you my honey be"?

The Bible Is Our Source

Jesus wants to save your soul but you must do your part.
You have to share with Him the love that's in your heart.
There is no better time than now to let Him know your plan.
He'll give you all the tools you need to help your fellow man!

When you look back into your life was there someone special there
Who always put your mind at ease and let you know they care?
You never forget those kinds of folks, you think of them each day.
These are the folks you missed the most when they passed away!

You must use the things you've learned from those folks that you admire.
When you add your voice to theirs you have joined the choir,
And soon sweet music fills the air as the choir begins to sing.
That's how you can do your part, how you can do your thing!

The Bible tells the entire story that God wants us to know.
He sent Jesus to teach us what it means and to give His life also
To save the entire human race if we believe in Him.
God and Jesus, what a team, we must believe in Them!

Those friends of Jesus, now known as Saints, they were a special breed.
They tried to do what Jesus taught, to help all those in need.
They preached and wrote about those things they learned from Him.
The New Testament provides the source where we can learn from Them!

There's something new we learn each day we'll never know it all.
If we should question what it means we know who we can call,
And we don't have to use the telephone we merely say "hello,"
For Jesus is always ready and willing to tell us what we need to know!

The Book

Dedicated to American Bible Society

Something bothers me today don't know what it can be.
I've racked my brain to find a cause but there's nothing I can see.
This leaves me in a doubtful mood with worries on my mind.
That's not healthy for my soul, the answer I must find!

I'm waiting now with my head bowed for Jesus to arrive.
When I'm in need I call on Him, He helps me to survive.
He always brings with Him a Book, it's filled with helpful hints.
It's a Book that we all need, it makes a lot of sense!

I hope that you will read this Book it's worth its weight in gold.
The stories that we find there-in are true and always bold.
They tell us all we need to know to make our lives worthwhile.
When we read of Jesus' birth it causes us to smile!

Just thinking now about this Book has put my mind at ease,
For Jesus moved into my heart and gave my soul a squeeze.
I know that you have felt His love He gives it free to all,
And Jesus always carries that Book, it's full of protocol!

Down through the ages the Saints have all read this Book of love.
It's full of history of the past with lessons from above.
The most read book in all the world this one of which I write,
In any language, any tongue, in Braille for those who've lost their sight!

I'm feeling better now at last my worries all are gone.
My doubtful mood received a lift for now I'm not alone.
Jesus came and brought His Book, the "Bible" don't you see
With these words, "This Book, Jacob, was written for you and Me!"

October 26.

The Earth In All Its Grandeur
Is Not Like Heaven

They say beauty is in the eye of the beholder and that's what it's for.
Beauty just for beauty's sake perhaps we might just ignore.
The dawning of a brand new day is beauty that all should see,
But the beautiful rays from a setting sun are first in popularity!

The beauty of my first born baby is something that I'll never forget.
I look for beauty in everything but nature has been my best bet.
There's beauty in all of God's creations but you have to look
And you won't find what you're looking for in any kind of book!

Jesus sent us flowers and rainbows for He loves the beautiful things.
That's why He made sure that the butterfly had those pretty wings.
My favorite flower is the rose which He made so all could see
Beauty for the eyes fragrance for the nose, pleasing to you and me!

Architects are trained to see the beauty in a simple curve,
But some of their creations surely must take a lot of nerve.
Yet all of us love to live where we are surrounded by beautiful homes.
We're so enamored by some like Monticello that have beautiful domes!

The earth was created with beauty in mind there is no longer doubt.
We have ravaged the countryside, there's still beauty, just look about.
For trees it's Palms and Weeping Willows and Dogwoods, but more,
The Oak the Elm the stately Pine the Walnut, Chestnut and Sycamore!

Some folks are heard to say that "Beauty is only skin deep,"
Then say, "but ugly is to the bone", and that makes us weep,
For we ourselves are housed in one of those, bodies if you please.
We are made in God's image, so thank Him while on your knees!

The Holy Trinity Is At Work

You cannot see Him but I assure you that He is there.
You see, my friend, the Holy Spirit is always everywhere.
He watches over all of us even when we sleep at night,
Just making sure that everything around us is perfectly alright!

You need not worry every night when you lay down your head.
The Holy Spirit is standing by in fact He's right beside your bed.
He'll be there to take your soul if you should die before you wake,
To guide you home to Heaven which He'll do for Jesus' sake!

The Holy Spirit does not intrude you never know He's there,
But you should thank Him when you pray for keeping you in His care.
You cannot hide from the Holy Spirit, no matter how hard you try.
That's why you always feel so ashamed when you tell a lie!

Every decision you make in life is either right or wrong.
The tendency to take the "easy" way is always very strong,
But that's not always the Christian thing that we should really do,
So just call on the Holy Spirit for He'll love advising you!

Jesus and the Holy Spirit are both as busy as they can be.
They stay in constant contact of course and their help is always free,
So if you feel that you need some Divine help just bow your head and pray
And you can rest assured that they will help to make your day!

I'm glad to know that I'm not alone as I face another day.
I'm not ashamed to call for help because I really love to pray.
I know that I can count on them for I know they're always there.
It's true that God so loved the world that He is always everywhere!

October 28.

The Man Upstairs

Today is just another day,
Or that is just what some folks say,
But for me today's a perfect gem.
That's because it comes from Him!

By Him I mean the Man Upstairs,
The one who answers all our prayers.
He's the one who makes our life worthwhile.
I've loved Him since I was just a child!

From Him I get such good advice.
I never have to ask Him twice.
Everything that comes from Him is free.
I'm so glad that He loves me!

I don't believe that I've ever been
In any place completely free of sin,
But I always walked upright and full of pride,
Because He was always there, by my side!

There have been times too when I was down and out.
Things could get real bad without a doubt.
Without Him there to pull me through,
I don't know now what I would do!

So if you think today is just another day,
With nothing exciting coming your way,
Call on Him and ask His advice,
He'll soon be there to treat you nice!

October 29.

The Master Of The Universe

When you're feeling down and out do you know where to turn?
As you seek to find your way you'll find there's much to learn.
There are places you can go and help is right nearby.
Just step outside and say "Hello Jesus" and look up to the sky!

"That sounds too simple" I know you'll say "for Jesus is far away."
Now that is where you're wrong my friend, He's nearby every day.
You will not see Him in the flesh but you can be sure He's there.
He's the Master of the Universe and He is truly everywhere!

When you speak to Him each day just tell Him what you need.
You don't have to get real fancy and you don't have to plead,
For Jesus wants us all to enjoy life and wants to help us out.
He's always listening for your call and you won't have to shout!

When you talk with Jesus just talk like you would with me.
Your reverence for His Heavenly Crown will show through instantly.
He'll understand that you're nervous and soon put you at ease.
He's a down to earth type friendly guy who really wants to please!

So if you're really down and out and truly want His advice,
Don't be afraid or bashful, but of course always be real nice.
Let Him know right off the bat you love Him, His love for you is pure.
When He learns you're down and out His help you will secure!

It's not real costly, for the help Jesus gives is free.
He will place His Hands upon your head when you're on your knee.
No longer will you be down and out and you can say a prayer.
Thank You Jesus for all Your help I'm so glad that You are there!

The Old And The New

There is a new year coming soon and not too soon you see.
The year gone by has not been fun, 'twas full of misery.
So many folks have lost their jobs and don't know where to turn.
Good jobs are needed in our land so folks can live by what they earn!

Our leaders spent the entire year debating health-care reform.
Republicans would not vote for change, the no vote became their norm!
Our new Congress set the pace with the majority on their side.
The Healthcare Bill which has been passed is one we view with pride!

Despite success we still must press, we can't sit back and crow.
The final Bill will be coming soon, but has a way to go.
The opposition continues buying votes to try to run the show.
They hope their purchases will maintain the dreaded status-quo!

Democrats who voted against the efforts to cover all,
Should lose their seat and be sent back home for failing to play fair ball.
Once the Bill is signed and the law is actively in force,
Jobs for everyone with fair pay, is next in line of course!

There are plenty of things across our land that really should be done.
Grab the horns of that old bull and give jobs to everyone.
The markets are just waiting for the opportunity to rise.
If banks will lend, folks will borrow to do something needed and wise!

Don't sit around and cogitate and wait for someone else to act.
Hop on the bandwagon as it builds up steam to move down the track.
It's certainly true as has been said, that "good things come and go."
Don't be the one that's left behind for acting much too slow!

October 31.

All Saints Day

Today is "All Saints Day" and I think of the Apostles band.
Twelve loyal, worthy men of God who gave Jesus a helping hand.
They weren't the only Saints of course there have been quite a few.
I've known a few quite well myself and I know that you have too!

What does it take to be a Saint, what do you have to do?
I guess there is no set of rules, but to Jesus you must be true.
A Saint is anyone who believes in God and helps his fellow man
In any way to save his soul and lends a helping hand!

I like to think of my Mom in Saintly terms, at least to me she was.
She never said an unkind word of anyone and it was because
She believed that everyone was good if given half a chance.
Almost everyone could be a Saint in a given circumstance!

Think of all your friends today and what they've done for you.
They do not "have" to be your friend it's something they want to do.
That makes them Saintly in a way and in a way they were
Like those friends of Jesus who were Saints and who we all revere!

I think that Jesus considers us all as Saints and wants us all to be
His helper among our fellow man to help save every soul you see.
The twelve Apostles, Saints indeed, helped Jesus spread the word.
For many people of that time it was the only way they would have heard!

When we look about us in today's world we ask "Where are the Saints?"
When it comes to helping others there are few cans and many "can'ts."
So on this "All Saints Day" is there something special that we can do?
Say a special prayer of "Thankfulness" to Jesus for all He's done for you!

Halloween

Contents *November*

1. Election Day Is Near 329

2. Memories Are Valuable..330

3. Look Forward To Tomorrow Let Bygones Fade Away 331

4. Just What Do You Believe? 332

5. Jesus Christ of Heaven...333

6. Is Anybody Listening...334

7. He Is Our Friend Indeed 335

8. Get On With It 336

9. Friends 337

10. A Special Day, A Special Way 338

11. Veteran's Day 339

12. Equivocation...340

13. Enjoy Every Day 341

14. Our Frame Of Mind 342

15. Education Is The Tree From Which All Knowledge Grows 343

16. Don't Worry, Don't Hurry, Time Is On Your Side......................................344

17. Don't Worry About It...345

18. Don't Wait, Don't Hesitate, You Don't Know The Date.............................346

19. Don't Be Discouraged..347

20. Beyond The Pearly Gates 348

21. Can Jesus Always Count On You? 349

22. Building Your Home In Heaven 350

23. Brotherhood..351

24. Brother Can You Share?..352

25. Be True To Yourself..353

26. Attitude..354

27. The Day Before The Day 355

28. Thanksgiving Day 356

    Thanksgiving Day 357

29. Farewell..358

30. The Truth Can Make Us Free 359

November 1.

Election Day Is Near

One week to go before we know who wins the biggest prize.
There is a real war going on right before our eyes.
We've heard so much and seen too much it won't be a surprise.
Whoever wins must show some "class" I hope they're very wise!

Politics has always been a somewhat "got'cha" game,
Some good folks and some not so bad, but we're the ones to blame.
It sometimes seems that no one in the race will play by all the rules.
I guess they think that all of us who vote are just a bunch of fools!

There's been enough unpleasantness for all of us to see,
That none of them are "squeaky clean" but dirty as can be.
Regardless of which side you're on, they're very much alike,
The stories sound similar in many ways when they're behind a mike!

Whoever wins, we must accept that they have a job to do.
They must represent both sides not just a chosen few.
They must stop playing politics and begin to govern well,
For otherwise our country will be on its way to hell!

I've been around a long long time I think I've seen it all.
Our country is much better off when Congress just plays ball.
It's known as "compromise" you see, a little "give and take."
"Half a loaf is better than no bread" is true for goodness sake!

We won't know for several years the damage that's been done.
Luckily, there will be another chance, some things will be undone.
Meantime we all can get together and still call each other friends.
We're all Americans who believe in a democracy that never ends!

Memories Are Valuable

Don't burn your bridges to the past they are a link you will need.
If you close your eyes right now you'll think of some good deed
That you either gave or you received and is a good link to the past,
Which is good to keep in mind since your life moves by so fast!

It's awfully nice to sit and reminisce about things good and bad.
It's pleasant to remember some happy times as the best we ever had.
We learned a lot from all the things we did as a part of life we love.
The kind of things we'll never forget even tho' we're in Heaven above!

Our memories form the basis for the lives we live today.
What we learned in yesteryear helps us now to make our way.
While we may not write a history book about our past, it's true,
You'll never want to forget those days because they involved you!

When you walk down memory lane put your brain in gear.
Sometimes it's hard to remember things that happened just last year.
Someone said that every moment of our past is in our brain 'til now.
To resurrect those moments is a chore but some folks do know how!

If I try hard I can remember things from very long ago.
It's evident to me that it's all there among the many things I know.
Sometimes I can't remember what I said yesterday but even then,
I can remember almost everything but just cannot remember when!

So as I say above keep all of those bridges close and intact.
You never know when you may want to bring those memories back.
As we age, our brain may want to sleep but never let it die.
If you lose those memories for sure the world will have passed you by!

November 3.

Look Forward To Tomorrow
Let Bygones Fade Away

This year is moving fast and it will soon be at an end.
That means a new year is coming and it is just around the bend.
Have you accomplished all the resolutions that you made back then.
Do you feel you're better off now than you were way back when?

Today is a good time to look back at the year that has just passed.
Let's all hope that we can improve on the year that has now past.
We're fortunate that our life unfolds slowly day by day,
Which gives us plenty of time to plan rather than to stray!

We can't start off the New Year until we complete the old.
Last New Years day the plans we made were quite bold.
There were lots of things that we all resolved to do.
Thank goodness that list we made then has dwindled to a few!

We must not begin to count our chickens until they hatch.
It's like going fishing when we don't know what we'll catch.
To be making plans in advance is a rather awesome task and chore.
Let's make sure this year is complete before we ask for more!

There's still time to wrap up those last few lingering details.
You've been able to do quite well in finding bargains at the sales.
The problem that we have is not a matter of what is needed,
The things that are still there on my list just haven't been completed!

My first resolution for the coming year is to complete my resolutions.
I put that one before all the others so that theres no confusions.
I thank Dear Jesus for guiding and protecting me all year long,
And as I start the New Year I pray He'll keep me from going wrong!

November 4.

Just What Do You Believe?

When Jesus died upon the Cross did He just disappear?
Some folks believe it's all a hoax and death is something to fear.
Does that mean I won't see Mom and Dad again, that it's all a sham?
Don't anyone ever try to tell me that, how dumb do you think I am?

Jesus comes to see me every day to find out how it's going.
He comes down, rain or shine, and even when it's snowing.
I reach out to Him each day to let Him know I'm fine.
Someday I'll sit and talk with Him and enjoy a glass of wine!

When people say they don't believe my heart always skips a beat,
For I know that person's life will always be incomplete.
If this life here on earth were all we'd ever know,
It's understandable why some folks would be very reluctant to go!

Folks who do believe in Him face their death without fear.
We all know that death will come for Jesus made that clear,
That He was preparing a place for all of us to live,
In comfort, peace and harmony, like that which only He can give!

No one can truly imagine eternity for our body would not last.
As we age we all become aware that our body declines real fast.
When we move into the Heavenly realm in the twinkling of an eye,
We become a Spirit like Jesus, but it won't happen until we die!

I hope these words don't frighten anyone, we all expect to die.
There may be some who expect to live forever so they are living a lie.
Please ask Jesus in your prayers today to save your soul from sin.
If you've been unable to say "I believe" it's not too late to begin!

November 5.

Jesus Christ of Heaven

We know more about the universe than we know about Heaven it seems.
It's awfully hard for human beings to have a lot of faith in dreams.
We do have faith in Jesus Christ and we know that He still lives.
We also know that He's in Heaven and that fact sweet comfort gives!

I love to read the Bible and all the things that Jesus said.
My favorite is the Easter story when God raised Him from the dead.
I always carry that story in my heart for He promised me the same.
He shed His blood and gave His life for me and that is why He came!

When I die and arrive in Heaven I often wonder how it will be.
Will Jesus and His Heavenly Hosts be waiting there for me?
I'm sure there are many things to learn about the protocol.
I'll just ask my friends who've gone on ahead, I'm sure they know it all!

The major thing that I'm sure about and Jesus told us that,
He has prepared a place just for me, it's a lovely habitat.
I'm sure some places here on earth are like Heaven in disguise,
But nothing can compare with Heaven that we'll see with our own eyes!

The short life that we have on earth seems long in earthly years.
As we begin using "eternal time" in Heaven we really must change gears.
Everything will assume a new dimension and that includes us too.
We must believe all that Jesus said for we know that it is true!

What can I personally do to be ready for that wonderful life ahead?
I don't know when but I know it's coming and it won't be 'til I'm dead,
So I must be ready at all times to meet Dear Jesus face to face,
For He's the One who gave His Life to save the human race!

Election Day

Is Anybody Listening

We never know when fate will strike and end our time on earth.
We know that Jesus is in charge and has been since our birth.
I learned early that Jesus loves me and He's with me every day.
He has given me a wonderful life and I thank Him when I pray!

I know that I'm a sinner and have done things I regret.
I confess my sins and ask forgiveness every chance I get.
I know my soul is in good hands and Jesus has the key.
It is to Him I owe everything for being so good to me!

I feel so sorry for anyone who says "I don't believe."
They're missing out on all of Jesus Love which they would receive.
Not that Jesus has abandoned them, He still loves us all.
He's in constant battle with the devil who has a lot of gall!

Our sins are all the devil's work, he knows that we are weak.
His sales pitch includes access to all the pleasures that we seek.
We must resist the devil's plan and follow Jesus' lead.
He'll see that we are happy and have everything we need!

There will come a time, we don't know when, our time on earth is done.
If we have followed Jesus day by day then He will be the One
Who will be waiting for us and take us by the hand
When we have crossed the bar and are headed for the Promised Land!

It makes me shudder to think of those who will never accept our Lord.
There will be some we don't see in Heaven for they never got on board.
So sad to think of anyone whose eternity will be spent in Hell,
It behooves us all to listen up and to listen well!

He Is Our Friend Indeed

Without Jesus I'd be lost, I'm glad He's there today.
It's not rare to need His help for I often lose my way.
He's always been there when I called He's never let me down.
I owe my very life to Him and I'm glad that He's around!

Jesus died so young, it is true, He was only thirty-three.
God sacrificed His Only Son for the sins of folks like me.
Every human has a soul and they also have free will.
All human souls are born in sin and without Jesus are sinful still!

Jesus offers us salvation but the devil covets our soul.
The devil offers us worldly goods for our soul, which he wants whole.
As humans we are given the choice of how to treat our soul.
Do we trade it for worldly goods or is Jesus in Heaven our goal?

Jesus suffered and died on the Cross, a young man in His prime.
He lived the only perfect life on earth and died before His time.
God loves every human soul and sent Jesus to die for them.
The greatest gift for all mankind, our sinful ways to stem!

We as humans are allowed each day to choose our way to live.
We are given access to worldly goods a share of which we should give.
The devil tries to lead us astray and fills our hearts with greed,
While Jesus gives us thankful hearts but we overlook those in need!

Get on your knees today and ask Jesus to be your guide.
Who better to lead you to Paradise, it was for you He died.
Don't trade your soul for worldly goods, be happy just to share.
When it's time for you to go to Heaven you'll be welcome there!

November 8.

Get On With It

Why can't I do what others can when I have set a goal?
I know you've heard it said before, can't do it to "save my soul."
The major reason that we all fail is because we do not try.
Procrastination blocks the road, "we'll do it by and by!"

That "project" sits upon the shelf and months and months pass by.
We have so many other things to do that we just let it lie.
We think, "Oh well, it can wait, I've got better things to do."
We let good ideas gather dust while we look for something new!

We often feel that we need to act and reach out for that goal.
That "project" sitting on the shelf it's worth its weight in gold,
It's just a little "project" and to solve it would be a cinch,
Down comes the "project" from the shelf and now it's on the bench!

In looking over the "project" now you see some things you missed.
As you examine it in more detail you begin to make a list.
By the end of the day you're underway, things are moving well.
The problems are solved, you need to act, it's something that will sell!

You take the list of things you need to build the prototype.
You head to town and to the store, the idea is getting ripe.
You walk down the center aisle looking here and there,
The store is full of new ideas, they're displayed everywhere!

Very soon you come upon a sight that takes you by surprise.
. It's a very large pyramid of "stuff", you can't believe your eyes.
The sign says, "Gizmo Of The Year", the hottest thing in town.
There sits your "project" sure enough your dream comes tumbling down!

November 9.

Friends

I have to say my life's been fun.
I get along with most everyone.
My friends have helped by being there,
They always let me know they care!

I've wondered how my life would be,
Without those friends who care for me.
I hate to think of my life alone
Without some friends that I could phone!

Don't think of life in terms of "worth,"
Or what you've "socked away" since birth.
All that is worthless without friends,
The kind who'll "cry" when your life ends!

You should think of friends each day,
More than just in a casual way.
Those friends are what makes life worthwhile,
And they're the ones who make you smile!

The saying goes "a friend in need is a friend indeed."
I prefer to say, "a friend indeed is a friend we need."
If you've got friends your life is blessed,
They'll keep you from feeling stressed!

Friends can help in your life today.
You can count on them when others stray.
Get on that phone, now, give them a call,
Tell them that, as a friend, they're best of all!

November 10.

A Special Day, A Special Way

Happy is the person who knows that Jesus is their friend.
They don't have to worry about when their life will end.
For they know that Jesus will be waiting to take them by the hand,
And lead them home to Heaven in the Promised Land!

There are a lot of people who don't know Jesus well at all.
They know there's something missing but don't know who to call.
Jesus loves each and everyone and wants all to follow Him.
For those who don't know Him well, we must be examples to all of them!

Don't be afraid or feel ashamed to let your allegiance to Jesus show.
The way we live our lives each day will let other people know
That Jesus is our friend indeed and we're happy that it's true.
We can live in peace and harmony as one of the chosen few!

Thanksgiving Day is coming soon, it's special in the USA.
Other places celebrate as well but in a different way.
While we are thankful every day we set one day aside
To show the whole wide world our patriotism has not died!

There are dangerous forces at work in our world today.
They are part of the devil's mighty army trying to have its way.
We can overcome these destructive forces for Jesus is on our team,
We must show the world at large that "freedom" is not just a dream!

Our nation is still evolving folks, there's still a lot to do.
We must not let the evil forces mislead the red, white and blue.
We all are patriots and we've played our part to save the USA.
We must continue to do what's right and not let it slip away!

Veteran's Day

To all our veterans on this day, God Bless you everyone.
While many fought and many died not everyone carried a gun.
There were jobs of every kind and each one must be done.
Each job as important as the next and each vet was someone's son!

Let's not forget our sister vets, there are many of them as well.
While they may not have carried a gun, all jobs in war are hell.
The jobs those brave women did was never done in vain.
Some died performing dangerous tasks their loss was no-one's gain!

What can we say about all those vets who went to hell and back?
Thank God who helped to save our nation when we were being attacked.
When we meet this Veteran's Day and offer thanks to all,
Let us not forget to praise the Lord, who did not let us fall!

The longest war we've ever faced continues to this day.
Young men and women must leave their home for battles far away.
Too many of them don't return alive and others aren't the same,
They suffer loss of limb and more, this war is not a game!

I'm one of those who still believe this war was politics.
The men in charge had never fought and placed us in a fix.
Not only have we lost too many troops we've lost our way as well.
We were not fighting in defense and the enemy got help from hell!

I did my part in World War II, it seems so long ago.
We all should have learned by now that peace is the way to go.
Intelligent leaders with gifted tongues solve problems as diplomats.
It matters not be they Republicans or faithful Democrats!

November 12.

Equivocation

Why use equivocation when you know just what to say?
I guess you'd say it's just a tool that we all use every day.
Many times it's useful when we can't make up our mind,
And sometimes too it serves us well as the best words we can find!

Sometimes its use is ambiguous when we are just not sure,
And at times it's to "beat around the bush" like a simple road detour.
If "Mama says, where've you been?" don't say, "Oh just here and there,"
She wants to know for your own good so tell her "fair and square!"

If you'd rather not commit yourself you can always equivocate.
When someone says "What've you been doing?" they want you to relate
Something about your activities so don't say, "Oh just this and that"
And if it's confidential ask them to "please keep this under your hat!"

Now I'm not one to advocate the use of equivocation,
But I find it useful myself at times in simple conversation.
And sometimes when it's over and has all been said and done,
Put two and two together and you can have some fun!

In arithmetic we learned to count with numbers, all precise,
But there are times when we equivocate like saying "once or twice."
If you say "once" that means just one and two is "twice" as much.
Numerical equivocation takes place a lot and can get you into "dutch!"

In using numbers in most cases, the difference in value is small,
But using the simplest one, "once or twice" it's largest of them all.
Keep the numbers consecutive and close, you'll see just where I've been,
Because saying "once or twice" means more than saying "nine or ten!"

November 13.

Enjoy Every Day

Today's a special day for someone, somewhere, could you be the one?
Do you have things to celebrate, some things you haven't done?
Perhaps you need to tell someone you love them, that's a lovely chore.
The older that we become in life it seems that we need that more!

Old guys and gals, like you and me, may not show our age,
But we've been around a block or two and it's time we turned the page.
Don't sit around the house all day and hope the phone will ring,
Get some good music on the "tube" and open up and sing!

You may not sound like Judy "G", but you can sing along.
Nothing brightens up our day quite like a lovely song.
No one's listening that's for sure, so who are we to care.
Maybe we can twist our hips and twirl a bit and dream we're Fred Astaire!

There are no deadlines we have to meet, all we've got is time.
The fact that we have lots of that is what makes our life sublime.
Turn the volume on the music up so we can hear it well.
Fred Astaire and Judy "G" are loud enough and we won't have to yell!

While we stay busy doing our thing and no one comes to call,
The major thing we celebrate is the fact that we're still around at all.
Our birthdays become historic dates and our families have a blast.
We "snuff" the candles, eat lots of cake and hope it's not our last!

"Oh yes, a special day" you say, for someone, I hope it never ends.
You see, even with all the fun I have I like to see my friends.
So come on by when you get the time, it sure will make my day.
We'll just sit and "chew the fat", that's special wouldn't you say?

Our Frame Of Mind

Happiness is a frame of mind it can make your day.
A sour puss does no one good it turns the folks away,
So why not put on a happy face and let folks see you smile.
Invite them in to chew the fat and visit for a while!

Things look gloomy down the road let's hope they work it out.
Both sides need to think of us and take a different route.
We the people are the ones whose ox is getting gored.
They must solve our problems by doing something all can afford!

I'm getting old, I've seen a lot, our leaders stir the pot.
They like to show how smart they are when things are getting hot.
The trouble is, we feel the heat and no one takes the blame.
They cannot get their act together and that is such a shame!

Let's face it folks our politicians have so little to lose.
They've got it made, no matter what they should be in our shoes.
Their nest is feathered, sink or swim, they never feel the pain.
They pass the laws which favor them from which they all can gain!

Our country has had its ups and downs over many years.
Too many downs and too few ups have lots of folks in tears.
Some folks bear the burdens while others eat the pie.
The rich folks feast on caviar which poor folks cannot buy!

Let's think about what makes us happy, that'll be more fun.
Let's get together with friends and enjoy the summer sun.
I've learned there's very little I can do to change the status-quo,
So I'm going to just sit and take it easy while rocking to and fro!

Education Is The Tree From Which All Knowledge Grows

Words are like children's blocks from which great poems are made.
Letters that form the structure are like an alphabet that's played
Much like a mighty organ that sends beautiful music our way.
The words bring the message and that is what makes our day!

Do you remember as a child you piled up blocks to spell a word?
You couldn't read but you spelled out words you'd never heard,
And now as you sit and search for words, they do come back again.
Everything that you ever learned is stored somewhere in your brain!

It's amazing how what you learn is something that you don't forget.
It's known as education and we never get too much, but yet
Too many young folks don't know its value and drop out of school.
They don't realize until too late that they're discarded their best tool!

My success in business hinged on being able to put words together.
Selling an idea many times was akin to trying to predict the weather.
That's when you organize your most beautiful thoughts into words,
And you make sure that everything you say isn't "just for the birds!"

What you have learned in Kindergarten or at dear Mother's knee,
Is the start of what you will become or just what you might be.
You learn to put words together and sometimes make them rhyme.
I realized I could do this quite well, but it took me a very long time!

We made sure that all our seven children were very well educated.
To them and to my six grandsons this poem is lovingly dedicated.
They've all done quite well for themselves as they are yet to be heard
So who knows but what their success may depend on one little word!

Don't Worry, Don't Hurry, Time Is On Your Side

If everything is going well be wary, your next move may be wrong.
It's when we think we know it all the likelihood to err is strong.
Don't write down all the answers until you know they're right,
And when you know that you are wrong give up without a fight!

Erasers were put on pencils for it was known they would be needed.
Using them is the only way that most could ever have succeeded.
That's why brakes are on cars, we have to stop sometime you know,
Curtains fall at the end of a play to announce the end of the show!

We spend our entire life learning for there is always something new.
That's how we keep ourselves busy for there's always something to do.
We have to learn, there's no other way, to be kept right up to date.
Our world's an ever changing place at an ever increasing rate!

Being created equal doesn't mean that all of us are the same.
Each one of us is different and that's why we're given a name.
It's true some folks do look alike since our genes do play a part.
We can't create a carrot from a turnip seed we just aren't that smart!

I'd like to caution everyone to please look well before you leap.
You don't want to wind up like so many at the bottom of the heap.
It's always wise to make some plans and follow them with care,
Just as when you're on a trip and the map lets you know you're there!

Trial and error is one method that smart folks like to use.
That way they can get the best results as they pick and choose.
As I've tried to emphasize herewith, we'll never be perfect you see,
But our friend Jesus, who is perfect, loves both you and me!

Don't Worry About It

They say it's darkest before dawn and that's true in a way,
But it could be darkest at midnight on any given day.
There's no exact time for it to be dark so why worry at all.
How do you determine how dark it is, who is to make that call?

The depth of the darkness has no relevance, it's about the same
From day to day like many other things that I can easily name.
Just take the temperature, it's variable but does stay within a range
And we misjudge how hot or cold it is but know that it will change!

That's just the way that our life is, we sweat the simple things.
We can't do much about those things so accept what each day brings.
It may be dark because there's no moon or clouds obscure the light,
But all in all just rest assured that it'll be darkest in the night!

The temperature is a little different we have thermometers of all kind
Which are around the house of course always where you can find,
How hot it is when you're flushed and deciding what to drink.
Will you need cold water from the fridge or tap water from the sink?

There are much more important things for us to think about.
I hesitate to use that word "worry" but by nature we do have doubt,
And yes, we question this or that although simple it may be.
We human beings are "worry warts" and not happy with simplicity!

So here we are in the midst of holidays, are you able to relax?
Don't let Uncle Sam know it, he'll want you to pay a tax.
All fun aside, let's show our "mettle", we really are okay,
But we've got a lot of things to do to be ready for Christmas Day!

November 18.

Don't Wait, Don't Hesitate, You Don't Know The Date

When I die, please don't cry but smile and shed no tears
For I'll be up in Heaven where Jesus will calm my fears.
I'll be talking to all our friends, all those who've gone ahead.
Still think of me as your good friend, don't think of me as dead!

I know that Jesus knows my name and He knows yours too.
He created all of us you know and that's why He loves you.
All those who say they don't believe are making a big mistake.
You are rejecting Jesus' love, the greatest error you'll ever make!

God created the Universe and all that there is there-in.
He's still at the head of it all and fighting against sin.
The human race has its origin and destination in Heaven on high.
Into each human being he places a soul that will never die!

The devil heads an army of non-believers who only deal in sin.
This group is hard at work at all times trying to suck you in.
God sent His Only Son Jesus to die for us and our souls to save.
Jesus and His Angels spend a lot of time teaching us how to behave!

As a human being there is no way we can escape this world alive.
When we die our fragile body decays but our soul will survive.
Our Eternal existence will depend on the mercy of the Judge.
The teaching of Jesus on the Earth unfortunately fail to get some to budge!

It's a shame that no matter how hard everyone may try,
There are those who profess they don't believe but are doomed to die.
Their souls may be cast into the devils fiery torment,
Or into the bleakness of outer darkness forever unless they do repent!

Don't Be Discouraged

I'm feeling extra good today, don't know why but that's okay.
A feeling of doom has been lifted and I feel victory's on the way.
Somehow I feel the tide has changed there's power in the air,
And I don't mean right here at home I think it's everywhere!

For some time now conditions across the globe make me want to cry,
But I awoke this glorious morning without a teardrop in my eye.
I still cannot explain the change, it's just a feeling but it's strong.
It couldn't come at a better time we've been suffering far too long!

The changes that I see coming will be subtle and won't arouse the foe.
It's like the changing of the seasons, some will come while others go.
We'll be ready for those changes you can bet on that,
It's been a long time coming but now our side is up at bat!

The reason that I have hope I know that Jesus is still alive,
And with that knowledge I know for sure that we will all survive.
We may have to bite the bullet and make changes all around,
But the one thing I know for sure is that Jesus won't let us down!

As I survey the landscape, most folks don't know just what they want.
They've been listening to the empty suits while others say please don't,
Things are almost out of hand I hope cool heads will prevail.
Those forces with the money bags will find our country's not for sale!

We've climbed up partway from the hole that others put us in.
We were led into that trap by subterfuge which certainly was a sin.
I think that the biggest problem that we face, the devil is still at large.
We need freedom "of" not "from" religion with Jesus still in charge!

November 20.

Beyond The Pearly Gates

There is nothing that can compare
With love we'll find out there,
In that lovely place that lies
Beyond the "Pearly Gates!"

Jesus told us all about that place
While He was here on earth,
And said that He would take us there,
When we each had met our fates!

I wish that I could have been
Among those folks of old,
Who saw dear Jesus in the flesh
And heard the stories He told!

He talked of Heaven in glowing terms.
He sure described it well,
And said that if we followed Him
He'd take us there to dwell!

God Himself is always there
Upon His Throne of Gold.
Along with Jesus, His dear Son
And all the Saints of old!

Now I don't know 'bout you my friend,
But I want you to know,
That I am working hard to be
Among those that get to go!

Birthdate of my Late Wife, Mother of my 7 Children
Joann Learu Yates Shepherd, 1930-2002

November 21.

Can Jesus Always Count On You?

Speak up everyone and let Jesus hear your voice.
He may hear what you have to say and make you His first choice.
He wants to capture everyone and add them to His team.
He's competing with the devil, your very soul to redeem!

You know of course that Jesus sent your soul to your Mom and Dad.
It was for sure the greatest gift that they had ever had.
What you are today has come from what they did for you.
With Jesus' help they set you on the course that He told them to!

Not all of us will be saved and that is a terrible shame,
But don't be mad at Moms and Dads they aren't the ones to blame.
You see, we all are given the thing that's known as "free-will."
We forget what Mom and Dad taught and start going down the hill!

All this while the devil's been lurking, yes that's the word to use.
He's been around the entire time just trying to pick and choose.
He'll find that some are willing targets it's safe to rope them in.
These are the ones he works on first and gets them involved in sin!

Meanwhile Jesus does not give up, He loves our very soul,
And even if it's tainted a bit, to save it is His goal.
So even if you've given in to the devil you can still be saved.
Jesus is very happy when you repent even though you've misbehaved!

Thank You Jesus for my very life, without You I wouldn't be.
Not even a gleam in my Daddy's eye as far as he could see,
But when you created my soul to be their little boy,
Mom and Dad said "Thank You" too, for you added to their joy!

November 22.

Building Your Home In Heaven

When you see someone having trouble, try to help them out.
That's what being a part of the human race is all about.
If we all would help others when they were in real need
The world would be a better place with Jesus in the lead!

I'm sure that there are times when we find ourselves in need.
That's when we all turn to Jesus hoping He will lead
All of us toward that wonderful place we call the Promised Land,
And help us make it through our earthly life by lending us a hand!

When you say your prayers each day do you thank Jesus for His aid?
Do you realize the part He played in all those plans you made.
Could you have been successful if you had been all on your own,
Or would you have been as hopeless as that person without a phone?

We should not be offended or upset when we are asked to share.
Whatever the Lord has given us He wants us to be fair.
If we have more than we really need, then help your fellow man.
Those gifts you give help to build your home in the Promised Land!

Being poor down here on earth means there are things we do without.
Being rich means having more than you need of that there is no doubt.
The poor and the rich arrive in Heaven with nothing to their name.
They won't be judged on what they had but how they played the game!

As we move into the twilight of life remember it's not the end.
The Gates of Heaven will lead us to Jesus our dearest Friend.
Let's pray that our record in His Book will help us pass His test,
And each of us can settle down to enjoy our Eternal Rest!

Brotherhood

The vastness of the Universe is hard to comprehend.
We don't know where Heaven is perhaps it has no end,
But God is there and Jesus too and all the Saints of old,
Along with all the human souls who've already joined the fold!

God began the human race with Adam and Eve ancestors of you and me.
That makes everyone a kindred soul, we're cousins don't you see.
Who would want to harm a cousin, rather they are friends.
As we travel around the globe we're at home, our family never ends!

I think of all those kindred souls when I'm walking down the street.
I can't help but smile and say "hello" to everyone I meet.
To be surrounded by family at all times is quite a thrill for me.
I had no brothers in my home, but now I have many you see!

If we're all cousins under the sun why don't we look alike?
I mean there's every color in the rainbow among the folks along the pike.
We also speak in many tongues as we move around the earth.
Now that's not a difference we can explain, it happened at our birth!

Let's just take a white man and a black lady as a way to start.
He speaks English, she speaks French, it doesn't affect their heart.
Their children may be white, may be black, or may be in between,
But you can rest assured my friend that they'll be squeaky clean!

These children speak both languages, one just as good as the other.
The fact that people don't sound like you don't make them less a brother.
It's time that we all faced the fact that we're members of the human race
And Jesus will call us by our name when we meet Him face to face!

November 24.

Brother Can You Share?

There always comes a time in life when we must make a choice.
If necessary we must act and sometimes even raise our voice.
While many others stand idly by we have to get involved,
And do our best in every way to get the problem solved!

It's true that in our world today so many are in need.
We see these people every day with families they must feed.
It's just not possible for us to know which one needs help the most,
So many times we just give up and then for that we cannot boast!

This is just one of those times when we must pick and choose.
We never know where our money goes it might well go for booze.
There are those who beg for food who should be in "A A",
But God is the only one who knows so what we should do is pray!

If you feel guilty you're not alone when passing beggars by,
Make your donations to a worthy cause and that's how we comply,
These agencies know just what to do and they do it every day,
Some even have a place where the homeless folks can stay!

We all know that Jesus wants us to help our fellow man.
I'm sure we also know the story of the Good Samaritan.
We should be ready to do our part to help the ones in need,
And do our best to bypass those who have a habit to feed!

Don't feel guilty or get upset when you have done your part,
When you have helped some needy soul with gifts straight from your heart,
Even though you may have passed some beggars on the street,
You'll feel good and sleep well at night after helping someone have food to eat!

November 25.

Be True To Yourself

It seems that sometimes we all feel the need to cheat.
It may be that's the only way that we can find to compete.
We like to think that we are smart and know our way around,
So we resort to cheating a little in subtle way's we've found!

We tell ourselves that it's ok if we just fudge a bit,
Like reading from a comic book and calling it English lit'.
But don't feel bad, we're not alone we all cheat just a little,
Like the guy with a Stradivarius in hand who can't even play the fiddle!

Oh my, now that's big time, I don't mean to impugn the art,
But making copies of Picasso's work I don't think is very smart.
Most people today who have a talent don't need to cheat at all.
They should exhibit their own work, that's proper protocol!

Most of us don't cheat a lot but we feel we must at times.
Consider a poet who searches all day to find a word that rhymes.
It happens in almost every way, it's just a fact of life.
When you go to a ribbon cutting, you always carry your knife!

Do you remember taking exams when you were still in school?
As you sat there scratching your head you remember the Golden Rule.
You wanted folks to do unto you as you would do unto them.
No one seemed to want to help so it was just "sink or swim"!

As we look back into our lives we think of times we cheated.
We tell ourselves it was necessary and was something that we needed,
But then we realize it didn't help, the answer we got was wrong.
The answer that we had on our own was the right one all along!

November 26.

Attitude

I'm feeling extra good today.
Why that is I cannot say.
It seems that's just the way it is.
To tell the truth it's no one's biz!

Feelings are fleeting, they come and go.
Don't always know what makes that so.
We must accept the hand we're dealt,
And not be influenced too much by how we felt!

Along with good things there will be some bad.
Accept the good things and don't get mad,
For attitude is the key that makes things click.
It can even keep us from feeling sick!

So many problems are of our own design.
We don't plan ahead and soon we're out of line.
Much time is spent correcting mistakes.
Have a good plan in mind, that's what it takes!

America is the greatest nation in the world today.
We must do all we can to keep it that way.
Start out each day with a good attitude, a good plan.
Above all try to benefit your fellow man!

Innovation and hard work made our nation complete.
We must not let jealousy and greed cause our defeat.
Every one of us who care, can have a part to play.
Let's all join hands and hearts and get things underway!

November 27.

The Day Before The Day

Don't wait until tomorrow to say "thank You" to the Lord.
We don't know what tomorrow may bring, to wait we can't afford.
We must say "thank You" every day for it is the thing to do.
Jesus gives us all we need and takes good care of me and you!

Oh yes, Thanksgiving Day is now just one day away,
But no one knows if they'll survive to see another day.
So we are thankful for today and we must let Jesus know,
And it should not take a special day for us to tell Him so!

The USA is a special place and we have much to be thankful for.
Oh yes, we have our problems but there is no one who has more
Of the worldly goods than our citizens with their big share.
We all must learn to give and take and to always do what's fair!

Many folks will travel today, most are homeward bound.
They can hardly wait to celebrate with their family all around.
We all should pause and think about the homeless folks today.
We should say a special prayer for them for they have lost their way!

Those who have family gatherings are in need of a special prayer
That those who travel from afar will be able to make it there.
The thanks we give will not be "just for food" but everything indeed,
For Jesus provides not only food but everything that we need!

So let's get ready for the big day just one more day away.
Everyone can rise and shine, dance and dine on Thanksgiving Day.
One of the very special days that come throughout the year.
We say a special prayer right now that they all make it safely here!

November 28.

Thanksgiving Day

Of all the things I'm thankful for there's one that's at the top,
But when I begin to offer thanks I don't know when to stop.
There is but One to Whom we owe the most, for our being here today,
So we must pray first of all, "Thank You Lord" for this Thanksgiving Day!

Our Nation was founded "Under God" by men of Christian faith.
We owe our thanks to all those men, we'll meet them at the "Gate."
There is no doubt that God still uses them as leaders in the realm,
And we are blessed to know that Heaven has such men helping at the helm!

I say a special prayer today for all those folks in need.
If Jesus were to come today imagine all the thousands He could feed,
But we have some "so called" leaders who are simply motivated by greed.
If they persist, our Nation will fall, so I ask Jesus to intercede!

We must use this Thanksgiving Day to ask the Lord for aid.
We cannot continue with the status quo, look at the mess we've made.
Those who have the most are striving to pile up more,
While those who need some help so badly are ushered out the door!

In years gone by our government has helped the common folk,
But now it seems that some in power want to use the yoke.
The down and out don't want a hand out, but they sure do want a chance,
Yet what they get from the party of "no" is a kick in the seat of the pants!

There is one consolation that we have on this Thanksgiving Day.
We know that Jesus will share His Love in a very non-partisan way.
He also made it clear to all that a wealthy man must strive harder to be saved.
The gold and silver from his vault form the bricks
of which the road to hell is paved!

Thanksgiving Day

It's customary to say a "Blessing" when we sit down to eat.
It doesn't have to be real long it can just be short and sweet.
We ask the Lord to "Bless" our food and other things beside.
We would have a whole lot less it's true if He did not provide!

There are a few days through the year when we gather to celebrate.
They can be birthdays or better yet the day we married our mate.
Christmas is the major holiday when we go "all out" each year.
Gifts are exchanged by one and all and almost everyone is here!

Another special day that comes before is Thanksgiving and it's today.
That's why we're gathered for a big meal and for that food we pray.
We say "Thank You Lord" for what we have and for our daily bread,
And we pause to give You thanks indeed as we now bow our head!

We also pause today to Thank the Lord for giving us this land.
Our forebears landed on these shores just as they had planned.
It was almost four hundred years ago when they came ashore.
That we are still alive and well, we all should give thanks for!

Of course it's true we do work hard each day to earn our daily living.
For that we need to bow our head and pray on this Thanksgiving.
The Lord will "Bless" all that we share and give us more besides,
And it's just not on Thanksgiving Day that He generously provides!

So yes it's true we need to offer thanks today and every day.
Our Heavenly Father's listening in and just loves to hear us pray.
Let's join hands now and think of family here and those who've gone.
Someday in Heaven we'll be together again a real big happy throng!

Farewell

There is a word we don't like to say, that word is just "goodbye".
It's not the word itself of course but by it what we signify,
For goodbye means the end is here and that's a sad event.
Some folks can't say it so they wave but we know what that meant!

I'd rather hug and give a kiss to those I bid farewell.
We may never meet again since there is no way to tell,
So be sure to let them know in every way you can,
That you will miss them very much and hope they understand!

There are some words that mean "goodbye" that you can use instead.
It's easy to just say "so long and best of luck ahead".
Others want to shake your hand and grab it with a squeeze.
Always avoid them if you can, if you can't just fake a sneeze!

When it's time to say "goodbye" there's more than one involved.
Someone's leaving that's for sure and they will be resolved,
To wish the best for all their friends, those who they leave behind,
And that's the hardest part of all, to break the "ties that bind".

Saying "goodbye" to a pal is hard but sometimes they must leave.
We drink a toast and wish them well they leave us there to grieve.
Some stand around and tell their jokes but we're crying deep inside,
And as our pal moves down the road the tears are hard to hide!

Sometimes our mate must say "goodbye", the final time has come.
They're moving to a better place, Jesus has called them home.
We must always be prepared and now let me explain.
At this time we don't say "goodbye", it's "'til we meet again"!

November 30.

The Truth Can Make Us Free

If everyone would tell the truth **and** everyone believed,
There'd be no trouble in our world today, we all would be relieved.
It seems that devil Satan reigns supreme, he's passing out the lies.
I can't find someone to really trust and that is no big surprise!

The sacred institutions of our land no longer do we revere.
You can't believe the things you read and nothing that you hear.
The radio is Satan's biggest outlet and it is his most potent tool.
I can't say for sure which talk show host is truly the biggest fool.

The devils target is of course, those folks like you and me.
We depend on what we hear and of course on what we see.
When we must question everything we're told, what are we to do?
How can we depend on anything when we don't know what is true!

Popularity today it seems is judged on who tells the biggest lie.
These garbage peddlers wouldn't tell the truth they wouldn't even try.
Their pay check, which is huge, depends on how many lies they tell.
You can be sure if they persist in lying they're headed straight to hell!

Lying and greed it seems really do go hand in hand.
If paid enough some folks will even "sell out" our beloved land.
There's plenty of money in our land for everyone to live real well,
But it's concentrating at the top the rest can just go to hell!

We must revise the way we think and everyone must believe.
The richest of the rich must give and the poorest of the poor receive.
Somewhere in between would be the "null", no receiving or no giving.
With cooperation from everyone we all would have a decent living!

Contents December

1. God's Golden Book Of Life 361
2. Always Watching Over Me 362
3. Be Gentle But Above All Be Strong 363
4. Once Born Your Soul Will Never Die.............................364
5. It Never Gets Late In Heaven 365
6. I'm Listening, Go Ahead 366
7. Remember When 367
8. Anytime Is Prayer Time...368
9. Are You Free, My Friend 369
10. But What Can You Do For Me 370
11. Do You Remember All That Your Mother Did For You 371
12. Have A Nice Day 372
13. He Who Feeds The Birds Is At Your Beck And Call.............373
14. Helping Others Is Really Helping Ourselves...................374
15. He's Got His Eyes On You..375
16. You Can Be A Humanist And Still Believe.....................376
17. I Think I Did But I'm Not Sure.......................................377
18. Santa Needs Our Help 378
19. It's Invisible But It's There 379
20. Love In Bloom In The Upper Room...............................380
21. Make Good Use Of Your Time.......................................381
22. No One Can Save Your Soul But Jesus 382
23. Our Yesterdays Are Never Forgotten..............................383
24. It's Christmas Time Again 384
25. Christmas Cheer For Christmas Is Here 385
    We All Have A Date With Jesus For Christmas 386
26. Some Things We Must Abide 387
27. Tell The Truth Even If It Hurts.......................................388
28. The Battle For Your Soul And Mine 389
29. The Facts Of Life Come Home To Roost........................390
30. Thoughts Of Jesus Comfort Me 391
31. To Some Eternity Is Just A Word....................................392

December 1.

God's Golden Book Of Life

When God created my soul He also created my Book Of Life.
He wrote there-in the details of my journey and the name of my wife.
My story made a lengthy tale and there-in is the date I'll die.
There must be something hidden there-in too, that I love apple pie!

You cannot change the facts at all that are written in your Book.
The life that God proposed for you will happen while you look.
You may think that what you do is something that you planned,
But everything that you've ever done was done at God's Command!

When I hear people say, "I don't believe", it makes me want to cry.
I'd rather hear an "I don't know", and then be saved when they die.
When you bow your head to pray, Jesus will open your Book.
In order to help you plan your day He'll take a real good look!

I'm sure that we all have moments and say "why did I do that?"
We're just following God's plan, but sometimes we fall flat.
That's to say that we must heed the answer to "What would Jesus do?"
Jesus has access to our "Book Of Life" and knows what's best for you!

There is a quotation, "The best laid plans of mice and men,"
But this absolutely does not apply to our Book Of Life, Amen!
God's Book Of Life for each of us has it's beginning and it's end.
We know of the beginning but the end is unknown and it will depend!

God wants everyone to come to Heaven it's in our Book Of Life,
But old devil Satan gets involved and leads us into strife.
Those of us who take his "bait" are lost unless we repent.
Jesus said, "Come unto Me", and we know just what that meant!

December 2.

Always Watching Over Me

Lord I saw You watching me from that tree today.
From that topmost branch You could hear what I had to say.
You looked so lovely sitting there I couldn't close my eyes.
That's when I knew for sure it was You in Your disguise!

I know You come in many forms to watch o'er me each day.
I feel Your presence most of all of course when I bow to pray.
Knowing that You are always near has been my constant guide
As I have traveled down the road of life with You by my side!

I'm just a simple man dear Lord but Your love for me is true.
I've been through some trying times and did not know what to do,
But You came and offered aid which always pulled me through!
I'm here today because You cared for me and I cared for You!

Where do people go for help when they don't believe in Him?
For most of us each day's a test and it's either sink or swim.
You don't appear to us in human form, t'would take away our breath
And seeing You in the flesh would scare us half to death!

Evidence of Your love for us surrounds us every day.
Sunshine and rain are gifts for which we need not pay.
All we owe is a thankful heart and there we must not fail
To show our gratitude each morn and every night as well!

Jesus doesn't need your I D to know just who you are.
Your life story is recorded in His Book preceded by a star
To indicate that you believe and will be ready when you die
To come and live with Him forever in Heaven in the sky!

Be Gentle But Above All Be Strong

Hell hath no fury like a woman scorned I have heard it said.
Whoever said it knows naught of hell and won't until they're dead.
When I think of women they are like Eve, the Mother of mankind.
Yes, they are gentle but they are strong, just what God had in mind!

Women bear the brunt of pain to bring babies into the world.
Mothers have a special bond with those babies, be they boy or girl.
A lifelong love affair begins when every child is born.
Could you imagine a brand new mother being a target of scorn?

We do not know why God picked Mary to bear His Only Son.
She was just a young teen aged girl who was picked to be the One.
When God's Son was born His Mother was still just a girl,
But was resolute and strong enough to raise the Savior of the World!

So when we think of women we must think of our own Mom first,
And yes we think of what she went through just to give us birth.
We never think of our Mom as weak we know that they were strong.
They were the ones who nurtured us and taught us right from wrong!

Now women can be mean of course, they are not free from sin.
Mean women can be very tough just like the real mean men.
I don't think that they must be scorned to show their ugly side.
Some women come about it naturally almost a source of pride!

I've had three lovely women for my wife and I am a better man.
Because of them at times when I was down they led me by the hand.
Women are the stronger sex and they know just what to do.
Without them, I wouldn't even be, and neither friend would you!

December 4.

Once Born Your Soul Will Never Die

Some folks have a hard time believing in something they cannot see.
Yet they are easily led by politicians who say "just believe in me."
We all make choices every day, for which there is no proof,
And we buy goods from shysters who have polished up the truth!

The most powerful microscope on earth has never glimpsed a "soul".
Yet, we all have one and it's our guide, to save it is our goal.
We'll need our soul in the afterlife it's the one thing that never dies.
Everyone believes in something but please don't believe in lies!

The only thing that's truly invisible is the "soul" of man.
It never leaves a living body because there's no earthly way it can.
At your death your soul will leave your body as it gives up the ghost.
Your soul lives on in the afterlife in a new form which is now the host!

Christianity is the pathway which Jesus wants us to follow.
Other beliefs may have merit but too often are too hollow.
They have no connection to the afterlife which our soul demands.
We are the guardians of our soul and must do as God commands!

If you're on the highway to Heaven, don't take the fork in the road.
The straight and narrow is the way down which to take your load.
Your soul's GPS will take you there 'twas loaded at your birth,
And it knows the way back home once you depart this earth!

Our soul is a mighty force its power must last forever.
Jesus helps us plot our course we must never leave Him ever.
Our soul arrives here in swaddling clothes but will go home to glory.
All of us know what we must do in life for it's that "age old story"!

December 5.

It Never Gets Late In Heaven

Lord, what can I do for You today, you've been so good to me.
I need to stop and think awhile so the answer I might see.
I know there's something that I must do and must do it everyday,
And before I do anything else dear Lord I need to stop and pray!

As a human being I must admit there are things I forget to do.
I know I need not ask my friends for the same is true with you.
We all are prone to let things slip and then we wonder why
Everything we start to do goes wrong and makes us want to cry!

We must start every day off right, in the presence of our Lord.
He will help you choose the course so that you can afford
To plan the day ahead without a crystal ball.
If you find you need more help then you know just who to call!

We all have our telephones our cell phones help so much.
We know that we must have those phones so we can stay in touch.
When we want to talk with Jesus the telephone is a no-no.
We just stop a moment, relax and bow our head and say "hello"!

Jesus' line is never busy, He's on duty twenty-four seven.
That's because time has no meaning in the realm of Heaven.
There's no need for a Rolex watch for Eternity will never end.
Measures of time will be a lost art and you'll never be late again!

We humans are bound by limits of time so we must plan our day.
Jesus is our dearest Friend and He's waiting for us to pray.
He will answer all our prayers and bless us with His Love.
He'll be waiting to greet us everyone when we join Him up above!

December 6.

I'm Listening, Go Ahead

If you can't get down on your knees that's no reason not to pray.
What's important is not how you do it but what you have to say.
Jesus listens to all our prayers and answers all indeed.
The answers may not be what we want but what Jesus feels we need!

Even though we have free will, Jesus wants to help.
He knows our every deed so we must be sure to watch our step.
Plan your activity to please the Lord for He is watching you.
When you need help just say a prayer, it's the thing to do!

Jesus keeps your records in the book of your life in deep detail.
He knows your faults, your good points too, He'll help you if you fail.
With Jesus' help you can survive, your troubles will disappear.
As you recover from the depths you'll know that He is near!

When I look back into my life I wonder what might have been.
Without Jesus in my life I would have been trapped in sin,
But with Him leading me I've been as happy as could be,
With ups and downs like everyone but I had help you see!

So many fall between the cracks and have no place to go.
They are homeless without a job, they have classic tales of woe.
We must do the best we can to help them get back on their feet.
For most of them the prime concern is having something to eat!

We as fortunate members of mankind must help our fellow man.
When we see someone in real need we must do everything we can.
If we see a needy person on the street but we just pass them by,
It could be Jesus in disguise and that would really make Him cry!

December 7.

Remember When

When your memory first gets bad and then it starts to fade,
Try hard not to ever forget all those good friends you've made.
There are many things you can do to stay in closer touch.
What that contact will do for you will always mean so much!

It's quite true that our memory does work both ways.
We're all a part of someone's past and think, "those were the days."
Meanwhile we forget to make that call just to say "hello."
We can't remember when we were last in touch it's been so long ago!

Those precious memories that we all have must be kept alive.
That's really the major part of all the things that help us all survive.
When all our friends and family too have gone we have no one to call,
We must rely on our memories to help us get along at all!

What we really need is a widespread telephone "party line",
In order that when your telephone rings, right then so does mine.
The first thing that you do of course is to call the roll for all.
If anyone fails to answer "present" give them a "hot line" call!

If we can just remember to make that call to let them know we care,
That will keep the "party line" busy with news from everywhere.
All our friends and family too will join in with lots of things to share,
And if anyone has a special problem then everyone will be aware!

We play a big part in our friend's life and need to let them know,
That we're all okay if only because Jesus loves us so,
But don't forget to stay in touch so make that phone call right now.
That will prove to one and all that you haven't forgotten how!

Pearl Harbor Day

December 8.

Anytime Is Prayer Time

Jesus lets us know He's near as we start out each day.
We feel His presence loud and clear when we bow to pray.
Don't miss this chance to say "hello" to your dearest Friend.
He's waiting now to hear your prayer, how will you begin?

You don't want to advertise that you say your prayers each day.
Your prayers are meant for God alone, He'll hear everything you say.
Be sure to pray with a thankful heart for what He's done for you.
He sets no limits on His time He'll listen 'til you're through!

Jesus knows we all are different, He should, He made us all.
He sees everything we do each day He needs no crystal ball.
Even though we try to ban Him from our schools today,
Do not worry He's always there and He's never far away!

The folks who tell you that you can't pray are forces of the devil.
They're in disguise as agents for good but they're never on the level.
We cannot pray that lovely prayer that Jesus taught us all.
The agents for good say "no Lord's Prayer for you but let's play ball"!

God set aside the seventh day as a day of rest.
It's also called the Sabbath day, and it's especially blessed.
A Holy Day around the world for us to worship God above.
We desecrate His Holy Name when we don't pray to show our love!

Do you feel you're going to Heaven or do you feel doomed to Hell?
It's not too late to ask forgiveness and that's one way to tell.
If you're forgiven of your sins then you can make some plans,
Knowing that your soul is now forever in His Hands!

December 9.

Are You Free, My Friend

Sometimes due to circumstances things get out of hand.
That may necessitate that you consider changing things you planned.
Once you've made that change you must get on the phone.
Which proves again that you must not set your plans in stone!

Keep your schedule flexible in case tomorrow brings
A golden chance for you to do one of your favorite things.
If you are free you can accept and go and have some fun,
Doing what you like to do and that's how things should be done!

Don't get so bound up in your plans that you can't change your mind,
If you renege on others plans that would be unkind.
Your friends should know you well enough to always depend on you,
And they will always buy your plan no matter what you do!

We've been around long enough to see almost everything.
When plans must change that's not so strange, just give me a ring.
I'll do my best to accommodate and do what must be done.
When we all do get together then we'll have lots of fun!

We're living in a changing world, nothing stays the same.
Of course that doesn't mean everything, I haven't changed my name.
I wouldn't even if I could, I like the sound of "Jake."
Others think my name is Jack and that is right hard to take!

They say what goes around comes around and that is true.
Wouldn't want it otherwise, wouldn't know what to do.
Keep on doing what you're doing until you're told to stop.
If you're real hard of hearing just quit before you drop!

December 10.

But What Can You Do For Me

Mankind is born with free will to choose what he will do.
We must make decisions everyday there's always something new.
Although some of us are old and gray there is still some life ahead
And we must keep on making choices like "should I get out of bed?"

Life itself is simple really, there's only good and bad.
It's the living that makes it difficult as decisions must be had.
Influence is a fancy name for telling us what to do,
And influence peddlers tell you that they know what's best for you!

Everything that you see and hear is a part of the influence game.
While entertainment is a worthy goal the result is still the same.
You can be led to believe this or that which may or may not be true,
And you can also be led to vote for one whose name sounds good too!

Do you feel that the influence business has its hold on you?
Do you ever do things just because someone told you to?
Do you feel free in every case to make your choice alone
Or can you not wait to say okay until you're off the phone!

There are many polls these days, influence of a kind.
Do you use results of polls to help you make up your mind?
The biggest influence game alive today is politics of course.
You'll know for whom to vote and a poll will be your source!

Ear plugs and blinders would be useful for all of us today,
Then we wouldn't know what anyone else had to say.
Are you confident that what you believe is good enough for you?
Just silence all the influence taps and look for that something new!

December 11.

Do You Remember All That Your Mother Did For You

Sadness on our Mother's Day comes from memories of the past.
She's been gone so many years and time goes by too fast.
Her smiling face is etched upon my heart and always will remain,
As a reminder of her untimely death which still can cause much pain!

On Mother's Day and other times as well I think of Mother Dear.
I know she loved me very much that message was so loud and clear.
She was who taught me right from wrong and helped me see the light.
She taught me how to say my prayers which helped me sleep at night!

Mothers have the hardest role on every family team,
She wouldn't trade it for anything for that's always been her dream.
She bears the pain to birth the babies be they boy or girl.
The most important job of all, to populate the world!

Mothers too must raise the brood and teach them the Golden Rule,
And all the other things they need to know so they do well in school.
Sometimes Mothers must do it all when Fathers flee the nest.
Those Mothers work from morn 'til night and never get much rest!

Who picks the young ones up when they cry out at night?
They may have been frightened by a noise so she holds them tight.
The soothing words from Mother's lips soon have it under control.
The big problem that Mother has is she must also lead "dawn patrol"!

They say that Mother's work is never done and you can bet on that.
She doesn't just wear a pretty "chapeau" but every kind of "hat".
My Mother was very talented and she could do anything.
The thing that I miss most about my "Mom" is listening to her sing!

December 12.

Have A Nice Day

Today is one of those perfect days, the kind you hear about.
The kind that makes you want to sing, maybe even shout.
Another day that Jesus sent that He wants us to use,
To do the kind of things that He would do if He were in our shoes!

Can't think of a more perfect day than one which Jesus made,
With plenty of time to find a tree and sit there in its shade.
Every day in its own way is good, it's made by Jesus' hands.
I look forward to working with him there in the Promised Land!

When I awake each early morn and open up my eyes,
Another beautiful day I see and that is no surprise.
One more gift from God our Father who wants us to have the best
Of everything that He provides so we can pass the test!

Let's spend today in useful pursuit of things to aid mankind.
There are plenty of things we can do they are not hard to find.
Just put on your "thinking cap" and list some things to do,
Then get to work and make it happen as Jesus would want you to!

How are you fixed for things to do as you plan your day?
Can you stay busy all day long and still have time to play?
If you are free and have time to kill why not call a friend?
They'll be glad to hear from you and wonder where you've been!

Perfect days and friendships are examples of God's Love.
They both are born in Heaven and come down from above.
When you receive these gifts be sure to pause and pray.
Let Jesus know that you are thankful for another perfect day!

He Who Feeds The Birds Is At Your Beck And Call

Don't neglect your time with Jesus we still have much to learn.
Never wait until you're forced to act with nowhere else to turn.
Jesus is never off the job, He's always at His Post.
If you need a helping hand, He is the One who can help the most!

If you are feeling down and out and need to bend someone's ear,
Just bow your head and call His name, He'll be sure to hear.
Jesus loves to talk with us, and He has so much to say,
Why not give Him a chance to help you out, He'll come right away!

You don't have to face life alone though no one may seem to care.
Jesus' line is never busy so why not go to Him in prayer?
He can brighten up your life when there's no one else who can.
You'll be glad you talked with Him and learned of the Promised Land!

Most people want to go to Heaven but Satan stands in the way.
Don't be surprised at all if he gets in touch with you today.
Satan will try to sign you up, he needs firemen and you will do.
Do not fall for his bill of goods which may sound awfully good to you!

If you will stay in touch with Jesus and talk with Him each day,
He will keep Satan from your door and give you time to pray.
Occupy any idle time by learning about Heaven where you will spend
Eternity in a glorious afterlife with friends, and it will never end!

Today is not too soon my friend to begin to make your plans.
Satan will be around at our death, pulling with both hands.
Jesus will battle him for our soul for which He has prepared a place.
He'll be waiting for us at the Gate, we'll finally see Him Face to face!

Birthdate of my #1 Wife, Lucile Smoot Shepherd, 1923

Helping Others Is Really Helping Ourselves

When you think you can't go on, that there's nothing left for you
Just bow your head and say a prayer, ask "What would Jesus do?"
We all have times when things look bleak, no answers do we see.
It's always dark before the dawn but Jesus is there with thee!

Too often we fail to think of Him, the One who made us all.
He always wants to help us out and He's waiting for you to call.
You'll have no trouble getting through, His line is never busy
Even though the calls he takes would make an earthly operator dizzy!

Not to worry, not to fret, He's the best friend that you've had yet.
If you haven't been in touch you've missed help that you could get.
It's true that we are all born much alike and equal to the task.
If we can't make the grade Jesus is waiting and all we need do is ask!

Smart folks aren't the only ones who make it on their own, some fail
And when they do they need some help to pull them out of the well.
None of us should ever forget that Jesus wants us to be a success
And when we are we should share with others what we possess!

Therein lay one of mankind's greatest failings the tendency for greed.
Too often we dwell on what we have and not on what others need.
That is where the sin comes in we always think of ourselves.
Tho' some folks find their pantrys bare there's no room on our shelves!

When you're feeling down and out look around you my dear friend.
You'll find that many others are worse off but they haven't given in.
You see there's such a thing as helping out by helping others
And that is what all of us should do for they are all our brothers!

He's Got His Eyes On You

I've never seen Him Face to face but I have felt His Touch.
He is my very best Friend and for me has done so much.
On the darkest days of my long life I knew that He was near.
Jesus, Guardian of my "soul" let me know that I need not fear!

In times of sorrow when sadness filled the air with gloom
Jesus led me to the garden where I could watch the roses bloom.
T'was in the garden years ago when Jesus said to me,
"I need you on My team to help the "blind" to see!"

Now that was a metaphor for those folks who don't believe.
To help those folks to see the light I hope that I can achieve,
For Jesus loves "every" living "soul" and offers us His Hand,
To help us board that final flight into the "Promised Land!"

The merchants of doom are building arms to blow the world apart.
Jesus teaches us that the greatest weapon of all is an open heart.
We must spread that message all around and deliver it with a smile,
Remember it was He who said our love must become like a little child!

You must make your case to go to Heaven while you're here on earth.
Jesus made sure we'd be equipped by providing all a "soul" at birth.
Your "soul" is the only thing in your body the force of evil cannot kill.
It will leave your body at your death and climb up Calvary's hill!

It's all related, can't you see, what you're born with you will keep
For all eternity your "soul" will exist, the sins you sowed you'll reap.
You have to make the choice here on earth, only Jesus can forgive.
In order that He can be a fair Judge He's watching how you live!

December 16.

You Can Be A Humanist And Still Believe

The greatest Humanist of all time is our Savior Jesus Christ.
He doesn't choose but loves everyone for whom He was sacrificed.
There are some who don't believe in God they say He doesn't exist.
They say that humans can make it on their own and on this insist!

Jesus does not forget these folks for He wants to save their soul.
He sent them here as a tiny baby and to save them is His goal.
Jesus the Master Humanist showers each of us with His Love,
And prepared a place to spend eternity with Him in Heaven above!

Humanists believe they don't need God and can make it on their own.
I'm sure that there are many times when they feel they're all alone.
Just as I am never alone, neither are they, for Jesus is always there.
That's important for our well-being for the devil is everywhere!

I am a Christian Humanist and try to love everyone I meet.
I try to maintain a happy outlook and for me life is sweet.
To pass that on to all my friends is a duty born of love,
Just as that Love that comes to me from Jesus up above!

It's true that we cannot go to Heaven unless Jesus lets us in.
That means that we have asked Him to save our souls from sin.
Jesus battles the devil for our soul with everything He can employ,
And every soul He saves thereby fills Him with so much joy!

Just because you're a Humanist don't abandon your Maker my friend
For He is the only One who can and will save your soul from sin.
Jesus knows how hard it is to fight the devil He's at it every day.
He will help you win that battle if you'll just let Him hear you pray!

December 17.

I Think I Did But I'm Not Sure

Are you forgetful, can't remember, sometimes don't know your name.
I know the feeling, I've been there, old age is not to blame.
A good memory is mandatory and something you must train.
We each were born with our own hard disk which is called our brain!

The human brain has many gigabytes in total no one knows the score.
No one has ever filled up their brain, there's always room to store.
Everything you ever see will be stored in your brain forever.
Those folks who have "instant recall" are thought to be quite clever!

If you sit around and "doze" your brain is always standing by.
That's why we have dreams as our brain is asking why.
Why do you send me lots of zzzzzz's , I need more ABC's,
Put your brain in second gear and send me more of these!

There are sometimes things we see that we would rather forget.
We can close our mind to them a bit, but they are still there yet,
And they will be there when we die, no matter how we try
To erase them from our memory which keeps on idling by!

In the very olden days folks wrote things in the sand.
Sometimes they wrote on dusty boards but always by hand.
Are you proud of your handwriting, can others read it well?
Another thing that helps a lot is knowing how to spell!

Education is the key to everything we will do in life.
If you act dumb you'll have big problems, even with your wife.
If you can't remember what she said, you're in trouble friend.
Jog your memory just a bit to bring that trouble to an end!

December 18.

Santa Needs Our Help

'Twas the week before Christmas and the roses were dead,
But the lights were all burning, and bells rang instead.
There was snow in the forecast but none on the ground.
Santa used an airplane to scout all around!

He was searching for poor kids with no playthings at all.
None of them came to see him at the big shopping mall,
And he wanted to be sure that they were not overlooked,
But signs of the times were evident as he was soon overbooked!

Santa was worried as he flew 'round the world.
Turmoil and conflict were keeping things in a whirl.
Many children were homeless and had no place to go.
It would be a bleak Christmas with no presents to show!

When Santa arrived back home the weather was nice.
The North Pole looked so different with the absence of ice.
There's no doubt "global warming" is taking its toll.
Even Santa's poor reindeer have no cool place to stroll!

Santa has mapped out a new plan for this year.
His new GPS is not helpful so he must plan things by ear.
He's anxious to visit those whose Moms or Dads are away.
Perhaps drive away some sadness and leave the children at play!

This Christmas it's possible for all mankind to get a lift.
On the birthday of Jesus let's all say a prayer as a gift.
Let's all pray that Peace and Goodwill will return soon to the earth.
That would be so appropriate on the anniversary of His birth!

It's Invisible But It's There

You can't see it, nor can I, it's not visible to the human eye.
It's yours to keep and you'll take it with you when you die.
Wear and tear may take its toll, but you can't trade it in.
The greatest thing that causes damage is when you engage in sin!

There is a market-place where some are sold, the devil runs the sale.
If you accept the devil's highest bid you get a ticket to hell.
There's no escaping the devil's lair, the sentence is "forever."
You must not sell your very "Soul" that's the worst thing ever!

God developed your body around your "Soul" and put it there to stay.
Tho' you can't see it and never have, you can be sure it's there today.
Jesus directs the actions of your "Soul" as long as you're alive,
And as your body draws its last breath your "Soul" will still survive!

Our "Soul" is all that goes to Heaven and there it has new birth.
Oh yes, we can be born again but it's hard down here on earth.
Our "Soul" will be cleansed of all its sins to become "as white as snow."
We'll inherit a "Heavenly" body and Jesus will show us where to go!

Jesus has prepared a place for us and wants us "all" to go.
He doesn't want to lose a single "Soul" and He even tells us so.
"Come Unto Me" He says and I will give you rest.
Please ask forgiveness for your sins and you will pass His test!

It seems our world becomes more sinful every single day.
We can't exist much longer if more people don't learn to pray.
No one knows the date and time when their "Soul" is released to fly,
But you must be well prepared for that is when you will die!

Love In Bloom In The Upper Room

Love is the mirror of our soul for they go hand in hand.
They will lead us at our death into the Promised Land.
Love provides the fuel for our soul while we are here on earth.
That's why babies are wrapped in much love at the moment of birth!

If we have all the superlatives but have not love, what then?
We may live an active life but we'll be prone to sin.
These folks who seem to have it all have a greater need.
The love that once was in their heart has been replaced by greed!

The Bible has another word that's a synonym for love.
That word is charity and it comes down to us from above.
Love and charity mean the same and they can co-exist.
To use the word charity does give love a little different twist!

If you are charitable toward your fellowman love abides in thee.
Jesus will note that in your book as part of your history.
Jesus loves a cheerful giver and of that you can be sure.
They have a place reserved in Heaven and their future is secure!

What about these folks who care not for others need.
Their piles of gold and stocks and bonds are a sign of greed.
Those signs of greed will disappear at death but leave no room for love.
Makes you wonder if they'll get charity up in Heaven above!

We know that Jesus loves everyone no matter who you are.
Will the love that's in your soul be able to carry you that far?
Did you share what came your way in love and charity?
Your reward will come in Heaven when you have been set free!

Make Good Use Of Your Time

Every day I spend with Jesus is a day well spent.
I try to tell all my friends what to me He has meant.
Things would be about the same if I never wrote a word.
If I could speak like Billy Graham I know that I'd be heard!

I know that Jesus primes the pump and tells me what to say.
In fact I know that He's telling me now just what to say today.
All I have to do is put His words together so that they will rhyme.
I hope that my work will be worthwhile and stand the test of time!

Going down the road of life we all make many choices.
We all have things we need to say and speak with many voices.
I love to read what others say or have said through the years.
It helps to soothe my trusting soul and helps to calm my fears!

I want to live as long as I can be of help to Him,
Right here on planet Earth where each day we must sink or swim.
We wake up every morning not knowing what the day will bring,
But there is something we all must face we have to do our thing!

We all know that Jesus wants us all to be happy every day,
And we also know that He wants us to follow as He shows us the way.
What do you plan to do today have you asked for His advice?
You know that He wants to help 'twas He that paid the price!

It isn't often that the words come so easily to mind.
I know that He is real nearby, as those words He helps me find.
If you have trouble making your plans just turn to Him in prayer.
You can be sure that He will want to help and He is always there!

December 22.

No One Can Save Your Soul But Jesus

The devil is lurking real nearby so please look all around.
You won't be free to go your way until his hideaway is found.
Most problems in your life today are caused by his recruits.
You will not recognize them all for most are dressed in suits!

The devil is not choosy and he's after everyone.
He needs a lot of help to get all of his dirty work done.
He's not interested in your IQ he's not looking for a friend.
He'll lead you down the beaten path but he's waiting 'round the bend!

If you will put your trust in Jesus He will keep the devil at bay.
Jesus wants to save your soul and He will lead the way.
The kind of things you'll do in Heaven are things you like to do
And you'll be living among good ole folks just like me and you!

I follow Jesus the best I can but I know I do some things wrong.
It's hard to reach perfection but I know Jesus will keep me strong.
I always know when I have sinned I know I need to pray.
I also know that He will forgive my sin when I talk with Him today!

So many wicked things occur they happen everywhere.
Evidence of the devil at work should make us all aware,
That we must walk hand-in-Hand with Jesus as through life we go.
He will keep us free from sin as long as we're down here below!

It's not hard to ask yourself, "What would Jesus do"?
You'll get your answer when you pray because He does love you .
He'll keep the devil from your door but you must join the fight,
To help your fellowman in every way to always do what's right!

Our Yesterdays Are Never Forgotten

It seems like only yesterday when I was just a child.
My Mother would let me play outside just a little while.
I was not prone to run away and I stayed close to home.
It wasn't long however before I began to roam!

Things were different in those years we weren't at all afraid.
There were always older kids nearby and with them we played.
Guy Robbins was my friend next door older by six than me.
He often took me to the movies and could get me in for free!

What fun we had on West Smith Street with lots of kids around.
We were lucky that our street was close to and near our downtown.
Out Moms did not have cars you see but they really loved to walk,
And when you walked with Mom downtown there was a lot of talk!

Our Moms all stayed in touch around the neighborhood.
You can be sure that all us kids tried to be real good.
If one of us did something wrong that fact soon hit the fan
And Mom would soon give us "what for" good with either hand!

Oh those were the days that I remember most of all.
We did not have a telephone so we had no one to call.
The front porch rockers were where the mothers chose to sit
They loved to watch us play "hide and seek" especially if we were "it"!

Our home life back then was fun but like a "homegrown" CIA.
We depended on the "grapevine" to tell us plans for the day.
Older sisters were the agents who kept Mom and Dad informed
And you can bet when we were bad our britches soon were warmed!

December 24.

It's Christmas Time Again

I love to write about Christmas for it's my favorite time of year.
It's a great time to contact friends and send to them "good cheer!"
Something strong would do them good but may leave them in a fog,
So I'll just raise my toast to all of you in "unfortified" egg nog!

It's that time of year when Rudolph is working overtime,
Helping Santa get all his reindeer ready for the climb,
As they depart the North Pole for points around the globe.
Santa settles in the driver's seat dressed in his fine red robe!

Giving and receiving is emphasized every Christmas Day.
For the little ones Santa brings beautiful gifts in his sleigh.
The tots can hardly sleep for the excitement offers surprise,
And they just can't wait 'til Christmas morning to open up their eyes!

We all know that Christmas is sacred it's the day of Jesus' birth,
When we received the greatest gift of all time to mankind on earth.
That gift comes to everyone with only our gift of love in return.
If we confess our sins we'll be forgiven, it's nothing we can earn!

So let's place all our trust in Jesus and ask Santa to join right in.
That sweet Santa that we've all known is also free of sin.
He couldn't be a role model for our kids if he did not believe,
And if he didn't think that it was much better to give than to receive!

Let's try not to get too confused on this coming Christmas Day.
We'll welcome Santa in early morning and then kneel down to pray.
While we have much to be thankful for there are some things we need,
To give and receive we must add our share, and overcome the greed!

Christmas Cheer For Christmas Is Here

I say "Merry Christmas" to everyone here on the planet earth.
Today we pause to celebrate our Glorious Savior's birth.
Two thousand years ago He came, a gift from God our King.
God sacrificed His only Beloved Son, which started everything!

How thankful are you on this day, for what God did for you?
Don't just celebrate today, because it seems the thing to do,
But open up your heart and soul and invite Jesus to enter in.
Let Him know that He'll always be your very dearest friend!

It's sad that Christmas comes but once a year,
We could use the joy it always brings to drive away the fear.
We do feel sorry for those unbelievers who somehow have gone astray.
What will they do as we celebrate this wonderful Christmas Day?

This Christmas Day it's sad to say our whole world's in a fight.
Even in our dear USA, not all will do what's right.
Bicker, bicker, that's the word, it seems no one can agree.
We all should pray and ask the Lord, to bring some harmony!

Everywhere you go today you see signs of Jesus' birth.
He's recognized in some kind of way around the entire earth,
But there are those who do oppose dear Jesus as our King.
The devil is alive and working hard to destroy everything!

Let's cover up the devil's work with holly and mistletoe.
Then when people look around they'll always be sure to know,
That Jesus' friends from far and wide, are gathered here today,
To celebrate the Savior's birth, a "Happy Christmas Day"!

We All Have A Date With Jesus For Christmas

My thoughts at this time are of all those lonely friends of mine.
So many dear friends have departed and left their mates behind.
I know they are all in Heaven making birthday plans,
The kind of celebration for Jesus impossible with human hands!

I know that Jesus wants to share His Birthday with us all.
And for all those lonely gals and guys who I know Jesus will call,
If for no other reason than to let each one of them know
That He's taking care of "you know who" and who says "hello!"

I'm so mindful today of all those who find themselves alone.
We must all join the Heavenly Chorus gathered around Jesus' Throne.
As we celebrate around the world the Day of Jesus Birth,
There'll be Christmas trees and Christmas lights all around the earth!

No matter who you are you must have something to be thankful for,
But for so many folks this year the wolf is at their door.
It makes me cry as I think of folks sleeping in the woods,
With a big black plastic bag containing all their worldly goods!

I wish that I could just wave a magic wand and cure all of our ills.
So many cannot get their act together and just depend on pills.
Holiday time is a most terrible time to be caught down and out,
While happy songs and cheerful music tell what it's all about!

In all your hustle and bustle please don't forget the lonely,
Especially all those this year who have lost their only
Major connection to happiness when their mate passed away.
May God Bless each one of you with His Love on this Christmas Day!

December 26.

Some Things We Must Abide

The taxman cometh, the taxman goeth, the taxman taketh away.
The taxman works for Uncle Sam and he's in town today.
Be sure your check is large enough to cover what you owe,
Then you can just relax and rejoin the active status-quo!

If you still have something left go out and have a blast,
But please go easy, take your time so you can make it last.
When your wallet is finally empty don't get caught off guard.
Be sure you brought along that precious credit card!

Oh aren't we lucky to live in the land of the free and of the brave?
Where we can have those beautiful things that we continue to crave.
We're the most fortunate people on the face of the planet earth,
Because Jesus was responsible for and present at our birth!

With all the resources that we have we don't all have the same.
There are many ways to participate and get into the game.
If everyone played by the rules and didn't rig the score,
Then everyone would have enough to keep "wolfie" from their door!

There are those driven by greed who take more than their share.
This leaves less for those in need but some don't seem to care.
It seems our taxes are not enough to pay off all our debt.
The more we owe, the interest grows and the deeper in we get!

Let's all agree to pay our fair share it's proper that we do.
It's not fair when I have less but pay much more than you.
The time is coming for all of us when we'll have to leave it all behind.
If we had shared the load in fairness we'd have more peace of mind!

December 27.

Tell The Truth Even If It Hurts

If I cannot trust your word you're a dead duck in my book.
If you would lie to anyone then you're nothing but a crook.
My integrity is built on your knowledge that what I say is true.
How could I call you a friend if I felt I couldn't trust you?

When you listen to a speaker can you tell if he's sincere?
You know problems do arise when you can't believe what you hear.
People are elected to high office based on things they've said.
Many people cast their vote right after they have been misled!

I cannot claim nor would I try to say "I've never told a lie."
I may get by while here on earth but I'll get caught when I die,
So I must get down on my knees and ask Jesus to forgive,
And help me to always be true to those with whom I live!

I get upset when someone says "May I please see your ID?"
When I've told someone my name that questions my integrity,
But that's the way it is today in everything we do.
Does your wife ever look askance at you when you say "I love you!"

Most of us think it's okay to tell a "fib" now and then.
The trouble comes when we don't remember what we said nor when.
It's always better to tell the truth and face the facts head-on.
That way you don't have to lie again in order to be left alone!

I trust my friends with all my heart believing everything they say.
If I even thought that they would lie to me it would ruin my day.
I will do the same for them of course, you can take my word.
Turn up your hearing aid my friend and believe what you just heard!

December 28.

The Battle For Your Soul And Mine

I feel sorry for those who say they don't believe.
How they can deny the existence of God is something I can't conceive.
Their soul must lead a lonely life languishing in the shade,
But Jesus will not let your soul rest that was a vow He made!

Jesus does love every soul no matter who you are.
He will fight to save your soul until you cross the bar.
The battle with the devil goes on, the soul of man the prize.
Those who don't believe trade their soul for the devil's merchandise!

The frailties of the human body show up in many ways.
The "I can't" crowd includes me as well for I've seen better days.
Although there are things that "I can't" do, my soul is alive and well.
Jesus battled the devil and won and saved my soul from hell!

I don't know how long I'll be around it may soon be time to go.
I don't worry about it a lot for I know Jesus loves me so.
He has a place prepared for me and all those who believe.
Unbelievers have a change of heart, repent and ask for a reprieve!

If you think it's been hot the last few days think again my friend.
The hottest place is not on earth but in hell with wicked men.
The devil wants a lot more souls to help fan the fires below.
Bow your head right now say "I love You Jesus" He'll be glad to know!

I've always been a believer, but the devil still works on me.
I often feel the presence of Jesus who from sin my soul sets free.
I'm always thankful that my Mother taught me how to pray.
Now when I say my prayers to Jesus I see her with Him each day!

December 29.

The Facts Of Life Come Home To Roost

When we look back into the past we often want to cry.
We think of someone that we loved, why did they have to die?
And yet, had they survived life for them would have been an ordeal.
Jesus took our loved one home with Him saying I know how you feel!

Our loved one has a happy home in Heaven, they're with friends,
And we look forward to being there too when our life down here ends.
Jesus tells us every day when we talk with Him in prayer
That our home in Heaven will be ready to spend Eternity there!

I often think of my good friends who have already crossed the bar.
Some of them were killed in battle in that dreaded thing called war.
They were much too young to die it's true but they made the sacrifice.
Hero's all they're settled now in Heaven where they're treated nice!

The older I get the faster it seems that the time on earth goes by.
I'm sure that most folks including me are in no hurry to die.
We have some things we want to do, we worked on them today.
The clock keeps ticking all the while and soon it's another day!

We hear a lot about Heaven and we're sure we want to go,
But most of us are happy with our life now and with the status-quo.
We're in no big hurry to make the change, a big one it will be,
But most of us old folks know it won't be long 'til Jesus we will see!

We give thanks to God each day for the life on earth we've led.
Jesus has made sure that we were well supplied with our daily bread.
Be sure you are well prepared to face death as life draws to a close.
We don't know when that will happen, for that only Jesus knows!

December 30.

Thoughts Of Jesus Comfort Me

I love to think of Jesus for it makes my spirit sing.
He lends comfort to my soul while I do my thing.
The life He lived while here on earth prepared Him for His role.
He saw the sinful nature of us all and He died to save our soul!

God sent John to tell the world that Jesus was the One.
He preached from the Old Testament stories of things to come.
John knew that His cousin Jesus was the Messiah that was foretold
And he spread the message loud and clear in stories that he told!

King Herod was a weak and wicked man like many leaders today.
Herod liked John and listened to him but hated to hear him say
Those things about him stealing his brother's wife, a terrible sin.
So Herod had John beheaded, the quickest way to do him in!

John the Baptist, went to Heaven, there is no doubt of that.
All of us will get to see him when we get to where he's at.
Be sure to make your aim in life the saving of your soul.
Ask Jesus to forgive you of your sins and that should be your goal!

We don't hear much talk about the devil but he hasn't gone away.
He was a thorn in Jesus' side and he's still around today.
We see the evidence of his work in all avenues of life.
There is no doubt he has a hand in causing all the strife!

Don't let someone mislead you and camouflage the facts.
It's up to you and you alone to protect your soul from stupid acts.
If you will place your trust in Jesus He won't let you stray.
Please tell Him that you love Him and please do that today!

December 31.

To Some Eternity Is Just A Word

When you start feeling down and out without a place to go
Turn to Jesus, He will help, for He loves you so.
So many seek relief that is good just for the day.
You can't depend on that alone for it will go away!

Quick fix is the name of the game, a kind of instant relief.
What we really need is a recharge of our Christian belief.
We should never forget that Jesus is always standing by.
He'll be there to help before you can "bat" an eye!

We know that some folks don't believe in God, too bad for them.
They miss out on that extra help which comes from Him.
Of course they'll get help from their friends but what about their soul,
That invisible "compass" that we have which never does grow old!

Too little time I have to spend with friends and family on earth.
I'm in the waning years of life, it's been a long time since my birth.
I look forward being with them in Heaven where life will never end.
We'll have plenty of time to talk about all those good times again!

I want to talk with Peter, James and John, all the Saints of old.
To hear stories from the "horse's mouth" the ones that we were told.
I want to trace my family trees the ones from which I came,
And find out exactly how I wound up with the Shepherd name!

In the meantime now there are some things that I must do.
I don't have a lot of time left and neither my friend do you.
Our time on earth is limited, but in Heaven it will never end.
To think that we will live there forever is hard to comprehend!

Happy New Year's Eve

Epilogue

To all the folks who've read my book,

I hope you've seen the light!

God's Love is shining from each page

To help us always do what's right!

I am the Shepherd referred to in

The title, and Jesus led Me by the hand

To help me "guide" you as you prepare

For your journey to the "Promised Land"!

Jake Shepherd

POET
2012

WWII B-17 Pilot
1944

BUSINESS EXEC
1985

Biographical Sketch

Jacob Nathaniel Shepherd, Jr. was born August 5, 1923 in Greensboro, North Carolina. The family's membership and participation in activities at First Lutheran Church led him to develop a deep and lasting love for Jesus.

He graduated from Greensboro Senior High School at the age of 15. As Captain and Pilot of a B-17 bomber he flew 25 combat missions over Germany! He received an Engineering Degree from N.C. State and retired from Blue Bell, Inc. as a Corporate Vice-President.

Happily married for 47 years to the mother of his seven children which ended tragically when she died from effects of lung cancer. He remarried in 2005 to a widow whom he met in a church program. They reside in Winnabow, N. C.

His poetic endeavors began in 2005 when he wrote a poem as a talk on Stewardship for his church.   That poem became a hymn , is registered, And included in the book under the title "I Have A Friend in Heaven"